The Metanarrative of Blindness

Corporealities: Discourses of Disability

Series editors: David T. Mitchell and Sharon L. Snyder

War on Autism: On the Cultural Logic of Normative Violence
by Anne McGuire

The Biopolitics of Disability: Neoliberalism, Ablenationalism, and Peripheral Embodiment
by David T. Mitchell with Sharon L. Snyder

Foucault and the Government of Disability, Enlarged and Revised Edition
by Shelley Tremain, editor

The Measure of Manliness: Disability and Masculinity in the Mid-Victorian Novel
by Karen Bourrier

American Lobotomy: A Rhetorical History
by Jenell Johnson

Shakin' All Over: Popular Music and Disability
by George McKay

The Metanarrative of Blindness: A Re-reading of Twentieth-Century Anglophone Writing
by David Bolt

Disabled Veterans in History
by David A. Gerber, editor

Mad at School: Rhetorics of Mental Disability and Academic Life
by Margaret Price

Disability Aesthetics
by Tobin Siebers

Stumbling Blocks Before the Blind: Medieval Constructions of a Disability
by Edward Wheatley

Signifying Bodies: Disability in Contemporary Life Writing
by G. Thomas Couser

Concerto for the Left Hand: Disability and the Defamiliar Body
by Michael Davidson

The Songs of Blind Folk: African American Musicians and the Cultures of Blindness
by Terry Rowden

Disability Theory
by Tobin Siebers

Fictions of Affliction: Physical Disability in Victorian Culture
by Martha Stoddard Holmes

Disability in Twentieth-Century German Culture
by Carol Poore

Moving Beyond Prozac, DSM, *and the New Psychiatry: The Birth of Postpsychiatry*
by Bradley Lewis

Bodies in Commotion: Disability and Performance
by Carrie Sandahl and Philip Auslander, editors

The Metanarrative of Blindness

A Re-reading of Twentieth-Century Anglophone Writing

DAVID BOLT

The University of Michigan Press
Ann Arbor

First paperback edition 2016

Published in the United States of America by
The University of Michigan Press
Manufactured in the United States of America
♾ Printed on acid-free paper

2019 2018 2017 2016 5 4 3 2

A CIP catalog record for this book is available from the British Library.

Library of Congress Cataloging-in-Publication Data

Bolt, David, 1966–
The metanarrative of blindness : a re-reading of twentieth-century Anglophone writing / David Bolt.
pages cm.— (Corporealities: Discourses of Disability)
Includes bibliographical references and index.
ISBN 978–0-472–11906–6 (cloth : acid-free paper)—ISBN 978–0-472–02958–7 (e-book)
1. Literature—20th century—History and criticism. 2. Blind in literature. 3. Blindness in literature. 4. People with disabilities in literature. I. Title.
PN56.B6B65 2014
809'.9335271—dc23
2013020496

ISBN 978-0-472-03654-7 (paper : acid-free paper)

As I set about writing this loving dedication, I am momentarily tempted to begin by researching the meaning of your name. Please forgive this rather impersonal, objective approach. I guess it is the habit of an academic. I am no poet, alas.

But instead I will venture my own definition, one that I know is certainly accurate in your case.

I dedicate this book, with love, to you, Heidi, the bringer of true happiness.

Acknowledgments

What a thrill it is for me to have this book published. For my work to become part of the field-defining Corporealities series is a great honor indeed. But after only a moment of pondering this prospect and bearing the unavoidable pride, I am struck by the sheer number of people to whom I am indebted. This list of acknowledgments is therefore long and yet surely incomplete—for which I apologize in advance.

Most obviously, David Mitchell, Sharon Snyder, LeAnn Fields, Alexa Ducsay, Marcia LaBrenz, the anonymous reviewers, and everyone at the University of Michigan Press must be thanked for their part in making my ideas a reality.

Given that a working version of chapter 1 has already been published as "Community, Controversy, and Compromise: The Language of Visual Impairment," in Paul McPherron and Vaidehi Ramanathan's *Language, Bodies, and Health* (2011), I must thank the publisher, Mouton de Gruyter, for permission to include that material in the present book.

Like anyone working in our field, I owe much to the dedicated academics and activists involved with the *Journal of Literary and Cultural Disability Studies,* including Clare Barker, Tammy Berberi, James Berger, Michael Bérubé, Brenda Jo Brueggemann, Lucy Burke, Simone Chess, Johnson Cheu, G. Thomas Couser, Michael Davidson, Lennard Davis, Helen Deutsch, Elizabeth Donaldson, Jim Ferris, Anne Finger, Maria Frawley, Chris Gabbard, Rosemarie Garland-Thomson, Martin Halliwell, Diane Price Herndl, Martha Stoddard Holmes, Richard Ingram, Jennifer James, Alison Kafer, Deborah Kent, Georgina Kleege, Miriamne Ara Krummel, Fiona Kumari Campbell, Petra Kuppers, Stephen Kuusisto,

Cynthia Lewiecki-Wilson, Robert McRuer, Madonne Miner, Mark Mossman, Stuart Murray, Felicity Nussbaum, James Overboe, Catherine Prendergast, Ato Quayson, Julia Miele Rodas, Ellen Samuels, Carrie Sandahl, Susan Schweik, David Serlin, Tobin Siebers, Anne Waldschmidt, James Wilson, and the rest of the editorial board, as well as the authors, loyal readers, and everyone at Liverpool University Press.

During the writing of this book I have also benefited from the work of my colleagues in the Centre for Culture and Disability Studies and the International Network of Literary and Cultural Disability Scholars, especially Owen Barden, Emmeline Burdett, Ria Cheyne, Liz Crow, David Doat, Pauline Eyre, Alice Hall, Alan Hodkinson, Claire Molloy, Marie O'Connor, Claire Penketh, Irene Rose, Will Southwell-Wright, Alex Tankard, and Laura Waite.

In addition, in recent years I have been lucky enough to work with, and thus learn from, Chris Atkin, Philip Bamber, Len Barton, Wendy Bignold, Peter Clough, Siobhan Garber, Dan Goodley, Elizabeth Green, Ann-Marie Jones, Essaka Joshua, Chris Lowry, Daniela Mangione, Bart McGettrick, Susannah Mintz, Kenneth Newport, Tessa Owens, Gerald Pillay, Shirley Potts, Alan Roulstone, Carol Thomas, Margaret Rose Torrell, Joan Walton, Nick Watson, and June Wilson.

I am eternally grateful for my undergraduate and postgraduate education at the University of Staffordshire, which was facilitated by literary and cultural scholars such as David Alderson, Aidan Arrowsmith, Christine Gledhill, Azzedine Haddour, Peter Heaney, Siobhan Holland, Edward Larrissy, Andrew Lawson, Susan McPherson, Martin McQuillen, Ann Parry, Laura Peters, Shaun Richards, and Barry Taylor.

From my undergraduate days to the present time I have put my trust in, and depended on, a select number of support workers—namely, Tom Coogan, Sarah Cooper, Heather Cunningham, Jane Goetzee, and Pippa Leddra. They have all become good friends whose advice has often been invaluable.

My oldest friends, Pete and Julie Bagnall, David Cuddy, and Kim Edge, as well as Chris Pearce, deserve a mention if not a medal for joining me so often in a much-needed beer at increasingly short notice and for tolerating my repetitious jukebox selections—long may it continue.

Finally, my family has always been supportive in all of my writing. Thanks to them I have come to believe that not one of my big ideas is too big and that in any case failure is just a change of direction. They should all be thanked, but especially my mum, dad, brother Steve, sister-in-law Gerry, and above all, my daughter Nisha.

Contents

An Embodied Introduction

The decision to write about blindness has hit some academics like the proverbial bolt from the blue. This is illustrated by, for instance, Jacques Derrida in *Memoirs of the Blind* (1990) and Naomi Schor in "Blindness as Metaphor" (1999).[1] Both were writing in a prompt response to the onset of their visual impairments, the one temporary and the other permanent. In my case, however, the decision was far more gradual, a culmination of reflections on personal, political, professional, academic, cultural, medical, and social encounters, a few of which I briefly outline and explore in this introduction. The rationale for allowing myself to draw on personal experience follows a point made in Sharon Snyder and David Mitchell's *Cultural Locations of Disability* (2006), which refers to this kind of approach as a means of showing "how a cultural model of disability provides an opportunity to reimagine the landscape of impairment as well as its attendant social contexts" (12). Indeed, in *Representing Autism* (2008), Stuart Murray goes so far as to assert that "the anecdote emerges as a tool every bit as useful as the studied analytical insight" (19).[2] But for the sake of readers from outside the discipline of disability studies, who may be unaccustomed to such applications of experiential knowledge, perhaps I should say right away that, though rife here, anecdotes are confined to the footnotes in the chapters that follow. The bulk of that all-important experiential knowledge is provided by the autobiographical work of Georgina Kleege, Stephen Kuusisto, and John Hull, among others.

To begin it is probably worth mentioning that, having failed in my first occupation as a singer/songwriter, I sought professional career advice when I was in my late twenties and, predictably, was directed to a three-year course in piano tuning. This advice was anticipated because I had been registered as blind since my teens, a fact that in the imagination of many professionals seemed a sufficient (if not necessary) condition of the piano tuner. I guess the idea must have gained some credence in my own mind, too, for though not even proficient at tuning the six strings of my guitar, let alone the hundreds inside a piano, I eventually enrolled at a residential college for the blind. After only half a term (that is, six weeks) I was convinced that piano tuning could be a highly rewarding career, but one in which I had neither ability nor real interest. Instead I found myself gate crashing classes in psychology, sociology, and creative writing, not to mention an art class that enabled me to begin making a short film about blindness that was ultimately, and perhaps fortuitously, abandoned. I think of this abandonment as lucky because the project would have surely followed many of the stereotypes that I have come to challenge.

When the term ended I was at a bit of a loss about my next move. I opted to leave the so-called special institution and enroll at the local college of further education in an endeavor to make up for a woeful lack of formal qualifications (having left school at the tender age of fifteen). It was my intention to concentrate on learning about prejudice and the social sciences, which is why I conducted a minor research project about attitudinal barriers and how I came across the classic studies to which I turn in a moment and throughout the book. But the access course was designed in a way that meant I also had to take something in the humanities. I chose literary studies, reluctantly at first, yet soon became interested enough to take the subject at degree level. I was thereby introduced to numerous representations of visual impairment, which I approached not only with the requisite tools of literary criticism but also with occasional reference to the social sciences and what seemed like rather sneaky allusions to my own experiential knowledge of impairment and disability.

During those much-enjoyed undergraduate years, I was struck by the absence of an informed approach to the literary representation of disability, subsequent research into which revealed that the state of affairs was far from unusual. I began to address the problem a little in my doctoral thesis on literary blindness and its resonance with the ancient Samson myth but felt somewhat isolated in the humanities until my superviser, Shaun Richards, spotted extracts from *Enforcing Normalcy* (1995) in *The Norton Anthology of Theory and Criticism.* I immediately contacted the author, Lennard Davis, who was both encouraging and helpful, directing me, as he did, to Georgina Kleege's *Sight Unseen* (1999), a book that became a point of reference in the bulk of my subsequent work.

As I became increasingly aware of literary disability studies in the American academy, completed my doctoral research at the University of Staffordshire in the United Kingdom, and published numerous related articles, the writing of the present book became more and more likely. But I noticed that there was no academic periodical that focused on literary disability studies and, before spending the necessary amount of time and effort on my own writing, felt driven to have a go at plugging the gap. That is to say, in an endeavor to make a much more significant contribution to the emerging field in general, and curricular reform in particular, I founded the *Journal of Literary and Cultural Disability Studies* (*JLCDS*). But if this undertaking was initially a distraction from my own research, the editorial board members and other contributors became by far the biggest influence when I started writing the book.[3] The other irony is that, thanks to the massive support of my colleagues in the Centre for Culture and Disability Studies at Liverpool Hope University, I began to make more progress when I had less time to spare, when my scattered sessional and part-time lecturing in English and creative writing was set aside in favor of a full-time academic post in disability studies.

Before and alongside these things were the perplexing attitudes toward visual impairment that I encountered on a regular basis. During the first year in my current post I found myself telling my students several anecdotes, reflecting on a number of rather mundane but relevant experiences. For instance, on one occasion I was standing in the university's Senior Common Room, waiting to satisfy my constant desire for coffee, when someone joined me in the queue. We chatted for a few minutes, and it soon became clear that he thought I was a student rather than a tutor. This assumption is noteworthy not just because our Senior Common Room is only open to staff but also because it has been made about me by other people and at other institutions. Perhaps it is simply the case that some people are thrown by my misleadingly youthful appearance. But then again, perhaps there is a more plausible explanation. Given the ubiquitous confusion between seeing and knowing, which is considered in chapter 1, perhaps it is more likely to be the case that for some people the idea of a tutor who has a visual impairment remains a contradiction in terms.[4] Whatever the reasons, this encounter leaves me pondering the complex array of details and dynamics invoked, the commonplace notions that are interrelated but nonetheless contradictory. I wonder, for example, why there is often a compulsion to gaze silently at those of us who have visual impairments as we pass by in the street, yet barely a glance is thrown in our direction during many conversations. Such encounters correspond with what I call the metanarrative of blindness, a concept that this introduction begins to explore with reference to a small selection of writing in and around the field of cultural disability studies.

The key point about cultural disability studies, according to Ria Cheyne's "Theorising Culture and Disability" (2009), is that it "seeks to contribute" to our "understanding of disability and its role in wider culture," as well as to our "understanding of the particular cultural form or artefact under consideration" (101). This is certainly an aim in the present book, the cultural form under consideration being Anglophone literature—more specifically, a sample of over forty twentieth-century short stories, novellas, novels, and plays. I make no overarching claims about this material—which after all encompasses numerous genres, from several distinct literary moments, not to mention different geographical locations—but draw on the sample to identify and examine a selection of recurrent tropes. My reading of these tropes informs, and is informed by, an understanding of disability that emanates from a myriad of directions and disciplines. Accordingly, entangled with my application of anecdotes, first- and second-wave works of cultural disability studies are the main focus of this introduction, work that, along with life writing, feminism, postcolonialism, critical theory, philosophy, and research from the social sciences, informs the literary criticism in the chapters that follow.

Theorizing Social Encounters

Brought together in Davis's first *Disability Studies Reader* (1997) are many authors who, like Derrida, in some ways grounded the field of cultural disability studies. The other names that spring to mind include Mikhail Bakhtin, Judith Butler, Michel Foucault, Sander Gilman, Kaja Silverman, Susan Sontag, and the sociologist on whom I now focus, Erving Goffman. I start here because of a posting on the DS-Hum mailing list in 2010 that enquired about the origins of disability studies.[5] The response was diverse, as we might hope and expect, but there was some agreement that (in part) disability studies grew from early work on stigma. Goffman is one of the authors of this significant work.[6] Most poignantly, he recognizes that "all human differences are potentially stigmatizable" and that "stigmas reflect the value judgments of a dominant group" (Coleman 217). Importantly, given that one of the terms coined in the present book is *ocularnormativism,* meaning the mass or institutionalized endorsement of visual necessity, Goffman's *Stigma* (1963) problematizes the very notion of the norm by asserting that there is just one unblushing male in America: "a young, married, white, urban, northern, heterosexual Protestant father of college education, fully employed, of good complexion, weight and height and a recent record in sports" (153). This profile may be said to represent the subject position of the American male, a narrow ideal by which those who judge themselves will inevitably emerge wanting. Despite this unattainability, it is paradoxically the so-called normals who occupy the dominant social position.

Goffman is particularly interested in what happens when normals and stigmatized people are in one another's company, be it in an intimate or a crowded setting. He goes so far as to assert that when we enter one another's immediate presence, especially if we attempt to engage in conversation, there occurs "one of the primal scenes of sociology; for, in many cases, these moments will be the ones when the causes and effects of stigma must be directly confronted by both sides" (24). It is in this primal scene of sociology that the present book detects the influence of cultural production.

So intense is the encounter between normals and the stigmatized that its very anticipation may lead to avoidance, the full significance of which is illustrated in Gordon Allport's *The Nature of Prejudice* (1954). Informed by the horrors of Nazi Germany, this classic study proposes that the behavioral component of prejudice has five incremental stages: antilocution, avoidance, discrimination, physical attack, and extermination. While the vast majority of the human race has always been opposed to extermination, the same cannot be said of antilocution or avoidance. The problem to which I return throughout the book is that the second stage of prejudice is predicated on the first, the third on the second, and so on, meaning that "activity on one level makes transition to a more intense level easier" (Allport 15). Most obviously, Hitler's antilocution led many Germans to avoid their Jewish neighbors, making it easier to enact laws of discrimination that, in turn, made anti-Semitic attacks seem somehow acceptable, the final stage being the concentration camps in which millions died. Along similar lines, it is too frequently forgotten that the T-4 program (among others) was predicated on disabled people being set aside, categorized as special. Of course avoidance does not necessarily lead to the more extreme forms of prejudicial behavior, but, like antilocution, it contributes to a divisive ethos of social exclusion that is often bolstered by cultural representations. In the present book I therefore amend Allport's model by making explicit that pejorative cultural representations are, at the very least, on a par with antilocution.

Not only anthologized in the *Disability Studies Reader,* Goffman's *Stigma* is also revisited in Rosemarie Garland-Thomson's *Extraordinary Bodies* (1997).[7] Though understandably critical of the assumption that femaleness has no part in the proposed normative subject position, Garland-Thomson expands on Goffman's conception of normals productively. She coins the term *normate,* thereby designating the "veiled subject position of cultural self, the figure outlined by the array of deviant others whose marked bodies shore up the normate's boundaries" (*Extraordinary Bodies* 8). This relatively widely adopted neologism denotes the "constructed identity of those who, by way of the bodily configurations and cultural capital they assume, can step into a position of authority and wield the power it grants them" (8). The sense of an elevated status is so ubiquitous that people often aspire desperately to accord with the normate subject position, trying to fit what constitutes a prohibitively exclusive ideal. After all, although (unlike Goffman) Garland-Thomson does not go so far as to invoke the idea of a single exemplary person, she does refer to a narrowly defined profile that describes only a minority of real people.

Goffman's primary scene of sociology becomes, for Garland-Thomson, more specifically an encounter between normate and disabled people. She acknowledges that in any initial meeting a large amount of information must be organized and interpreted, that each person "probes the explicit for the implicit, determines what is significant for particular purposes, and prepares a response that is guided by many cues, both subtle and obvious" (*Extraordinary Bodies* 12). However, she writes, if one person has an impairment the interaction tends to be particularly strained because the other may feel fear, pity, fascination, repulsion, and/or surprise, feelings that cannot be expressed in a society that has, what I for one regard as, laudable aspirations of political correctness. As well as experiencing this cognitive dissonance it is extremely likely that those of us who do not have impairments will not know how to act toward those of us who do, "how or whether to offer assistance; whether to acknowledge the disability; what words, gestures, or expectations to use or avoid" (12). It is acknowledged that the person who has an impairment may anticipate and perhaps fear subsequent avoidance, but the encounter is deemed especially stressful for the person who does not have an impairment, given that he or she is likely to be less skilled when dealing with such situations.[8]

The social encounter is considered with an emphasis on sexuality in Robert McRuer's *Crip Theory* (2006), although it is acknowledged that all normalizing moments depend "on identifying and containing—that is, on disciplining—disability" (178). The "more flexible gay or lesbian body" enables what McRuer calls "heteronormative epiphanies" that are underpinned by "compulsory able-bodiedness" (12). Moreover, distinguished by their ability, flexible heterosexual bodies tend to be overtly differentiated from people who have impairments, meaning that "heteronormative epiphanies are repeatedly, and often necessarily, able-bodied ones" (McRuer 13). From this perspective, the normate subject position marks a "critically disabled capacity for recognizing and withstanding the vicissitudes of compulsory able-bodiedness" (McRuer 197).[9] This relationship between sexuality and compulsory able-bodiedness is, as I argue throughout the book, but especially in chapter 3, particularly strong in cultural constructs of blindness.

Described by McRuer as an "indispensable theoretical concept" (197), the normate is also one of the main sources for Ato Quayson's *Aesthetic Nervousness* (2007), wherein the encounter between someone who has an impairment and someone who does not have an impairment becomes a "primary scene of extreme anxiety" (17). Of particular interest are the various relational elements that disclose themselves not as power, but as anxiety, dissonance, and disorder. Following Garland-Thomson, Quayson recognizes corporeal difference as part of a structure of power that is based on the normate's unmarked regularities, but it is stressed that the impulse to categorize during interpersonal encounters is part of an assumed ideal of order. As we explore the metanarrative of blindness, it proves especially important to remember that, for Quayson, what Garland-Thomson calls the probing of the explicit for the implicit constitutes part of a quest for an order that is thought to lie elsewhere. That being so, the impaired body may be ascribed metaphysical or divine significance. But because impairment is often deemed a manifestation of disorder, the normate impulse for order must be revaluated, and aesthetic nervousness results.[10] It might be, for example, that someone who is disabled (or, worse/better still, someone who is seen as blind) stares back at the starer, thereby disrupting the supposedly normal order of things. Indeed, the normate position is necessarily insecure, given that everyone is subject to radical contingency, and people who have impairments tend to be perceived socially as reminders of that fact. This is why those of us who have visual impairments will be more than a little familiar with the phrase *there but for the grace of God go I.*

The other source for Quayson's notion of aesthetic nervousness is the reformulation of literary history from a perspective informed by disability studies, such as that found in Mitchell and Snyder's *Narrative Prosthesis* (2000). The consequence of this field-defining work is that disability is now increasingly recognized as the "crutch" on which narratives "lean for their representational power, disruptive potentiality, and analytical insight" (Mitchell and Snyder, *Narrative Prosthesis* 49). While the concept of narrative prosthesis is illustrated fruitfully with reference to works of literature in both the eponymous monograph and the many derivative studies, it should be stressed for the purpose of this introduction that such examples are by no means exhaustive. After all, pretty much any discourse may be placed under the rubric of narrative, from which it follows that any discursive dependence on disability may be understood in terms of narrative prosthesis. That is to say, the term is applicable to any instance of a narrative in which impairment or disability is inserted for effect. Of course we might bring to mind the work of William Faulkner, J. D. Salinger, Harper Lee, Ken Kesey, and so on, following the lead of Mitchell and Snyder. But it might also be the case that a student unnecessarily invokes her or his tutor's visual impairment when querying a grade. It might be that political parties are described as shortsighted in their policies. It might be that someone is deemed blind to the facts. Indeed, when thinking of disability as a device on which authors depend for their "disruptive punch" (Mitchell and Snyder, *Narrative Prosthesis* 49), it might well be ableist jokes about, say, the American singer/songwriter Stevie Wonder or the British politician David Blunkett that spring to mind.[11] The list of familiar examples could go on and on, the key commonality being that nothing informed is said about the lives of the people invoked.

Given this unawareness of (or disregard for) experiential knowledge and agency, it is perhaps not surprising that when normate thoughts do turn to impairment, as pointed out in Davis's *Enforcing Normalcy,* it is often associated with a story, placed in a narrative. Thus, in encounters between those of us who have visual impairments and those of us who do not have visual impairments, according to Davis's account of the ways in which normalcy is enforced, the impairment may be rendered part of a Bakhtinian chronotope—that is to say, it may become embedded in a story, part of a time-sequenced narrative. Irrespective of the facts of the matter, a person is assumed to have been born blind, or to have been blinded in an accident, or to have become blind as a result of some illness, and so on. He or she is thereby objectified, framed in a narrative that bolsters the normate subject position. I say this because, in effect, the person who has a visual impairment is written into the story of the person who does not have a visual impairment—a point developed in chapter 6. The person who does not have a visual impairment assumes a kind of authorship, indeed authority, as the person who has a visual impairment is told rather than asked about her or his own life.

When thinking of discourse that bolsters the normate subject position we should not forget the way in which those of us who have visual impairments are often in danger of being left out of our own conversation. Does he take sugar? Does she take sugar? Do they take sugar? The questions are now clichés, but the underpinning attitude is by no means a thing of the past. Again I think back to the first year in my current post for a brief illustration, to a day on which a colleague and I accompanied one of our disability studies classes on a visit to a resource center for people who have visual impairments. Our intention was to facilitate a wider understanding of practical matters, to inform the students about various solutions to inaccessibility, but something far more profound was demonstrable within a few minutes of entering the center. Once the brief introductions were over, having noticed my visual impairment, the person who seemed to be in charge turned to my colleague and asked if she would be taking me around. On this occasion I was not that bothered about the erroneous assumption that because I was using a guide dog I would necessarily be unable to browse unassisted. In fact, the assumption happens to be quite correct in my own case (which is why my colleague had already indicated to me that she was more than happy to provide any necessary assistance). Nor did I give that much thought to the issues raised by the problematic application of the verb *taking*. Rather, the point of interest was my exclusion from the normate discourse, especially as it was initiated by someone we all expected to be fairly appreciative of disability. The resource center, by definition, is meant to empower people who have visual impairments. However, the person who seemed to be in charge unwittingly subjected me to a discursive form of avoidance—something else the book deems pertinent for a place in Allport's model of prejudicial behavior.

The critical point about such interpersonal encounters is that when one person has a visible impairment it tends to dominate the other's processing of perceptions, having a disruptive influence on her or his initial reactions: "Perhaps most destructive to the potential for continuing relations is the normate's frequent assumption that a disability cancels out other qualities, reducing the complex person to a single attribute" (Garland-Thomson, *Extraordinary Bodies* 12). This normate reductionism may explain my encounters in the resource center and Senior Common Room, where communication skills and indeed my very agency were obscured by the apparent significance of visual impairment. Of course, like many of us who have visual impairments, I could list innumerable examples that are far more important and/or interesting. I tend to refer to the encounter in the resource center largely because it was witnessed by several budding disability scholars (effectively during a lesson) but also because the context was overtly supportive of people with visual impairments.

What I must stress about such interpersonal encounters is that as well as the normate assumption that impairment cancels out other qualities, thereby reducing the complex person to a single attribute, there is a consequential but apparently immediate invocation of extraneous details. Not simply reduced to the facts of visual impairment, the complex person is lumbered with what may be called the "old vestments" of blindness (Kuusisto and Kuppers 74). In other words, those of us who have visual impairments are frequently keyed to an extensive metanarrative of blindness that is shaped by cultural representations.

The Metanarrative of Blindness

What I mean by a metanarrative, here, is the story in relation to which those of us who have visual impairments often find ourselves defined, an overriding narrative that seems to displace agency. Even for those of us who have visual impairments, as pointed out in Julia Miele Rodas's "On Blindness" (2009), "blindness is always a mediated experience, informed, even defined by language and culture" (129). With reference to what I class as one element of the metanarrative of blindness, for instance, it is asserted in Michael Monbeck's *The Meaning of Blindness* (1973) that, although the "number of blind beggars is rather small, it is the image of the beggar that is most commonly called to mind by the words 'blind man'" (8). This association is bolstered by two aspects of cultural production, one that relates to the content of the present book and the other to its premise. First, there is the recurrent use of tropes such as the blind beggar, which reaches far beyond the literary and indeed cultural imagination. Second, there is critical avoidance, the general lack of informed tropological criticism in the humanities (Bolt, "Social Encounters"). That is to say, the absence of critical readings that are appreciative of disability effect a covert perpetuation of recurrent tropes. After all, while there is no denying that stereotypes "in life become tropes in textual representation" (Garland-Thomson, *Extraordinary Bodies* 11), is it not the lack of profound if not general engagement with those tropes that ensures their return?

Having cited Monbeck, a source from the twentieth century, I should perhaps emphasize that like the sugar cliché, alas, the image of the blind beggar cannot yet be dismissed as a thing of the past. Just a few days before my visit to the resource center, I encountered another pertinent instance of normate reductionism. I had arranged to meet someone for a few drinks at a bar in the city center. I allowed half an hour for the journey but, owing to an unexpectedly low volume of traffic, arrived twenty minutes early. Because the bar was very noisy, making it difficult for me to order a drink and/or find somewhere to sit (relying in part, as I often do, on auditory cues), I decided to wait outside. After ten minutes or so someone walked passed, paused, and then turned back. I stepped forward very slightly in case it was the person for whom I was waiting, but it was a stranger who indicated in a friendly tone that he was trying to hand me something. I imagined it must have been a flyer of some description. Such material has not been readily accessible to me for many years, so I did not raise my hand. This has become my standard little expression of protest. He seemed perplexed at my lack of engagement, pausing again before asking if I was not collecting for the blind. At that point, though not in a can or a hat, a proverbial penny dropped for us both. I explained that I was just waiting for someone, and he apologized convincingly as he walked away. It was 2010, but in the mind of this kind stranger, I was reduced to the characteristic of visual impairment and, by extension, keyed to a metanarrative in which the blind beggar and sighted donor have become stock characters. My very presence was implicitly explained by a cultural construct.

The influence of this cultural construct does not exclusively reach the minds of those of us who do not have visual impairments, as considered in chapter 6 and chapter 7. Indeed, from interactionism and labeling theory to Fiona Campbell's relatively recent work on internalized ableism, there is a range of material to suggest that, as well as by others, those of us who have visual impairments may be keyed by ourselves to the metanarrative of blindness. For instance, though reasonably aware of the stereotypical possession of extraordinary senses (as I hope is apparent in chap. 4), I cannot help feeling a little pleased when someone notices if I am first to hear the arrival of a taxi at the end of an evening with friends. Because in such situations I am accustomed to listening for the sounds of the engine and closing door, it is not really surprising if I am aware of the taxi's arrival before the driver makes her or his presence known. That is the bare fact of the matter, but for a fleeting moment I may secretly embrace the so-called positive stereotype and all its cool mysteries. What is more, I am then likely to save myself from the internal displacement of identity by nervously cracking some joke about the extraordinary hearing of the blind. In other words, albeit through irony, I invoke the metanarrative of blindness overtly as well as covertly. Of course I soon regret my part in this social process when reporting a suspected gas leak, a problem with a sound system, or whatever, for in such instances it is not unusual for my supposedly extraordinary senses to be rather frustratingly invoked as the most likely explanation.

Before putting these introductory anecdotes aside, I should add a few details to expand a little on their context. For more than twenty years my visual impairment has been visible insofar as I have used guide dogs for mobility. In that time I have only experienced two of the blind-beggar encounters, and just for the record, in neither was I holding a can or a hat or anything that could have been mistaken for a begging bowl. The other situations, however, are far more common. I am certainly spoken about, rather than to, on a weekly if not daily basis and must admit to internalizing various stereotypes from time to time. Although in such instances I tend to be reduced not only to the characteristic of visual impairment but also to my own laughter (within if not without), thereby demonstrating the point that "real social relations are always dynamic" (Garland-Thomson, *Extraordinary Bodies* 11), I do appreciate that cultural representations may have a profoundly disturbing and disabling influence on those of us who have visual impairments. After all, is it not the idea rather than the lived reality of acquiring such an impairment that has the greater pejorative impact on the person? Are these ideas not frequently given currency in cultural representation? These questions remain relevant throughout the book.

Summary

So in these pages I argue that the metanarrative of blindness is invoked and thus potentially explored nowhere more than in twentieth-century

Anglophone writing, sometimes referring and sometimes alluding to what Snyder and Mitchell call the "quintessentially modernist project" (4). In so doing I explicate a key aspect of the cultural propagation of current problematic attitudes toward those of us who have visual impairments. To begin I provide a rationale for my choice of terminology, considering, as I do, a selection of concepts, models, and critical approaches that in relatively recent years have informed debates about the language of visual impairment. On the downside, terms such as *blindness* and *the blind* are deemed fundamentally problematic, but the radical social model of disability is recognized as something of a cardinal concept—notwithstanding its important criticisms and complexities.

The focus moves to literary representation in chapter 2, the central concern being how and why problematic terminology is used in character designation. The labels *blind girl* and *blind man* are explored with reference to two subsamples of texts that range from Rudyard Kipling's "They" (1904) to Stephen King's *The Langoliers* (1990), and from D. H. Lawrence's "The Blind Man" (1920) to Rupert Thomson's *The Insult* (1996). Selected from the early, mid-, and late twentieth century, these various examples chart ways in which the reductive labels key characters to the metanarrative of blindness, thereby raising issues of gender, empowerment, and sexuality on which the subsequent chapters expand. Because a relatively wide range of work is briefly introduced, the chapter also provides contextual detail for those that follow.

The metanarrative itself becomes the focus in chapter 3, as the sexualization of eye symbolism and imagery is considered in relation to the cultural construction of blindness. Psychoanalytic and pornographic classics are read for their insistence on what I call the ophthalmocentric notion that eyes and vision are fundamentally sexual, that they are necessary conditions of normative sexuality. The twentieth-century psychosocial manifestations of this ocularnormative notion include masturbation mania, asexualization, and emasculation. Various related definitions of castration are explored with reference to Henry Green's *Blindness* (1926) and Susan Sontag's *Death Kit* (1967). These two novels are used to illustrate the castrated figures of the blind man and the blind girl respectively. What also emerges from the analysis is the way in which the metanarrative of blindness is underpinned by the independence-dependence binary, the modernist denial of the rewards and realities of interdependence from which the disturbing eugenic term *useless eaters* derives.

Probing beneath the trope of blindness-castration synonymy, chapter 4 reveals notions of hypersexuality that correspond with the eugenic anxieties personified in the figure of the groping blind man, a parasitic dependent who poses a threat to the sighted normate position. In exploring some of the extraordinary senses from which this grotesquely haptic figure emerges, the chapter turns to James Joyce's *Ulysses* (1922) and James Kelman's *How Late It Was, How Late* (1994), novels that differ in many respects but nonetheless unify in their Modernist praise for independence. Because this state, indeed this myth, is embedded with the pseudo-science of eugenics, the chapter also draws on science fiction in the shape of H. G. Wells's short story "The Country of the Blind" (1904) and John Wyndham's novel *The Day of the Triffids* (1951). Common to all four works are assumptions about extraordinary powers of perception, ranging from the hypersensitivity of the sixth sense to the monstrous grip that epitomizes the eugenic rendering of lecherous Otherness. The result is the hegemony of what (with allusion to Goffman, Davis, Garland-Thomson, and McRuer) I refer to as ocularnormativism. If ocularcentrism is thought of as the baseline of assumptions, the very foundation of the metanarrative of blindness perhaps, then this neologism *ocularnormativism* denotes the effect: the perpetuation of the conclusion that the supreme means of perception is necessarily visual.

The significance of science fiction becomes still more profound in chapter 5, where the groping blind figure is considered on a macrocosmic level, as a personification of contagious blindness. In order to explore this recurrent motif as it occurs in works of the early, mid-, and late twentieth century, John Varley's "The Persistence of Vision" (1978) and José Saramago's *Blindness* (1995) are juxtaposed with "The Country of the Blind" and *The Day of the Triffids.* Though separated by decades in their publication, all four works portray the blind as a social majority that imposes blindness on the sighted minority. The motif of contagious blindness is, therefore, considered for its resonance with the prejudicial behavior of avoidance and, more specifically, issues of institutionalization.

Instrumental in working out who should and who should not represent human society, the eugenic gaze is a visual means of evaluating so-called good and bad stock but becomes still more concerning when its object does not perceive by visual means, when the gazer remains unseen, and it is this scenario that chapter 6 investigates. Of course the objectification might be thought of in relation to the Samsonean trope of the blind spectacle that can be traced back to ancient times, whereby blindness effectively becomes a source of pleasure for the sighted beholder. But the inclusion of this dynamic in twentieth-century literature is particularly noteworthy because of the resonance with the controlling force in

George Orwell's *Nineteen Eighty-Four* (1949) and Michel Foucault's work on panopticism in *Discipline and Punish* (1975). With reference to Brian Friel's *Molly Sweeney* (1994), as well as a couple of the texts introduced elsewhere in the book, and aiming to supplement Garland-Thomson's work on staring, the chapter considers how the controlling power of the gaze is utilized to bolster the normate subject position of the sighted.

Following the binary logic of the sighted and the blind to its terrible conclusion, chapter 7 illustrates some of the ways in which Joseph Conrad's *The End of the Tether* (1902) invokes the metanarrative of blindness by situating sight loss in a causal relationship with suicide. However, attention is also paid to counternarratives that portray the restoration of sight as the root of despair—such as J. M. Synge's *The Well of the Saints* (1905). These early twentieth-century texts prove noteworthy for their resonance with various contemporaneous and subsequent research projects in which both visual impairment and visual restoration are deemed explanations for suicide. This apparent contradiction is considered with reference to polarized notions of the sighted subject position and the blind, cultural constructs between which a chasm is conceptualized that may seem daunting from either side.

Conclusion

So the story to which those of us who have visual impairments may often find ourselves keyed is frequently invoked and/or explored in twentieth-century Anglophone writing. Readers are implicitly directed to a place in the cultural imagination where the metanarrative of blindness resides. This array of notions is often bizarre but may nonetheless make sense of the text in question. The scenario is in itself problematic but becomes infinitely more so when the same metanarrative is invoked socially, in an endeavor to understand those of us who have visual impairments. It is as though in some minds, in some groups, in some social settings, people become displaced in favor of characters. Through the medium of literature, then, this book explores the metanarrative of blindness, from the underpinning assumptions of ocularcentrism and opthalmocentrism, to the normate subject position of the sighted and the resulting perpetuation of ocularnormativism.

Community, Controversy, and Compromise

The Terminology of Visual Impairment

On the topic of terminology, as noted in David Mitchell and Sharon Snyder's introduction to *The Body and Physical Difference* (1997), there has been "much debate within the disability community" (25), from which we may infer a couple of things that are germane to this chapter: first, that there has also been much debate without the disability community and, second, that the community is not undermined by debate. Indeed, in part, it is because there has been so much debate without the disability community that the debate within is now inevitable.[1] The language we use is institutionally ableist, from the etymology to the most sophisticated of metaphorical applications, meaning that our choice of terminology is inherently problematic. Explored at some length in this chapter, these are the conditions in which we work, and I, for one, must admit to arriving at nothing better than a terminological compromise, even while departing from my learned colleagues in literary and cultural disability studies—and, more specifically, from those in the field of representing visual impairment.

The chapter considers a selection of concepts, models, and critical approaches that, for the past three or four decades, have informed various debates within the disability community about terminological typology. Attention is paid to dominant terms like *blindness* and *the blind,* the usage of which went largely unchallenged until the 1960s but was, and is, fundamentally troublesome. Consequently, several critical responses were ventured as the disability movement gained momentum in the 1970s. Most important, as pointed out in Colin Barnes and Geof Mercer's *Disability* (2003), the radical social model of disability challenged the idea that disability was an "inescapable biological destiny" (12); it drew a line between biological impairment and social disability. Given this empowering shift it is perhaps ironic that many academics and activists have endeavored to strengthen the disability community by problematizing the radical model, that some have endorsed a move toward a diverse cultural model in which the use of language plays a no less important part. Indeed, the terms used in this book, *people who have visual impairments* and *people who do not have visual impairments,* assist the deconstruction of the metanarrative of blindness by ascribing lack to the normate subject position.

Ableist Traditions

When considering the terminological typology of visual impairment, not to mention the effect of ocularnormativism and the representation of people who have visual impairments in general, a concept with which we should be familiar is ocularcentrism. This term denotes a perspective—and, by extension, a subject position—that is dominated by vision, as is illustrated with reference to language and metaphor in Martin Jay's *Downcast Eyes* (1994):

> Even a rapid glance at the language we commonly use will demonstrate the ubiquity of visual metaphors. If we actively focus our attention on them, vigilantly keeping an eye out for those deeply embedded as well as those on the surface, we can gain an illuminating insight into the complex mirroring of perception and language. Depending, of course, on one's outlook or point of view, the prevalence of such metaphors will be accounted an obstacle or an aid to our knowledge of reality. It is, however, no idle speculation or figment of imagination to claim that if blinded to their importance, we will damage our ability to inspect the world outside and introspect the world within. And our prospects for escaping their thrall, if indeed that is even a foreseeable goal, will be greatly dimmed. In lieu of an exhaustive survey of such metaphors, whose scope is far too broad to allow an easy synopsis, this opening paragraph should suggest how ineluctable the modality of the visual actually is, at least in our linguistic practice. (1)

The paragraph is steeped in explicitly and implicitly visual terms and phrases, unashamedly playful language that informs and is informed by the central figure. This metaphor uses sight as a vehicle, while the tenor of its meaning pertains to knowledge. The result is a positive perpetuation of ocularcentrism that I deem ocularnormative, for the use of visual terms to make epistemological points invokes the notion that seeing is synonymous with knowing, that visual perception is necessarily the normal way of gathering knowledge.[2]

A negative perpetuation of ocularnormativism is demonstrable, too, most obviously in Jay's use of the word *blinded,* the meaning of which pertains to epistemological diminishment. In "common usage today," as Georgina Kleege points out, the word *blind* "connotes a lack of understanding or discernment, a wilful disregard or obliviousness, a thing meant to conceal or deceive," being "far more commonly used in its figurative than its literal sense" (21). The trouble is that the figurative has some bearing on the literal sense because common metaphors such as "turn a blind eye," the example provided by Barnes and Mercer, reinforce an "impression of incapacity and abnormality" (17). These metaphors also form a basis for the antithetical impression—namely, the capacity and normality of sight. Thus, the word *blind* and its variants effectively ground the ubiquitous seeing-knowing metaphor. To this end, blindness is used as a vehicle, the tenor of the meaning being the lack of knowledge. That is to say, the seeing-knowing metaphor is profound because embedded in its foundation is the idea that not seeing is synonymous with not knowing.

The word *blind* is problematic because it denotes much that bears no intrinsic relation to visual impairment. For example, Lennard Davis points out that the word *blind* contains "moral and ethical implications" (*Enforcing Normalcy* 5) and as such resonates with the religious models of disability that interpret blindness as a punishment for sin. Other extrinsic and extraneous meanings are evident in the *Encarta World English Dictionary* (*EWED*) (1999), which contains no fewer than thirteen entries for the adjectival form:

> **blind**
> **blind** [blīnd] *adjective*
> **1. unable to see:** unable to see, permanently or temporarily
> **2. unable to recognize:** unwilling or unable to understand something • *blind to the consequences*
> **3. uncontrollable:** so extreme and uncontrollable as to make somebody behave irrationally • *blind rage* • *blind fear*

4. **unquestioning:** not based on fact and usually total and unquestioning • *blind prejudice*
5. lacking awareness • *a blind stupor*
6. **not giving a clear view:** not giving a clear view and possibly dangerous • *a blind corner*
7. SEWING **made on underside of fabric:** hidden from sight on the underside of a fabric
8. **without doors or windows:** without doors or windows, or not enclosing an open space
9. **closed at one end:** closed off at one end • *a blind unused tunnel*
10. **done without looking:** done without looking or while unable to see • *blind taste tests*
11. **done unprepared:** done without preparation or the relevant information • *a blind presentation*
12. **with information concealed for unprejudiced result:** used to describe scientific experiments or similar evaluations in which information is withheld in order to obtain an unprejudiced result
13. BOTANY **without a growing point:** used to describe a plant in which growth stops because the growing point is damaged. It may be caused by pests, nutrient deficiency, waterlogging of the soil, or drought.

While the first definition pertains to those of us who have visual impairments, the third evokes the ancient myth in which the angered Samson shakes an inhabited temple to the ground, as it defines blind rage and blind fear as so extreme and uncontrollable as to make somebody behave irrationally. Similarly, though botanical in its usage, the reference to a plant's lack of a growing point might be said to resonate with the myth in which Oedipus symbolically cuts off his generative power by gouging out his eyes, thereby illustrating the blindness-castration synonymy on which I focus in chapter 3. Informing and informed by the foundation of the seeing-knowing metaphor (the idea that not seeing is synonymous with not knowing), the ten remaining definitions are all ocularnormative but can be divided into the categories of ignorance and concealment. In the first category, a person is rendered blind to the consequence of her or his actions if unwilling or unable to understand something; to be in a blind stupor is to be lacking awareness; blind prejudice is an attitude that is not based on fact and is usually total and unquestioning; a blind taste test is done without looking; and a blind presentation is done without preparation or the relevant information. In the second category, which pertains to concealment, a blind corner does not give a clear view and is possibly dangerous; a blind stitch is hidden from sight on the underside of a fabric; a blind wall is without doors or windows; a blind experiment is one in which information is withheld in order to obtain an unprejudiced result; and a blind tunnel is closed off at one end. In brief, the dictionary offers thirteen definitions for the adjective *blind,* but twelve are negative, and only one pertains to visual impairment.

The same problematic pattern occurs elsewhere in the *EWED.* A list of synonyms for the adjective *blind* includes *in the dark, benighted, insensible, screened, inattentive, indiscriminating, misjudging, biased, ignorant, unwise, involuntary, obstinate, impassive, unastonished,* and *dead drunk.* Three definitions are provided for the adverb:

> *adverb*
> 1. **without prior examination or preparation:** without previously thinking about or preparing for something • *You shouldn't buy livestock blind.*
> 2. AIR TRANSPORT **using instruments:** using information from aircraft instruments, without being able to see
> 3. **totally:** totally or utterly (*informal*) • *robbed his clients blind*

The obvious problem is that all three of the definitions are negative, while not one refers to visual impairment. The reference to doing something "without previously thinking" or "preparing" is problematic, too, because as well as chiming with the ocularnormative implications of the seeing-knowing metaphor, it associates blindness with irrationality, an implication sustained by two of the four definitions of the verb:

> *transitive verb* (*3rd person present singular* **blinds,** *present participle* **blinding,** *past* **blinded,** *past participle* **blinded**)
> 1. **make permanently unable to see:** to make somebody permanently unable to see
> 2. **make temporarily unable to see:** to make somebody temporarily unable to see • *blinded by the lights*
> 3. **make unable to judge properly:** to make somebody unable to judge or act rationally • *blinded by rage*
> 4. **confuse:** to make it difficult for somebody to understand something • *Stop trying to blind us with statistics.*

In this instance one of the definitions does refer to those of us who have visual impairments, but otherwise the meanings are again predominantly negative. The image that emerges from the combination of all seven definitions is one of someone who is unprepared, unable to judge or act rationally, someone who is confused. Add to this the adjectival definitions, not to mention the synonyms, and the result is undeniably complex, undeniably ocularcentric, undeniably pejorative toward those of us who have visual impairments, and thus undeniably ocularnormative in its implications.[3]

The etymology, too, is problematic because, illustrating what Donald Kirtley's *The Psychology of Blindness* (1975) refers to as the way in which the "anti-blind prejudices of society are built into our very language" (41), the *EWED* states that the word *blind* derives from an Indo-European expression of confusion and obscurity, which is also the ancestor of *blunder.* The "underlying idea" is of "someone wandering around in darkness," an ocularcentric premise that informs the thesaurus entry that offers "in the dark, benighted" as yet another synonym for the adjective *blind* (*EWED*). As is illustrated in Rudyard Kipling's "They" (1904), when Miss Florence asserts, "I'm all in the dark" (257), and in André Gide's *La Symphonie Pastorale* (1919), when Gertrude is said to reside in a "little universe of darkness" (25), the etymology becomes manifest in many twentieth-century representations of blindness.[4]

For all the fictional examples and their resonance with the etymology of the word *blind,* no degree of visual impairment can place the bearer in a world of endless darkness.[5] Jessica Langworthy's "Blindness in Fiction" (1930) does go so far as to complain that few people "learn to think of normal persons without sight as merely men and women in the dark" (270), but later twentieth-century social studies (e.g., Monbeck) are far more critical of the proposed synonymy. After all, is it not only from the normate subject position of people with vision that darkness *looks* like blindness and vice versa? The thing is that for people who have no experience of visual perception, darkness, by definition at least, is no more relevant than light. Even for people who have past experience of visual perception, observes Deborah Kent's "Shackled Imagination" (1990), subject to "a period of adjustment," the "lack of sight is not comparable to darkness" (par. 3). Coming from a subject position that accommodates the whole spectrum of visual limitations, to accept the notion of blindness-darkness synonymy would be to do likewise with the bizarre notion that when someone without sight sunbathes in the blaze of noon, switches on a lamp, stands in the glare of headlights, a spotlight, flashlight, or whatever, he or she does so in complete darkness. The reality is that the light does not cease to exist, but simply remains unseen by a minority of people whose visual limitations are classed as impairments.

Only in ocularnormative terms does the lack of visual perception induce oblivion to the knowledge that at midday it will be light, at midnight dark, times that in fact may be determined via technology such as talking or tactile watches and clocks, not to mention radio, television, telephone, and so on.

Terminological Modification

All this considered, we might assume the word *blind* and its variants have long since been condemned to the past. Yet the National Federation of the Blind (NFB) assembled in Dallas, Texas, 9 July 1993, and adopted a statement of policy against the iconoclastic avoidance of "such straightforward, respectable words as *blindness, blind, the blind, blind person,* or *blind persons;* others (such as *visually impaired,* and *visually limited*) being undesirable when used to avoid the word *blind*" (Resolution 93-01, qtd. in Jernigan, "Pitfalls of Political Correctness"). I refute this assertion of straightforwardness and respectability here, and elsewhere, with the amassing of pejorative denotations and connotations, but must, of course, acknowledge that while the word *blind* and its variants are typical of the dominant discourse, appropriation is indicative of a response. "Perversely championing the terms of their own stigmatization," assert Mitchell and Snyder, "marginal peoples alarm the dominant culture with a canniness about their own subjugation" (*Narrative Prosthesis* 35).[6] In the terms of the present book, we might say that those of us who have visual impairments may, in some instances, deliberately key ourselves to the metanarrative of blindness by terminological means. Accordingly, although Kleege acknowledges that the word *blind* causes many "problems" (14), that it "has always meant more than merely the inability to see" (21), bearing "a burden of negative connotations and dreaded associations" (19), she also asserts, "Today I am likely to identify myself as blind" (1). Along similar lines, in *Eavesdropping* (2006), Stephen Kuusisto remembers that as a child he was ashamed of his disability, a sadness compounded by his mother's militant rejection of the words *blind* and *blindness:* "I became a soldier of denial and lived in nervous self-absorption. The Americans with Disabilities Act was thirty years away in an unimaginable future. My job was to live in the open without words for my circumstances" (viii).[7] Notwithstanding the problematics of traditional terminology, then, the NFB's, Kleege's, and Kuusisto's declarations of ownership clearly constitute a response to ableism from within the disability community.

The term *the blind* warrants a little more attention, for Kenneth Jernigan's "The Pitfalls of Political Correctness" (1993) makes the charge that the blind "have had trouble with euphemisms for as long as anybody can remember," but the "old notions of inferiority and second-class status still remain." It is my contention, however, that these negative notions are implicit in the very term *the blind,* which contains a tacit nod to the sighted and thus perpetuates the ocularnormative binary logic to which division is intrinsic. We might say that, much as the metaphorical ignorance associated with blindness grounds the epistemological construct of sight, the alterity evoked by the term *the blind* grounds the normalcy of the sighted.[8] The result is that the two constructs are antithetical to each other, and within the dominant ableist discourse the sighted take political precedence over the blind. What is more, as we find in chapter 2, the homogenizing term keys people who have visual impairments to the metanarrative of blindness; it points to an array of universals and grand assertions.[9]

Contemporaneous with Jernigan's "The Pitfalls of Political Correctness" and its endorsement of the NFB's opposition to terminological modification, Colin Barnes's "Political Correctness, Language and Rights" (1993) reminds us that "discussions of language and disability" arise because "disabled people experience discrimination daily and are denied the same rights and opportunities as the rest of the population" (8). Pointing out that in Nazi Germany oppressive "words and phrases were used to justify the attempted genocide of disabled people" (8), Barnes probes the perplexing right-wing notion that political correctness constitutes an argument against, rather than for, terminological modification. This perplexity is illustrated by the way in which the *EWED* defines the adjective *politically correct* as "deliberately inoffensive: marked by language or conduct that deliberately avoids giving offence," yet it is frequently loaded with negative connotations—even within the disability community. Peter White's *See It My Way* (1999), for instance, claims that the "tortuous debate about correct terminology" is a blatant example of "the idea that the best way for disabled people to assert their independence is to make non-disabled people uncomfortable at every turn," a process that adds "absolutely nothing to the sum of people's understanding," having only one aim—namely, "joyously to wrong-foot people who use the wrong words by changing them as rapidly and regularly as possible" (306).[10] Indeed, Kleege uses the term *visually challenged*—listed in the *EWED* thesaurus as a synonym for the adjective *blind*—when "poking fun" at what she calls the "current mania to stick a verbal smiley face on any human condition that deviates from the perceived norm" (10). The trouble is that the charge of political correctness is made not only by persons who appropriate ableist terminology but also, as James Valentine's "Naming and Narrating Disability in Japan" (2002) points out, by "those who want to retain the right to be freely abusive" (219). Obviously it would not be the intention of anyone within the disability community to use language that would cause offense to those of us who have visual impairments, but it should be acknowledged that a side effect of appropriation is expropriation, as the newly legitimated term returns to its original owners, resuming its original purpose.

Before considering some of the alternatives that have been posited in response to ableist terminology, it is necessary to answer the charge that any change causes confusion. Most important at a personal level, according to Caroline Roaf's "Le Mot Juste" (1992), is the "speed and naturalness with which one can adapt one's language to fit one's developing thought," but until a "form of words has been fully internalised, practised, corrected and recorrected, there will be hesitation and clumsy circumlocution" (340). For this reason it is argued that euphemisms and politically correct language can "obscure clear thinking and damage the very people and causes they claim to benefit" (Jernigan, "Pitfalls of Political Correctness"), from which we are bound to infer that traditional terminology does not cause confusion. However, in practice the terminology of, for example, the late twentieth-century British registration system created the juxtapositions of a blind person who could and a partially sighted person who could not read print, or a partially sighted person who required and a blind person who did not require assistance with mobility. Such scenarios may cause confusion because, as Kuusisto puts it in *Planet of the Blind* (1998), blindness is often perceived as "an either/or condition: one sees or does not see" (5).[11] In fact, in the late twentieth century, only about 10 percent of "legally blind" people are reported to have a "complete absence of any visual experience," but most people think the word *blind* "should be reserved to designate this minority" (Kleege 14). Some attitudinal progress is documented in "The Wind Gets in My Way" (1999), where Sally French writes, "I have used a white stick for 30 years and have noticed a change in people's responses especially in recent times. It used to be the case that people assumed total blindness, but now the question 'Are you partial?' is common. Similarly, if I am treated as a totally blind person and I say 'I can see a bit' this does not give rise to surprise" (24). That said, French recognizes that even in the late twentieth century people would have been confused if, having used a white cane to cross a busy road, she were to fold it up and read a book, and in our own century the fact that "the blind see anything at all" remains "often surprising to many people" (Kuusisto, *Eavesdropping* xii). So it is evident that, wherever we position ourselves in the terminology debate, there can be no denying that the word *blind* causes confusion.

Because this book focuses on Anglophone literature, the examples used are largely Western, but the debate about new terminology is global. In Japan, the original term *mekura* has been recognized as discriminatory and given way to the alternative *mōjin,* which is itself coming to be replaced by *me na fujiyū na kata* and *shikaku ni shōgai no aru kata,* equivalents of the English terms *people with a visual handicap* and *people with a visual disability* (Valentine 219). Similarly, as observed in Shridevi Rao's "'A Little Inconvenience'" (2001), the colloquial term *inconvenience* is used in Calcutta, India, to reduce the psychosocial burden of pejorative meanings that are attached to conceptions of impairment and disability. Far from anticipating this discursive social strategy, though, Kirtley doubts that terminological modification can appreciably mitigate negative attitudes: "New terminology is not likely to be effective unless such attitudes have already improved, for without this change, the older, prejudicial meanings would simply become reattached to the liberalized vocabulary" (41). I endorse this point in various American, British, German, and Spanish publications[12] but continue to pose the same questions. How can attitudes improve through the use of ableist terminology to which prejudicial meanings are inherent? Though admittedly not a solution in itself, can terminological modification really be cited as part of the problem?

Based on the word *sight,* the most obvious of alternative terms are *the unsighted* and *the sightless.* The first problem with these terms is their application of the definite article, which denotes the homogeneous group that is deconstructed throughout the present book. But what I must stress here is that, although less loaded with extraneous meanings than *the blind,* as umbrella terms *the unsighted* and *the sightless* are manifestly erroneous. The term *unsighted* implies congenital sight loss, which is relatively rare and not a necessary condition of blindness in any sense of the word (legal or otherwise). The term *sightless* denotes the absence of sight, yet as Kleege, Kuusisto, and French illustrate, this is another unnecessary condition of blindness. Even the 18 percent of "registrably blind" persons who, according to Ian Bruce, Aubrey McKennell, and Errol Walker's *Blind and Partially Sighted Adults in Britain* (1991), had nothing more than light perception (6), were not sightless. To so consider themselves, strictly speaking, these people would have been keying themselves to the metanarrative of blindness, illustrating the traditional ableist attitude, as would someone who had adventitious sightlessness but considered herself or himself unsighted.

Though now deemed offensive, and so defined in the *EWED,* the term *visual handicap* is posited as the least contemptuous alternative to *blindness* in Jacob Van Weelden's *On Being Blind* (1967). Derived not from the stereotype of the cap-in-hand blind beggar, as is sometimes thought, but from a mid-seventeenth-century hand-in-cap betting game, the sporting implication of the term is literally that superior competitors are allocated a visual impairment in order that they become equal to their inferior counterparts. This evocation of beneficial blindness, or compensatory powers, is problematic due to its ascription of alterity, but a late sense "switched from the idea of a superior competitor being weighed down to a newer sense of an inferior unduly burdened with a disability" (Davis, *Enforcing Normalcy* xiii). Accordingly, when in 1980 the World Health Organisation (WHO) commissioned Philip Wood to classify *handicap*—alongside *disability* and *impairment*—it was defined as a "disadvantage for a given individual, resulting from an impairment or disability," that limited or prevented the "fulfilment of a role" that was "normal (depending on age, sex and social and cultural factors) for that individual" (27–29). This definition is problematic on various counts, one of which pertains to the underpinning binary logic, how the implicit representation of abnormality grounds the meaning of the word *normal.* This meaning will obviously vary from person to person but, according to Wood's definition, does not involve disadvantage, impairment, disability, limitations, and so on. Given that it is not really possible for anyone's normality to be so defined, this scenario amounts to another invocation of the normate subject position explored in the introduction to the present book.

Published a decade or so ago in the *Journal of Visual Impairment and Blindness* (*JVIB*), some of my own initial responses to ableist terminology were based on the transitive verb *inhibit*—from the past participle stem of the Latin *inhibere,* "to hinder" (*EWED*).[13] The suggestion of terms like *visual inhibition* soon proved wholly inadequate but nonetheless provocative when Stuart Wittenstein, the superintendent of the California School for the Blind, entered the debate through a letter to the *JVIB* editor. Evidently unaware of my own visual impairment, Wittenstein's retort was that "the blind" should "lead the terminology decision making" (133), an assertion that was obviously well meant but problematic insofar as it implied, and depended on, homogeneousness. A more productive contribution to this discussion appeared in the form of Scott Lunsford's "The Debate Within" (2006), a Bakhtinian analysis of terminological typology that sited authority in an intertextuality of authorities, rather than in any one person or organization. Lunsford raised the germane point that conflict does not dissolve the notion of community, to which I return later in this chapter.

Another of my tentative contributions to the debate, "Terminology and the Psychosocial Burden of Blindness" (2004), followed the example of various disability scholars in America, taking, as it did, the term *people with disabilities* to the more specific level of *persons with visual disabilities*. The proposition was that with no ascription of homogeneity or other such inaccuracies, this term might be applied to the group of people who are, after all, of no particular class, gender, ethnicity, sexuality, age; people with and without multiple disabilities; people who, with varying degrees of severity, have numerous congenital and adventitious eye conditions. There is a drawback, however, according to proponents of the British social model of disability, because the preposition *with* implies that people carry, or are accompanied by, disabilities, meaning that environmental factors are intrinsically ignored. While a solution to this terminological problem can be found in French's "The Wind Gets in My Way," insofar as the author refers to herself not as a person with a visual disability, but a visually disabled person, it must be acknowledged that the word and variants of the word *disability* are products of ableist ideology, that, as Davis points out, even when seized on in an endeavor to control their usage, they still serve "at least two masters" (*Enforcing Normalcy* xv). This dichotomy is demonstrable when the *EWED* states that the adjective *disabled* is "used to describe somebody with a condition that makes it difficult to perform some or all the basic tasks of daily life," defining the noun *disability* as a "medically diagnosed condition that makes it difficult to engage in the activities of daily life," the erroneous implication being that at the time of the dictionary's publication, in 1999, the medical model was universally accepted. In fact, within the disability community, social models had been endorsed for decades.[14]

The Radical Social Model and Debates Within

Before considering the radical social model in more detail, it is worth reminding ourselves of the problems with previous approaches. The individual and medical models, as acknowledged in Mairian Corker and Tom Shakespeare's *Disability/Postmodernity* (2002), perceived and classified disability in terms of a metanarrative of deviance, lack, and tragedy, assuming it to be "logically separate from and inferior to 'normalcy'" (2). This reification of normalcy and emphasis on lack were evident in Wood's *International Classification of Impairments, Disabilities and Handicaps* (1980), which defined *impairment* as "any loss or abnormality of psychological, physiological or anatomical structure or function," and *disability* as "any restriction or lack (resulting from an impairment) of ability to perform an activity in the manner or within the range considered normal for a human being" (27–29). The trouble is that in these terms progress would necessarily involve rehabilitation if not cure, an assumption that does not recognize or even accommodate the achievements of people who have permanent impairments. These achievements had little purchase with the charity and medical models of the past, whereby, as observed in Lennard Davis's *Bending Over Backwards* (2002), people who had impairments were "seen variously as poor, destitute creatures in need of the help of the church or as helpless victims of disease in need of the correction offered by modern medical procedures" (12). Indeed, the "value" of the "healing professions" was "largely secured by their willingness to attend to populations seen as inherently lacking and unproductive within the social circuit" (Mitchell and Snyder, *Body and Physical Difference* 1). In a nutshell, there was a culture of ableism from which the disability community had to rise, a dominant discourse that fostered the retort that a medical solution was being sought for a social problem.

This medicalization of disability was frequently challenged from within the disability community in the second half of the twentieth century. In the "Proceedings of the First World Congress" (1982), for example, the Disabled People's International (DPI) redefined *impairment* as the "limitation within the individual caused by physical, mental or sensory impairment" and *disability* as "the loss or limitation of opportunities to take part in the normal life of the community on an equal level with others due to physical and social barriers." This definition was an improvement on its precursors insofar as it recognized the potential for progress in the removal of social barriers, rather than locating it in rehabilitation and cure. Indeed, the radical social model was developed in Britain by activists and academics such as the Union of the Physically Impaired Against Segregation (UPIAS) in the 1970s, Vic Finkelstein in the 1980s, and Mike Oliver and Colin Barnes in the 1990s. Comparable American models were emerging at the same time—namely, the civil rights model, which was based on the struggles of African Americans, holding that people with disabilities were "minority citizens deprived of their rights by a dominant ableist majority," and "the social model, which saw disability as a constructed category, not one bred into the bone" (Davis, *Bending Over Backwards* 12)—but the more radical British model was perceived from outside the disability community as the most controversial.

That is the potted history, the terminological distinction of the radical social model being more fully explicated in the work of, among others, Colin Barnes. In "Visual Impairment and Disability" (1996), for instance, Barnes asserts that in practical terms his impairment has caused him few difficulties: "it causes me no pain and, hitherto, has and is likely to remain relatively stable. The problems I have encountered have all been socially created" (37). The idea is that we may use the term *impairment* with reference to the effects of retinitis pigmentosa, retinal detachment, cataracts, diabetes, glaucoma, macular degeneration, tumors, injury to the optic nerve, and so on, but the word *disabled* denotes the consequence of living in an ocularcentric, ableist society. That is to say, those of us who have visual impairments become disabled as a result of society's continual assumptions about visual acuity. It might be that important mail and other documentation is only provided in standard print, or that audio description is not available at events or with multimedia texts, or that websites cannot be navigated using keystrokes, or that job application forms cannot be completed electronically, or that guide dogs are not allowed into certain establishments or vehicles, or that pavements are blocked by parked cars or unkempt trees, and so on.[15] Pertaining to employment, housing, transport, education, training, and leisure, the diverse list of examples goes on and on, the common factor being that in each instance disability can be avoided through some kind of social reform.[16]

The radical social model has been an invaluable resource in the United Kingdom for decades, but following the work of Jenny Morris, Liz Crow, and Sally French, among others, conflict and yet more controversy within the disability community became increasingly apparent at the turn of the century. The main criticism that some disabled people made of the model, according to Mike Oliver's "Defining Impairment and Disability" (1996), concerned the disjunction between disability and the experience of impairment. While arguing that there is still a great deal of mileage to be gained from the social model, Oliver illustrates the counterposition with reference to Sally French's work, which claims that visual impairment can impose social restrictions that are not resolved by the principles of the social model, such as the inability to recognize people and read or emit nonverbal cues in social interactions. Likewise, Tom Shakespeare and Nicholas Watson's "The Social Model of Disability" (2002) argues, on the grounds that people are disabled by their bodies as well as by social barriers, that the model has "outlived its usefulness," that the time has come to "put the whole thing to one side and start again" (sec. 1). Indeed, according to Shelley Tremain's "On the Subject of Impairment" (2002), the strict division between the categories that the radical social model is "claimed to institute is in fact a chimera," because advocates argue that while impairment is not sufficient, it is a necessary condition of disability: "Proponents of the model do not argue that people who are excluded, or discriminated against on the basis of, for example, skin colour, are by virtue of that fact disabled, nor do they argue that racism is a form of disability" (42). More than being outdated, then, according to Tremain, the radical social model of disability is fundamentally flawed. The result of this debate is that endorsements of the radical social model are deemed controversial in some quarters, as are criticisms in others, a state of affairs that is sometimes considered damaging to the disability community but, for me, merely goes to demonstrate that notions of homogeneousness are purely mythical.

There can be no denying that society is frequently disabling in relation to employment, housing, transport, education, training, leisure, and so on, the moot point being only that there are instances in which a person's cognitive and/or physical limitations are more significant. To venture an example, it is pointed out in French's "The Wind Gets in My Way" that, for those of us who have visual impairments, going out is more difficult on a windy day because the wind makes a noise that obscures the small auditory cues that can be so helpful (21).[17] Postmodern theory recognizes the epistemological value of such experiential knowledge and so values a multiplicity of "discontinuous and fragmentary" narratives (Macey 236). One postmodern concern is that the social model seeks to "explain" disability universally, creating, as it does, totalizing narratives that exclude important dimensions of disabled people's lives and knowledge (Corker and Shakespeare 14). Metanarratives "claim to have a universal status, and to be able to explain all other narratives. They therefore attempt to translate alternative accounts into their own language and to suppress all objections to what they themselves are saying" (Macey 167). For instance, in Tom Shakespeare's most controversial work, *Disability Rights and Wrongs* (2006), it is pointed out that although the term *people with disabilities* is generally used in an endeavor to promote social inclusion, expressing the common humanity that disabled people share (chap. 3), the extent to which an academic, organization, or policy uses the terminology of the social or medical models has become a litmus test of their value (chap. 2). In other words, although the radical social model has troubled the metanarrative of deviance, lack, and tragedy into which the previous models translated disability, a postmodern concern is that the grand assertion that people are disabled only by society may be indicative of yet another metanarrative.

It is quite evident that recent debate within the disability community has been informed by postmodern theory, but this relationship is by no means parasitic. Considering the "range of impairments under the disability umbrella," the "different ways in which they impact on individuals and groups over their lifetime," the "intersection of disability with other axes of inequality," and the challenge that "impairment issues to notions of embodiment," Corker and Shakespeare argue that disability is the "ultimate postmodern concept" (15). Disability, according to Davis, can be thought of as the "postmodern subject position" and "may turn out to be the identity that links other identities," ultimately replacing postmodernism with what he calls "dismodernism"—a notion that "ushers in the concept that difference is what all of us have in common"; that "identity is not fixed but malleable"; that "technology is not separate but part of the body"; and that "dependence, not individual independence, is the rule" (*Bending Over Backwards* 13–14, 26). This conception of disability as the identity that links other identities heralds a cultural and, by extension, social model that addresses Tremain's point about the strict division on which the radical model is based because, according to the assertion that "we are all disabled by injustice and oppression of various kinds" (Davis, *Bending Over Backwards* 31–32), biological impairment is not a necessary condition of social disability.

The implication in this brief account may be that medical and individual models were displaced in favor of revolutionary social models, and that medical and individual models themselves displaced moral and religious models, yet, according to Patrick Devlieger's "Generating a Cultural Model of Disability" (2005), these modes of thought are intertwined more often than juxtaposed. This claim is indicative of the cultural model, as Devlieger describes it, recognizing existing modes of thought that confirm the complexity of disability as an existential, technical, and social phenomenon. As well as evoking Davis's notion of dismodernism, not to mention the corpus of Mitchell and Snyder's work, Devlieger's approach chimes with Shakespeare's rejection of the radical social model in favor of an alternative that recognizes the predicament of bodily limitation and difference without reducing disability to a medical problem (*Disability Rights and Wrongs*).[18] With the benefit of such work, along with this chapter's opening discussion of ocularcentrism and ocularnormativism, we can return productively to French's contention about the inability to recognize people and read or emit nonverbal cues. If unresolved by the principles of the social model, these restrictions may be appreciated in cultural terms. I say this because when the cultural assumptions of social interactions are rejected, we soon discover that the inability to recognize people arises from a lack in verbal rather than visual communication, the essence of the problem being that the dominant social convention is to acknowledge a person by speaking to her or him, but not to identify oneself nominally. The person who breaks this ocularnormative convention and offers her or his name when greeting people who have visual impairments contributes to a culture of difference and dependence, rejects the privileging of visible identity in favor of a new social convention that is not, in these circumstances at least, disabling.[19] The salient detail about the cultural model, according to Devlieger, is that it points to an identity, community, and worldview that embraces disability. This perspective reduces the significance of eye contact, a form of communication that is irrefutably, yes, irrefutably valuable, but the privileging of which is an example of the ocularnormativism perpetuated by language on many levels (from etymology to metaphor and beyond).[20]

Conclusion and Compromise

The aim in this chapter is not to dictate which terminology should be used by or about those of us who have visual impairments, but to provide some rationale for the choice of terminology that is used throughout the book. Barnes, French, Jernigan, Kent, Kirtley, Kleege, Kuusisto, and White are already emerging as some of my mentors in the field of representing visual impairment, yet their approaches to terminological typology are diverse and frequently differ from my own. What is more, on the topic of terminology, there is much debate within the disability community about the very need for a debate, for although some assert that the study of terminology, sentence use, and discursive language should take a more central role in disability studies (e.g., Devlieger), others warn against becoming fixated with such matters (e.g., Shakespeare, *Disability Rights and Wrongs* chap. 2). Lunsford's Bakhtinian analysis accepts that authoritative discourse is fixed, that it demands acknowledgment and helps to solidify the ideologies of a community, but Lunsford concludes that if we cease debating about words and their meanings, we lose authority over them; they will continue to have authority over us. It is in this spirit that I admit to having no fixed solution to the problem, although the term *people who have visual impairments* is adopted as a compromise throughout the book.[21]

In accordance with the ethos of the cultural model, this terminological compromise is informed by various approaches, the most obvious being the person-first strategy that the NFB considers not only controversial but "totally unacceptable and pernicious when used as a form of political correctness to imply that the word *person* must invariably precede the word *blind* to emphasize the fact that a blind person is first and foremost a *person*" (qtd. in Jernigan, "Pitfalls of Political Correctness"). I must depart from Jernigan and the authoritative discourse of the NFB on this issue because, for me, person-first terminology does not emphasize; it merely reflects the fact that someone who has a visual impairment is primarily a person; it embodies Kleege's point that if she were to list adjectives to describe herself, "blind would be only one of many, and not necessarily the first in significance" (4). I proceed, therefore, on the understanding that person-first terminology discursively acknowledges a simple, uncontroversial fact—namely, that the personhood of those of us who have visual impairments is on a par with that of those of us who do not have visual impairments.

The shift away from the adjective and variants of the adjective *blind* is explained comprehensively in this chapter; the term *visual impairment* emerges as a viable alternative. More specifically, the noun *impairments* is adopted for three reasons: first, because it alludes to the radical social model from which I remain reluctant to depart entirely; second, because it denotes plurality and thus reduces implications of homogeneousness; and third, because it accommodates the continuum of visual limitation, being defined in the *EWED* as a "lessening or the absence of a particular physical or mental function." This continuum from absent to lessened is significant because Kleege, Kuusisto, French, and Bruce et al. all problematize the simplistic notion that people are either sighted or blind. Following Davis, Shakespeare and Watson, and others who recognize the universal experience of the body's limitations, my choice of terminology reflects the fact that because vision has inherent limitations, everybody is visually limited, nobody can see everything, meaning that a continuum exists between people who have high visual acuity and people who do not perceive by visual means. A legal distinction may be drawn somewhere between people who have visual impairments and people who do not have visual impairments, but in practice it will always be problematized by eye conditions that are complex, temporary, variable, and so on.

Finally, it should be clarified that the book is not indicative of a refusal to use variants of the word *blind,* or hackneyed labels such as *the blind, the blind girl,* and *the blind man,* for this terminology is newly appropriated in a strategy of cultural dissociation. Given the continuum of visual limitation and the various terminological issues, a conceptual distinction is posited between those of us who have visual impairments and the blind that is comparable to the distinction that has been drawn between impairment and disability: the latter in both cases is a cultural construct.[22] If only for the duration of this book, then, I refer to various autobiographers, novelists, poets, academics, social scientists, and participants in research projects as people who have visual impairments, reserving the application of the adjective *blind* and its variants for references to literary characters, tropes, motifs, stereotypes, and the mythos of blindness in general. Indeed, I go so far as to argue that it is frequently the word *blind* that refers us to a metanarrative of blindness, a state of affairs I now explore with reference to character designation.

Character Designation

Normate Reductionism and Nominal Displacement

So disability may be understood as a malleable identity that links other identities, and because we are all visually limited a continuum may be identified between those of us who have high visual acuity and those of us who do not perceive by visual means. This postmodern, indeed dismodern perspective recognizes that complex, temporary, and variable eye conditions problematize the distinction between those of us who are and those of us who are not identified as having visual impairments; it marks a departure from notions of the sighted and the blind that, as binary oppositions, are embedded in the Modernist project of the twentieth century. If we ignore the continuum of visual limitation, then we implicitly endorse the normate subject position that, narrowly defined as antithetical to the whole range of deviant Others, contrasts starkly with the subject position envisaged in dismodernism. That is to say, in a conceptual clash that reveals the very essence of social prejudice, the dismodern subject position is all accommodating, whereas the normate represents a prohibitively exclusive ideal.[1]

Manifestations of the resultant normate reductionism can be found in twentieth-century writing if attention is paid to character designation—that is, to the ways in which literary characters are named and otherwise denoted. Most obviously, the sense of subjectivity is reduced when authors paradoxically fail to ascribe proper nouns,[2] as is demonstrable in many characters known only as the blind man.[3] But a more complex variant is the device of spoiled nominal identity, the actual or effective use of an adjective as part of a character's name.[4] In such cases blindness is overtly posited as a key characteristic. Indeed, flying in the face of the person-first tenet considered in chapter 1, the problematic adjective *blind* is used as the primary component in the naming of several literary characters.[5] In accordance with the process of normate reductionism, this method of designation reflects that a character is, first and foremost, blind.[6]

The specific form of character designation on which the chapter focuses is nominal displacement—by which I mean the strategic setting aside of names in favor of labels.[7] With this device in mind it is worth setting the historical scene, regressing to where early twentieth-century institutions foreshadow the death camps of Nazi Germany in their numeric displacement of nominal identity. Of course the psychosocial significance of this displacement is profound, a person's name being "part of the central core of the self-image" (Gross 619). But selfhood was of no concern to the authorities in 1923 when, as documented in Steve Humphries and Pamela Gordon's *Out of Sight* (1992), the nine-year-old Ted Williams became an inmate at Sheffield's Manchester Road School for the Blind. On the day of his arrival he was required to change into the school uniform, and his own clothes were stored in the wardroom. He was allocated a number, forty-three, by which he was to be known for seven years. The number appeared on all of his possessions and even indicated where he had to stand in queues and so on. The objective, according to Humphries and Gordon, was to crush the personalities of the children and "shape them into a narrow and rigidly conformist mould" (68). This process of putting normate reductionism into practice on an institutional scale was bolstered if not enabled by the policy of discarding names. After all, if nominal identity is central to the self-image, then disruption of the one may result in disruption of the other. The numeric displacement of nominal identity betrays a blatant denial of selfhood and indeed personhood, an objectifying scenario that, as this chapter shows, resonates in numerous representations of blindness.

"No One Marries a Blind Girl"

In exploring character designation we can chart the progression of nominal displacement with reference to a sample of early, mid, and late twentieth-century literary texts. Analogous to the way in which names were discarded in favor of institutional numbers, many blind characters are ascribed names that are strategically displaced by labels that refer to blindness—most obviously, *the blind girl* and *the blind man.*[8] Corresponding with an assertion made by Jacques Derrida, that the "illustrious blind of our culture are almost always men, the 'great blind men,' as if women perhaps saw to it never to risk their sight" (*Memoirs of the Blind* 5), the male variant is the more common. But because the aim, here, is to chart progress, and the label *blind girl* is more consistently disempowering, it makes sense to begin the survey by considering a subsample of texts that illustrate nominal displacement in relation to female blind characters.

The earliest of these texts, Rudyard Kipling's "They" (1904), is an eerie tale told by an unnamed man who becomes lost when driving through a rural landscape of wooded hills. He soon finds himself on the grounds of a house to which he is repeatedly drawn. This apparently alluring estate belongs to Miss Florence, who has been blind since she was just a few months old and yet, for some reason, remains preoccupied with visual perception. Accordingly, although considered beautiful and manifestly maternal, she cannot imagine a blind person married or raising children, as noted in Kenneth Jernigan's "Blindness: Is Literature against Us?" (1974). It is as though blindness negates the very prospect of procreation, her solitary comfort being that she has the psychic capacity to mother the many infantile phantoms by whom she is surrounded—that is, the ghosts of locally deceased children.

The details for us to note pertain to the ways in which Miss Florence's name is discarded when the narrator hears the "voice of the blind woman crying" (245); when Mrs. Madehurst, the keeper of a nearby sweetmeat shop, exclaims that her grandchild is gravely ill and "the blind woman" steps forward (248); and then again when "Mrs. Madehurst and the blind woman" are convoyed to the child's sickbed (249). The last of these examples is particularly revealing because it contains a counterpoint, nominal displacement being emphasized by the narrator's adjacent use of Mrs. Madehurst's name. This use, moreover, represents a designation shift because, in the narrator's tongue, the "fat woman" (244) becomes Mrs. Madehurst, whereas Miss Florence, on the contrary, is always referred to as the blind woman. Some labels are evidently more adhesive, or socially acceptable, than are others.

Emphasized by means of repetition and contrast, Kipling's application of nominal displacement raises a couple of intriguing questions. Why is Miss Florence's name only ever used in reported speech? Why does the narrator always refer to her as the blind woman? Whatever Kipling's intention may have been, the effect is that, unlike the sighted character

Mrs. Madehurst, Miss Florence is implicitly distanced from the narrator. This maneuver illustrates what Ato Quayson refers to as the "interaction between a disabled and nondisabled character, where a variety of tensions may be identified" (15). The nature of the tension in Kipling's example becomes evident if we take a somewhat Freudian approach to the haunted existence and consider the possibility that there may be the ghost of a chance for Miss Florence's procreation, that her implied asexuality is merely a distraction from the narrator's latent desire. That is to say, it may be argued that she is distanced from him in a disavowal of attraction that ultimately protects his normate subject position.

Though defined in no small way by her various responsibilities, Miss Florence is deemed infantile by the narrator, a detail that contributes to the conscious distraction from his unconscious desire and therefore resonates with André Gide's *La Symphonie Pastorale* (1919). Superficially this novel is about a pastor who adopts a newly orphaned blind girl, but we soon recognize it as a far more sinister exploration of sin, religion, and hypocrisy. The narrative opens with the eponymous pastor retrospectively but quite obviously worming himself into the role of the blind girl's sighted savior. He reminisces about his first meeting with, or rather discovery of, Gertrude, whom he was compelled to save from the workhouse on pious grounds. He sets out to visit the house of a dying woman in good faith, but the central hypocrisy is implicit when Gertrude is found crouched at the corner of the hearth, her last remaining relative having just died, for the pastor's moral obligation only becomes imperative when he learns she is about fifteen years of age, soon after which he notices her fine, regular features. Her age becomes more ambiguous as the story progresses, especially when the pastor suggests she may have been a "good deal older" than was initially supposed (35), but the specter of pedophilia cannot go unnoticed. Gertrude is repeatedly referred to as a child—and, what is more, likened to the pastor's own young daughter, Charlotte. Indeed, initial suspicions that the pastor is moved by something other than sympathy are eventually confirmed.

The thing for us to note is that the pastor's desire may be traced in a designation shift from the label *blind girl* to the name *Gertrude*—a name that is not her own but is chosen by Charlotte and adopted by the rest of the family. Nominal displacement is recurrent in the opening pages, as illustrated when the pastor recalls how a neighbor seemed barely aware of Gertrude's existence, let alone her name, referring to her thus: "The blind girl there. She's a niece, the servant says" (11). The pastor also remembers turning "towards the blind girl," informing the neighbor of his ostensibly honorable intentions, and how the "blind girl allowed herself to be taken away like a lifeless block" (12). More than to objectify Gertrude, then, her name is discarded to evoke a sense of distance and, more specifically, to ascribe infantile and thus asexual qualities that disguise the pastor's attraction, as is illustrated once more when he remembers arriving home, placing his hand on "the blind girl's head," and telling his family that he had brought back the proverbial lost sheep (14). Thereafter Gertrude's name takes precedence over the label as she is systematically humanized in accordance with the pastor's design. Thus, the unknown name is displaced in favor of the label, which in turn is displaced by the adopted name, the salient detail being that the narrator stops referring to Gertrude as the blind girl when admitting his desire.

What happens as the story unfolds is discussed later, the point for us to note at this juncture being that Gide's application of the label *blind girl* has objectifying, infantilizing, and asexualizing connotations that can also be found in more recent texts such as Mary Norton's "The Girl in the Corner" (1951). This short story tells of a train journey that brings Pippa and her daughter Mary together with a group of fellow passengers, of whom one, the title character, Ivy, happens to be blind. The various attitudes toward this fact create the underpinning tension, yet Ivy's name is used only once. Instead, we are informed that the "blind girl leaned her head against the upholstery," that the "blind girl's eyes had turned towards the kitten," that Mary "leaned across to the blind girl," that the "blind girl looked startled," that the "blind girl began to smile," and finally that the "blind girl sat in the stationary train under the light, in the corner—as she had been told" (12–15). Her name is repeatedly displaced in favor of the objectifying and infantilizing label that seems even more noteworthy than in Gide's example, for although Gertrude is in her midteens, Norton's Ivy is in her late twenties. But irrespective of Ivy's age and indeed marital status, the asexualizing connotations of the label seem curiously pertinent. I say this because although her maternal nature, if not longing, is implicit when she holds the kitten, "guarding it, checking it, directing it," before "laying her cheek against the soft fur" and asking her husband, "Why couldn't we have one of these?" (14), actual motherhood seems no more a possibility for Ivy than it is for Gertrude, whose sexual activity is deemed null and void until her sight is restored. In fact, for neither Ivy nor Gertrude does the prospect of procreation seem any greater than for their solitary forebear Miss Florence.

A noteworthy successor of Norton's Ivy can be found in Susan Sontag's *Death Kit* (1967), the story of a businessman, Dalton Harron (or

Diddy for short), who spends much of his time trying to figure out whether or not he has battered to death an obstinate railroad worker. He believes the incident took place while his train was stuck in a tunnel, but according to fellow passenger Hester, this can be nothing more than a daydream. While Hester's version of events is tinged with doubt on account of her blindness, it is she with whom Diddy strikes up a romantic relationship. Nominal displacement is nonetheless illustrated when the narrator expresses Diddy's sweeping opinions about blindness, asserting that if "one is blind one is compelled to trust everyone" or "no one" and that he "wished he had fewer alternatives, like the blind girl" (27). We are also informed that Diddy is unnerved by "the blind girl's infinite enclosure in herself" (87) and that a "blind girl couldn't stroll on the streets late at night" (202). That these assumptions derive from the metanarrative of blindness can be inferred from the way in which Diddy tells rather than asks about Hester's experience, her character being surpassed by a preconceived notion of what it is to be a blind girl.

The objectifying connotations notwithstanding, Hester differs from Miss Florence, Gertrude, and Ivy in at least one respect. The "helpless, passive" Hester is, as Deborah Kent puts it, "not only sexually active, but also aggressive and uninhibited. Within half an hour of meeting Dalton on a train, she leads him into an empty washroom for a scene of passion" (par. 17). The marked difference between Norton's and Sontag's notions of how a blind girl might pass the time during a train journey is illustrative of Kent's point about blind characters benefiting from the sexual revolution, for Ivy is a product of the early 1950s and Hester of the late 1960s. I argue in chapter 3 that the scene of passion is not entirely at odds with the infantilization motif, but the detail for us to note here is that Hester's fervor is beyond the symbolically castrated character whom Diddy conjures up, that when he applies the label *blind girl* his meaning is consistent with those of Norton's narrator and Gide's pastor, as well as with Kipling's characterization of Miss Florence.

Evidently, the label *blind girl* keys numerous characters to the metanarrative of blindness, but as noted in chapter 1, the question of ownership is paramount. Not only the meaning but also the application of the label *blind girl* remains the same throughout Sontag's and Norton's examples insofar as it is applied *to* rather than *by* Hester and Ivy, much as Kipling's narrator applies the label *blind woman* to Miss Florence. It is worth us thinking a little more about Gide's *La Symphonie Pastorale*, though, for the label is ultimately used by Gertrude herself. She claims that "no one marries a blind girl" (48), from which it seems to follow, in accordance with the twisted logic of the story, that her relationship with the pastor need not concern his wife. Without sight, as asserted in Jacob Twersky's *Blindness in Literature* (1955), Gertrude "cannot consciously know sin"; she is "blissfully ignorant like Adam and Eve before eating of the forbidden fruit" (47). Accordingly, though pursued by not only the pastor but also his son Jacques, Gertrude internalizes the received identity of the blind girl, not appreciating her sexuality until her sight is restored.

In keying herself to the metanarrative of blindness, Gertrude's character may be said to herald an important shift that is found in Stephen King's *The Langoliers* (1990). This work of science fiction depicts an airplane journey to Boston during which everyone who is awake mysteriously disappears. The survivors, of whom one is the blind character Dinah, make an emergency landing at Bangor, only to discover that the whole planet has become deserted. What ensues is a race against time and the apocalyptic threat of the eponymous creatures that devour everything in their path. The fact that the infantilizing label *blind girl* displaces the name *Dinah* thirteen times is appropriate at least insofar as the character is only ten years old, but a more progressive aspect of this novella pertains to self-image. Granted, the label is applied *to* Dinah again and again, as we are informed that the pilot can hear "the little blind girl crying out for her aunt" (81), that Laurel had to "jerk sharply on Dinah's hand to keep the blind girl from running into" someone (145), that Craig thought "perhaps the little blind girl knew something about the Langoliers" (147), and so on. At one point, however, the locus of control shifts to Dinah: "I won't scream, she told herself fiercely. I won't scream and embarrass Aunt Vicky. I won't scream and wake up all the ones who are asleep and scare all the ones who are awake and they'll all come running and say look at the scared little girl, look at the scared little blind girl" (22). Thus, in the first subsample of texts, Dinah is the one character who demonstrates awareness of the assumption that blindness cancels out other qualities, knowing she is perceived in the terms of a preconceived label, as the blind girl above all else. She invokes the metanarrative of blindness but frames it within her own narrative, recognizing it as something outside her experiential knowledge—a scenario that reveals empowerment more commonly found among applications of the label *blind man.*

"The Power of the Blind Man"

The effects of displacing characters' names in favor of the labels *blind man* and *blind girl* are consistent in some respects. This comparison becomes evident when the survey is extended to my second subsample, which includes D. H. Lawrence's "The Blind Man" (1920). This short story depicts an evening in the life of war-blinded Maurice Pervin and his wife, Isabel, who share a relatively isolated but largely contented existence that is disrupted by a visit from her old friend and distant cousin Bertie Reid. There are vague connotations of an eternal triangle, but we are promptly informed that there is neither history nor prospect of anything romantic between Isabel and Bertie. Indeed, it is at Maurice's suggestion that Bertie is invited to visit.

Nevertheless, a sense of friction is implicit in the character designation, as is illustrated if the narrative is divided into four episodes, all of which follow the precedent set by the title insofar as Maurice's name is repeatedly displaced in favor of the label *blind man*. First, prior to Bertie's arrival, it is claimed that "life was still very full and strangely serene for the blind man" (347) and that, during his conversation with Isabel, not Maurice but the "blind man replied" (350). Second, when the three characters are together in the house, we are informed that the "blind man stuck his hand out into space, and Bertie took it" (357); that Bertie "watched the static figure of the blind man" (358); that "the two watched the blind man smelling the violets" (358); that the "blind man was silent" (358); and that the "blind man" only "replied, as out of a negligent, unattentive thinking" (360). That is to say, we are presented with an unbalanced image of "Isabel and Bertie chatting gossip and reminiscence, the blind man silent" (360). Third, when the two men are alone in the barn, we are told that a "large, half-wild grey cat was rubbing at Maurice's leg"—for his name is often used—but that the "blind man stooped to rub its sides" (362); that Bertie "suffered as the blind man stretched out a strong, naked hand to him" (363); and that the "hand of the blind man grasped the shoulder, the arm, the hand of the other man" who was "under the power of the blind man" (363–64). Finally, when the three characters are reunited in the house, Isabel's gaze falls on Bertie because she knows that his only desire is to escape from the intimacy: "He could not bear it that he had been touched by the blind man" (365). These applications of the label *blind man*, especially in the closing scene, are indicative of social friction—what Quayson means by the aesthetic nervousness of an interaction between disabled and nondisabled characters.[9] Maurice's name is used more than fifty times, but nominal displacement repeatedly evokes a sense of distance, and it is in this respect that Lawrence's application of the device is akin to those already discussed, those of Kipling, Gide, Norton, Sontag, and King, among others.

Something similar may be said of Rosamond Lehmann's *Invitation to the Waltz* (1932), which—set in the year of Lawrence's publication, 1920—portrays the emotional shift from childhood to adulthood as it is experienced by a middle-class adolescent, Olivia Curtis. The action of the novel begins with her seventeenth birthday and ends a week later, following a much-anticipated dance at the country house of her aristocratic neighbors, the Spencers. Though set just a couple of years after World War I, the historical context is largely (if not purely) implicit in the first instance, as Olivia and her sister Kate struggle to find male partners to accompany them to the dance. But the brutal realities of war eventually erode the bourgeois façade, not least because of the meeting with Timmy Douglas, the war-blinded character to whom the label *blind man* is applied both indirectly and directly. The indirect application is illustrated when Timmy is led to the dining room by Olivia and said to have "walked with a light quick step straight on his course, his touch on her arm almost imperceptible; not at all like one's idea of the shuffle and grope of a blind man" (257). That is to say, not only a received understanding *of* but also a departure *from* the metanarrative of blindness is implied. Yet Timmy is later seen sitting back, "his head slightly bent, the muscles taut in his face, waiting," and we are informed that "now he looks like a blind man" (258). The indefinite article in this observation is clearly indicative of a totalizing scheme, denoting, as it does, the idea of an identity that is common to all blind men, from which it follows that the character in question is in danger of being displaced. Accordingly, in spite of their introduction, dancing, and intimate conversation, when Olivia later spots Timmy it is not his name that springs to mind; she is said to have "noticed the blind man sitting by himself in the little room that opened on the ballroom" (285). This direct application of the label contributes to the connotations of distance and loneliness—a poignant image that resonates with the ending of Norton's "The Girl in the Corner," when the blind girl clings to a kitten for company in an otherwise empty train.[10]

While the identities invoked by the labels *blind man* and *blind girl* are similar in some respects, there are noteworthy differences, as illustrated in Henry Green's *Blindness* (1926).[11] The central character, John Haye, a budding young writer, is blinded when a stone smashes the window of his homeward train after a term at the Public School of Noat. He aspires to practice his chosen profession in the towns but, following the accident, feels trapped in the family's country home. His sense of hopelessness is worsened by attitudes toward blindness that are epitomized when Emily Haye, John's stepmother, supposes that he "would not meet any nice girls now, he could never marry. A girl would not want to marry a blind man" (61). This pessimistic supposition echoes the claim of Gide's Gertrude (that no one marries a blind girl), but by the end of Green's novel hope is restored insofar as John has moved to London and is set to start writing again.

Where Green's application of the label *blind man* differs from those already considered is in the connotations of empowerment. The novel informs us that, as "all blind men," John "would do everything by touch, and he would have tremendous powers of hearing" (50), a claim that is bolstered with reference to a "tiny sound, miles away," that "no one but a blind man could possibly have caught" (75).[12] Notwithstanding the generalization of these remarks and the problematics of compensatory powers that are analyzed in chapter 4, Green may be said to provide an early literary representation of what David Mitchell and Sharon Snyder call "the moment when the derided object embraces its deviance as value" (*Narrative Prosthesis* 35). "I will be a great writer one day," says Green's John, "and people will be brought to see the famous blind man who lends people in his books the eyes that he lost" (161). We might say that, unlike the texts considered thus far, *Blindness* applies the term *blind man* as a source of pride rather than shame, a badge rather than a label.[13]

Thomas Wolfe's novel *You Can't Go Home Again* (1940) also uses nominal displacement to evoke empowerment, but the formulation is overtly pejorative, based, as it is, on fear. The story is about another fictional author, George Webber, whose first novel is a great success but renders his hometown of Libya Hill in a way that is deeply offensive to the residents. On this level and many others, home becomes a place to which George can no longer return. He does, however, revisit the town for the funeral of his aunt Joyner, who raised him after the death of one parent and the desertion of the other, and it is then that he meets the feared blind character Judge Rumford Bland.

It is worth us noting Quayson's comment that the "embarrassment, fear, and confusion" with which disabled people are confronted on a daily basis become "translated in literature and the aesthetic field" as a "series of structural devices that betray themselves when the disability representation is seen predominantly from the perspective of the disabled rather than from the normative position of the nondisabled" (19). I raise this point because, coming from a perspective that is appreciative of disability, it is clear that Wolfe—like Norton and Sontag—portrays a train journey during which a blind character is scrutinized from an ocularcentric subject position. The name of Judge Rumford Bland is displaced a couple of times when the train in question begins to move, and the narrator observes that "a blind man appeared at the rear of the car. The other people were talking, reading, or dozing, and the blind man came in so quietly that none of them noticed him enter. He took the first seat at the end and sat down" (55). Exemplifying what Quayson calls the primary level of aesthetic nervousness (15), Judge Bland fills George with fear:

> [George] stopped and spun round. The blind man was seated there before him. He had almost forgotten about him. The blind man had not moved as he spoke. He was still leaning a little forward on his cane, his thin, white face held straight before him as if he were still listening for something. George felt now, as he had always felt, the strange fascination in that evil shadow of a smile that hovered about the corners of the blind man's mouth. (64)

The third-person narrator may be said to occupy the subject position, but the implication is that the point of view aligns with the protagonist George, rather than with Judge Bland, because it is the former's feelings and the latter's appearance that are being described. Biased in this way, the narrator repeatedly displaces Judge Bland's name in favor of the label *blind man,* the result being a mocking malevolence, with which the fascination continues as we are informed that the "blind man, never moving, in his terrible toneless voice that carried to all ears, broke in" (64); that in a "simple phrase, spoken by the blind man, there was the suggestion of a devilish humour" (65); that the "blind man cackled thinly to himself"; that there was an "evil ghost-shadow of a smile at the corners of the blind man's mouth"; and that the "smile still played about the blind man's mouth" (66).[14] Moreover, George is said to have "soon learned that his fear and panic in the blind man's presence were shared by all the people in the car" (67), emotions that are very different from the implicit and sometimes explicit pity felt by, for instance, the fellow passengers of Norton's Ivy and Sontag's Hester.

Nominal displacement is indicative of a comparably biased narrator in what has been described by Georgina Kleege, among others,[15] as Raymond Carver's retelling of Lawrence's "The Blind Man" (Kleege 87), namely, the short story "Cathedral" (1983). Like Lawrence's "The Blind Man," Carver's "Cathedral" depicts a married couple's attitude toward the wife's close friend. Again there are vague connotations of an eternal triangle, again we are made aware that there is no extramarital romance, again there is a sense of friction between the men, and again the label *blind man* is applied to create a sense of distance. But "Cathedral" is different because the visitor rather than the husband is blind, and, more significantly, the application of the label *blind man* is overtly problematic. From the outset we are positively encouraged to disapprove of Robert's objectification, for the narrator reveals his prejudice unambiguously. We are well aware that, regarding the visit, the narrator's lack of enthusiasm derives not just from the fact that he and Robert have never met: "His being blind bothered me. My idea of blindness came from the movies. In the movies, the blind moved slowly and never laughed. Sometimes they were led by seeing-eye dogs. A blind man in my house was not something I looked forward to" (292). So even before their meeting, the narrator reduces Robert to the identity of the blind man that in turn signifies an array of universals. Indeed, Carver's use of the indefinite article suggests that the narrator has issues with blind men in general, regarding them as a homogenous group, a sentiment that is reinforced when he says he "didn't want to be left alone with a blind man" (300). The implication is that the narrator is afraid of blind men, but, importantly, it is made clear that this fear has no experiential basis.[16]

The unreliability of Carver's narrator is underscored by his overt manipulation of nominal identity in general. Though remarkable that Robert's name is displaced so many times in fewer than sixteen pages, it is even more so that the narrator's wife remains nameless throughout. She has no nominal identity to displace. The resentment implied by this omission may be said to have an implicit sexual basis because the narrator complains that he and his wife "hardly ever went to bed at the same time" (302). But whatever the motivation, the omission must be interpreted as a sign of resentment because we are made aware of the narrator's attitude toward nominal identity and its manipulation. For example, he refers to his wife's previous husband, the air force officer, as her officer, asking, "Why should he have a name? He was the childhood sweetheart, and what more does he want?" (294). To ascribe a name would be to acknowledge the subjectivity of the officer in a way that is beyond the overtly jealous narrator, the implication being that nominal displacement and nominal omission are employed as defense mechanisms, that the resultant objectification is psychologically beneficial. By referring to his wife, her officer, and the blind man, rather than using their names, the narrator reduces the pain of his jealousy and thereby reveals the significance of nominal identity. This significance is further illustrated when Robert jokes about the gray in his beard and asks if he looks distinguished, and the narrator articulates his wife's response: "'You look distinguished, Robert,' she said. 'Robert,' she said. 'Robert, it's just so good to see you'" (297). The narrator relates this repetition with a growing sense of disturbance, thereby revealing that he resents his wife's use of Robert's name because initially, like the officer, he is perceived as a sexual threat. It would seem, therefore, that the label *blind man* provides the narrator with a comforting distraction from Robert's sexual capacity. In other words, the normate narrator has a clear agenda for keying Robert to the metanarrative of blindness.

While Carver's narrator is unreliable because of his overt prejudice and sexual jealousy, Martin Blom, one of the narrators in Rupert Thomson's *The Insult* (1996), is manifestly delusional, even if we never have it confirmed (in a postmodern way his very unreliability is unreliable). In this psychological thriller, Martin is shot in the head as he walks to his car in a supermarket car park, the apparent result being permanent blindness. Defying medical science, however, Martin soon discovers that he can see in the dark. He begins to lead a nocturnal existence, parodying the motif of blindness-darkness synonymy considered in chapter 1, chapter 5, and chapter 7. Though not unusual for this motif to expand into the nocturnalism that spells danger in the cultural imagination, Thomson's approach is atypical insofar as Martin can, or thinks he can, or at least says he can see in the dark, and it is on this basis that he becomes more active at night.[17] But the consequence is bittersweet because, although Martin meets and has an exhilarating relationship with the lustful and alluring Nina Salenko, he also becomes a suspect when she is brutally murdered.

Akin to Carver's "Cathedral," Thomson's *The Insult* is quite candid in its illustration of normate reductionism when Martin roams the hospital in the early hours. He puts on his dressing gown and reaches for the white cane that he now carries at all times, regarding it as part of a disguise.[18] "If I was caught," he says, "I was just a blind man who'd got lost on his way to the lavatory" (31). Martin's overt acknowledgment that he would be seen as *just* a blind man may be read as an allusion (if not a response) to normate reductionism that is bolstered when a woman working as a prostitute later shouts, "Hey, blind man. I'm fucking beautiful and you can have me for twenty-five" (71). When Martin is so addressed, nominal displacement is illustrated vehemently; it is unabashed and thus quite likely to elicit a reaction from the late twentieth-century readership.[19] That the reductive label functions as a key to the metanarrative of blindness is still more apparent during an audacious sexual encounter in a public library, when Martin warns Nina that such meetings would not be possible with a sighted man. "What are you telling me?" she murmurs. "You're the only blind man in the city?" (126). This exchange shows that Martin's charm has no specificity, deriving, as it evidently does, from beyond his character.[20]

It would be misleading, however, to suggest that the most recently published text in the sample is necessarily the most appreciative of disability. I say this because, notwithstanding the criticisms of ableism that are apparent in Martin's narrative, questions are raised by the uncertainty of his blindness. Being seen as *just* a blind man in the hospital setting is certainly significant, as though, in the medical environment, normate reductionism can be taken as a given (a reading that chimes with contemporaneously published criticisms of the medical model of disability considered in chap. 1). What is more, Martin's sight may well be read as a refreshing departure from the problematic binary system, as an allusion to the fact that most people who have visual impairments have so-called residual vision, and many are affected by night blindness, sensitivity to light, and so on, meaning that variable vision is relatively common. But the trouble is that Martin's clash with his medical diagnosis and prognosis deters us from reading him as an empowered blind character. After all, when he assumes control of the nominal displacement, it is precisely his apparent sight that complicates any inference that may be drawn about appropriation: the reluctant Martin expresses disbelief that Inge would want to dance "with a blind man" (82); when caught trying to flee from the police he defends himself by saying, "A blind man? Making a run for it?" (142); and the neurosurgeon Bruno Visser, when held at gunpoint and warned not to "try anything," says he "wouldn't dare," laughing nervously at the notion of "a blind man with a gun" (247). In so deflecting awkwardness from various situations, Martin's narrative refers to the blind man in ways that draw on tacit inadequacy. Of course we must not ignore the fact that the effect of Martin's remarks is manifestly ironic.[21] In terms of the disability movement, as Mitchell and Snyder point out, the "embrace of denigrating terminology forces the dominant culture to face its own violence head-on because the authority of devaluation has been claimed openly and ironically" (*Narrative Prosthesis* 35). The complication in *The Insult* is that Martin's embrace may or may not be considered ironic, depending on the authenticity of his blindness. Given that irony is based on opposites, Martin's assertion of inadequacy constitutes an acknowledgment of capability, but is the effect not canceled out if and when blindness is being used to mask his sight? With allusion to dismodernism I would say that perhaps the real irony is that, in the absence of a reliable medical diagnosis, this apparently postmodern text endorses the metanarrative of blindness.[22]

Conclusion

In this chapter the focus is largely (if not purely) nominal, stopping short of any profound analysis but revealing much about how the terminological issues discussed in chapter 1 impact the designation of literary characters. The social sciences tell us that a name is neither chosen arbitrarily nor neutral in its function as a label, having various associations and the capacity to stimulate numerous responses (Gross 619). This psychological insight is germane to the literary study because the labels *blind girl* and *blind man* are employed to evoke a sense of distance. The scenario can be explained with reference to aesthetic nervousness, which, as Quayson states, is not limited to tense interactions between disabled and nondisabled characters, being "augmented by tensions refracted across other levels of the text such as the disposition of symbols and motifs" (15). This chapter illustrates that character designation can function in a way that is akin to these symbols and motifs and, though focusing on nominal displacement, repeatedly exposes tensions between blind and sighted characters. It follows that these tensions resonate with labels such as *the blind girl* and *the blind man*. But I would go as far as to say that these labels are indicative of the tension between blind and sighted characters, often providing the very means by which the relation is short-circuited.

While the survey is by no means definitive, it is reasonably representative of twentieth-century texts that contain representations of blindness and nominal displacement. Within these texts female blind characters are underrepresented, a state of affairs that accords with Derrida's claim about familiar blind figures being nearly all men, as though women are somehow less likely to be, or become, visually impaired. In part, this imbalance can be said to reflect the fact that an increased number of men became visually impaired as a result of warfare in the first half of the twentieth century, cultural concerns about which manifest in the characters of Lawrence's Maurice Pervin and Lehmann's Timmy Douglas.[23] Judging by this chapter's study of character designation, however, the prevalence of the blind man continues in the second half of the twentieth century, a detail that illustrates Mitchell and Snyder's assertion that the "repetition of a representational formula (or anti-formula) draws out the often discomforting 'fit' between literary disability and the 'real' of disabled peoples' historical experiences" (*Narrative Prosthesis* 9). After all, Anglo-American records from the second half of the twentieth century state that in fact visual impairment is more prevalent among women.[24] In other words, the chapter's sample of literary texts concurs with Derrida's assertion about the masculine prevalence among well-known blind figures but contrasts harshly with the documented numbers of people who have visual impairments contemporaneously.

Finally it should be emphasized that qualitative as well as quantitative factors add to the gender imbalance. While the label *blind girl* consistently invokes a disempowered figure, the more common masculine counterpart is evocative of both empowerment and disempowerment. That is not to say that the corresponding female characters are necessarily flat in relation to their male counterparts, for the chapter's focus is on the symbolism of the labels rather than the content of the characters.[25] Even on this level, though, the sexual connotations cannot be ignored. In Thomson's *The Insult,* for example, nominal displacement effects a hypersexualized distraction from Martin's subjectivity that is very different from the examples set by Gide's *La Symphonie Pastorale* and Kipling's "They," whose invocations of the blind figure serve precisely to disguise desire. This distinction is indicative of the fact that the metanarrative to which the characters are keyed contains a hypersexual/asexual binary that I now begin to explore with reference to literary depictions of symbolic castration.

Come-to-Bed Eyes

Ophthalmocentrism, Ocularcentrism, and Symbolic Castration

As we consider the mechanics of the way in which labels such as *blind girl* and *blind man* invoke the metanarrative of blindness, it becomes clear that blindness-castration synonymy is something of a cardinal motif. Though easily traced back to ancient times, the motif is used in many ways and afforded new significance by Modernism, especially in relation to eugenics and psychoanalysis. In fact, Charles Rycroft's *A Critical Dictionary of Psychoanalysis* (1968) states that the word *castration* frequently denotes things other than anatomy, surgery, the removal of the testes, things such as masturbation, asexualization, and emasculation. That all three of these denotations accord with the metanarrative of blindness is the starting point for this chapter.

The first thing to note about the trilogy of denotations is that masturbation and asexualization are often interrelated. Rather than anatomy, the word *castration* may pertain to the loss of the penis, as in "threats used to deter little boys caught masturbating" (Rycroft 15). This definition corresponds with an institutionalized anxiety, masturbation mania, that was experienced by many people who had visual impairments in early twentieth-century Britain.[1] It has been documented, for instance, that at the Royal Manchester Road School for the Blind, one pupil was bemused by the severity of the punishment incurred when caught play fighting with another boy: he was given hundreds of lines about being rude to himself, was ignored for days, and had a reprimanding letter sent to his father (Humphries and Gordon 103). Such was the preoccupation with masturbation that any sign of dormitory activity was deemed suspicious. Hence, at the Birmingham Royal Institution for the Blind, another boy was not only falsely accused but also taught that masturbation would lead to the loss of his remaining vision (Humphries and Gordon 104).[2] The underpinning assumption at the time was that people who had visual impairments would not have sexual partners, that masturbation was the only available means of expressing erotic desires. But despite this reductionism, while neither sterilization, marriage restriction, nor compulsory segregation became formal government policies in early twentieth-century Britain (Snyder and Mitchell 120–21), sex segregation was pursued with vigor in most of the institutions where disabled people lived (Humphries and Gordon 101). "We would go back to school in January," recalls a former pupil at the Royal Manchester Road School for the Blind, "and we weren't supposed to speak to any girl until we went on holiday in July" (Humphries and Gordon 102). This regime, in its endeavor to reduce the capacity for erotic pleasure, corresponds with the second of Rycroft's definitions of the term *castration.* I say this because in effect, as with the numeric displacement of names considered in chapter 2, both sex segregation and masturbation mania keyed people to the metanarrative of blindness on an institutional scale.[3]

Like masturbation and asexualization, asexualization and emasculation are often interrelated. The "social role of men is to be starers," observes Rosemarie Garland-Thomson in *Staring* (2009), and looking masculinizes (146, 42), from which it follows that the inability to look emasculates, an inference that invokes Rycroft's definition of castration as demoralization in respect of the masculine role.[4] In the second half of the twentieth century, according to Allan Dodds's *Rehabilitating Blind and Visually Impaired People* (1993), some men suffered severe identity crises, wishing to be recognized as women when presenting for rehabilitation. Dodds's explanation is that the profound and powerful emotions unleashed by visual impairment bring some men face to face with aspects of themselves that they have previously deemed too feminine and wished to develop, perceiving, as they do, that masculinity can no longer be easily expressed (3–4). But another explanation is that the emasculating castration motif has become part of the metanarrative of blindness to which men who have visual impairments are keyed, largely (though not solely) by others. Man's social role is starer, woman's social role is staree; looking masculinizes, being looked at feminizes; and we all internalize and identify with the requirements of the system (Garland-

Thomson, *Staring* 146, 42). In accordance with this ocularnormative system, it is rendered crucial not only that a man can look, stare, and/or gaze but (given the seeing-knowing synonymy considered in chap. 1) also that a woman can see that she is the object of the look, stare, and/or gaze. Either way, visual perception is necessary if we are to avoid psychosocial castration.

In this chapter, all three of Rycroft's definitions of castration are explored with reference to blindness in twentieth-century writing. More specifically, returning to a couple of the novels introduced in chapter 2, Henry Green's *Blindness* (1926) and Susan Sontag's *Death Kit* (1967), the analysis focuses on literary examples of masturbation mania, asexualization, and emasculation. But first, in order to explicate some of the ways in which blindness-castration synonymy was perpetuated in the last century, attention is paid to psychoanalytic and erotic examples of eye symbolism. This symbolism is underpinned by ocularcentric notions of desire, a cultural focus on eyes and vision to which blindness-castration synonymy is antithetical. The ocularnormative result is that the blind, as a culturally constructed group, are placed beyond erotic desire and vice versa.

The Story of the Eye

When considering blindness-castration synonymy a concept with which to be familiar is ophthalmocentrism. Though related to *ocularcentrism,* the neologism *ophthalmocentrism* is distinct insofar as it describes fixations not on vision but on the instrument of vision, as in notions of eyes that are sexy, innocent, hot, cold, hard, soft, kind, evil, honest, lying, and so on. The term has certainly proven useful in my own work,[5] following the remarks made by Georgina Kleege about eyes being the most frequently mentioned feature in love poetry:

> Beautiful themselves for their gemlike color and liquid sheen, eyes not only are windows into the soul, but they also can send elaborate messages of love. They glow with affection, smoulder with passion, dilate with emotion. When we gaze into the eyes of the beloved and see a reflection of ourselves, our narcissistic tendencies are gratified. Now, as in the past, women spend more time and money accentuating, highlighting, lining, defining, and emphasizing their eyes than any other feature. (*Sight Unseen* 23)

Given this cultural construct of attractiveness I am tempted to begin by saying that, whereas ocularcentrism aligns with scopophilia, ophthalmocentrism aligns with exhibitionism, the one with the look, stare, and/or gaze, the other with the object of the look, stare, and/or gaze. But this binary distinction proves simplistic as consideration is given to the diversity of the eye symbolism that permeates the twentieth-century cultural imagination.

In a century whose first year is marked by the publication of Sigmund Freud's *The Interpretation of Dreams* (1900), psychoanalytic interest in eye symbolism is apparent from the outset. Of the erotogenic zones, as is pointed out in Freud's *Three Essays on the Theory of Sexuality* (1905), while "liable to be the most frequently stimulated by the particular quality of excitation whose cause, when it occurs in a sexual object, we describe as beauty," the eye is "perhaps" the "most remote from the sexual object" (130), but the contrary is frequently said to be the case in the unconscious. In "The 'Uncanny'" (1919), for instance, Freud asserts that a "study of dreams, phantasies and myths has taught us that anxiety about one's eyes, the fear of going blind, is often enough a substitute for the dread of being castrated" (352). In the unconscious, agrees Karl Abraham's "Manifestations of the Female Castration Complex" (1920), the "fixed stare" is "often equivalent to an erection" (352). These assertions are indicative of the fact that early twentieth-century Freudian writings allude more and more to the ancient myth in which Oedipus, upon discovering that his lover is in fact his mother, symbolically castrates himself by gouging out his eyes.

Following Freud's return to Oedipus, Sandor Ferenczi's *First Contributions to Psychoanalysis* (1916) refers to several case studies that link eyes with genitalia (270–74). There is a woman who has a phobia of sharp objects and frequently injures her eyes with needles, Ferenczi's interpretation of which points to the fact that she is sexually intimate with a male friend but avoids penetration for fear of rupturing her hymen. There is a man whose small-penis complex is said to become manifest in the shame of his myopia. There is a family whose members suffer an exaggerated fear of eye injury, supposedly a reaction to their wish to injure the eye, a wish that is said to be a displacement of sadistic coital desire (as one vulnerable organ is substituted for another). There are several anxiety dreams, featuring eyes that grow alternately larger and smaller, about which Ferenczi writes, "From the total context I have had to regard these eyes as symbols of the male sexual organ in its changing size" (273). There is another series of dreams in which eyes, as paired organs, are said to represent testicles: "Each part of the face thus becomes the representative of one or more genital areas. The face is especially well adapted (nose in the middle between the eyes and eyebrows, with the mouth below) for representation of the penis, testicles, pubic hair, and anus" (273). Finally, there is the case of a boy who, on learning the course of his parents' sexual relations, turns against his father, fantasizing about paternal castration and displaying intense anger. But the boy's feelings are always followed by remorse and self-punishment, as is illustrated when he inflicts damage to the eyes in his portrait, an act interpreted, predictably, as a disguised castration of the father.

That Ferenczi links eyes with genitalia in many ways is apparent, but the variety is not as wide as it may seem. Most of the referents are biologically masculine, both testicular and penile, and as such betray the phallocentrism of the analyses. I use the word *phallocentrism* because not only the erect penis but also the testes are generally equated with the phallus as a symbol of the reproductive force of life: the erect penis on account of its form and the testes because they are supposed to bear witness to a man's virility. But the masculine bias may be disrupted if the cultural grounding of blindness-castration synonymy is further explored.

The eye symbolism considered by Ferenczi resonates with Georges Bataille's *The Story of the Eye* (1928).[6] Bound to be classified as pornographic, given that it depicts a male narrator's account of his many and varied sexual ventures with the central female character, Simone, this novella is nevertheless often read in philosophical terms. It "features a number of named characters with an account of their sex play" in Madrid, Seville, and elsewhere, but according to Roland Barthes's "The Metaphor of the Eye" (1963), it "really is the story of an object" that passes "from image to image" (119). In one of the many graphic episodes, Simone attends a bullfight and on her request is presented with a "white dish containing two peeled balls, glands the size and shape of eggs, and of a pearly whiteness, faintly bloodshot, like the globe of an eye: they had just been removed from the first bull" (51). Connotatively, the testicles become eggs and then eyes, changing yet again when "two globes of equal size and consistency" are later propelled in opposite directions: "One, the white ball of the bull, had been thrust into the 'pink and dark' cunt that Simone had bared in the crowd; the other, a human eye, had spurted from Granero's head" (54). Indeed, when Simone's request for a human eye is answered, she is said to have "instantly amused herself by fondling the depth of her thighs and inserting this apparently fluid object" before slipping it "into the profound crevice of her arse" (66).

That is to say, in part, the story is one of an object that connotes testicular, ocular, and penile images, linking them together, and as such corresponds with the bulk of the case studies cited in Ferenczi's summary of eye symbolism.

Unlike Ferenczi's summation, however, Bataille's applications of eye symbolism are not centered on masculine biology. The "imaginary world" in *The Story of the Eye,* according to Barthes, does not have as its "secret" a sexual fantasy; otherwise the "first thing requiring explanation would be why the erotic theme is never directly phallic (what we have here is a 'round phallicism')" (122). It is more fitting to think in terms of what Nancy Etcoff's *Survival of the Prettiest* (1999) calls the "Fertility Goddess" (71), in which case it becomes evident that, while not directly phallic (in one sense of the word), Bataille's erotic theme certainly relates to the reproductive force of life. The object of the story takes on the form of eggs again and again and as such is directly related to fertility, but in a biologically feminine rather than biologically masculine way. Indeed, so pervasive in the cultural imagination is the egg as a symbol of fertility that Lauren Hutton is compelled to summarize the career trajectory of a model by asserting that as soon as a woman is "out of eggs," she is "out of business" (Etcoff 73). In these terms it is also relevant that Bataille's narrator remembers Simone sucking his eye "as obstinately as a breast" (34) and that "each of her buttocks was a peeled hard-boiled egg" (34–35). Globularity, pairing, whiteness, and alliteration are characteristics that superficially justify Bataille's substitutive relation among eyes, eggs, breasts, and buttocks, features that signify feminine fertility, which in accordance with Etcoff's reading of Darwin constitutes the key component of what makes a woman sexually attractive to heterosexual men.

What is more, while most of Ferenczi's case studies render the symbolism of the eye biologically masculine, the exception that proves the phallocentric rule may also be read in terms of the fertility goddess. In the example of a woman whose preoccupation with eye injuries Ferenczi interprets as fear of losing her virginity, the referent of the eye symbolism becomes the hymen, which, ironically, may be considered a sign of sexual attractiveness (along with the various cues for reproductive capacity). Men talk about "preferring big breasts or buttocks," as Etcoff notes, and are, according to evolutionary psychologists, "automatically excited" by signs of a fertile, healthy woman who has never given birth (71). In this respect, the hymen appeals to a proprietary interest in a woman's fertility, a man's innate desire to be the father of all her babies. In other words, a necessary condition of his complete satisfaction is that he may potentially father her firstborn, which is why the hymen, as a supposed signifier of virginity, has been attributed such cultural significance.

Illustrated in this reading of Ferenczi's and Bataille's classic texts, the one psychoanalytic and the other erotic, is the fact that whether the point of reference be the fertility goddess or the phallus, eye symbolism is frequently considered sexual. In the work of repression, as Ferenczi points out, the eyes "have proved to be specially adapted to receive the affects displaced from the genital region, on account of their shape and changeable size, their movability, their high value, and their sensitiveness" (275), a unisex representation of which we have found in Bataille's *The Story of the Eye*. But following Freud, Ferenczi also considers a more fundamental aspect of the symbolism, adding that the displacement "would not have succeeded so well, had not the eye already had from the beginning that significant libidinous value" (276). That is to say, according to classic psychoanalysis, eyes may unconsciously substitute genitalia for several reasons, not least the frequency at which they are likely to be stimulated by the object of sexual desire. There is no denying that, for some people, the mere sight of someone can elicit arousal, and in the case of voyeurism watching the sexual activities of others becomes the preferred sexual activity. It follows, therefore, that ophthalmocentric constructs of sexual attraction are grounded in ocularcentrism, that notions of sexy, hot, passionate, come-to-bed eyes are underpinned by the cultural significance of the look, stare, and/or gaze.

Blindness as Castration

The cultural construct is ocularnormative because not only ocularcentric but also ophthalmocentric renderings of sexual attraction theoretically place men and women who have visual impairments at a relational disadvantage, given that, in psychoanalytic terms, the removal of or visible injury to the eye or eyes may be unconsciously perceived as a form of castration, as may any severe loss or lack of sight. Indeed, according to H. Robert Blank's "Psychoanalysis and Blindness" (1957), the main "factors of psychoanalytic interest underlying the maladaptations and personality disturbances" of people who have visual impairments are the unconscious significance of three things: the eye as a "sexual organ, including the equation of eye with mouth and with genital"; the eye as a "hostile, destructive organ, including the equation of eye with piercing phallus and with devouring mouth"; and "blindness as castration, as punishment for sin" (1). Of these factors the first and second are manifestly ophthalmocentric, while the third is ocularcentric, the overall implication being that people are symbolically castrated whether their impairments be visible, visual, or both.

Blank's taxonomy of unconscious significance is illustrated with reference to his interpretation of a number of case studies, including that of a woman who is informed that one of her eyes must be removed. She has no vision in the eye, but active disease and unsightly appearance render enucleation necessary. The woman agrees with her doctor but also expresses serious concerns: "Even though the eye is useless and I will look better with a glass eye I don't want any part of me cut out" (Blank 17). This assertion is interpreted as a manifestation of the woman's castration complex. The ophthalmocentric concern is that while the glass eye may be considered preferable aesthetically, it would not function as a cue for her reproductive capacity. In other words, the woman's impairment may well become less visible, but she has developed a profound fear of feeling less attractive, as though the removal were of some vital aspect of her sexuality.

Blank's case studies also provide overtly ocularcentric renderings of personality disturbances associated with visual impairment. For example, there is the case of a woman who is said to reveal unconscious disdain for her femininity, masking it with "masculine strivings" that are contrived to attract maternal love (Blank 3). Because this love has always been given freely to her brothers, the woman is said to associate the deprivation with her lack of a penis, which is why the death of one son and, more noteworthy for us, the visual impairment of another are both interpreted as recastrations. From an ocularcentric point of view, the symbolic status of the boy who has a visual impairment is nullified; he is equated with his deceased brother and paradoxically does not testify to their mother's reproductive capacity.

Echoing Freud's and Ferenczi's ideas about symbolism, Blank's study betrays a link between notions of eyes as unconscious symbols of sexual organs and blindness as castration. That is to say, ophthalmocentric constructs of sexuality are not only grounded in ocularcentrism but also contain implicit evocations of blindness-castration synonymy. Ultimately, therefore, blindness-castration synonymy proves integral to the ocularnormative assertion of sexy, hot, passionate, come-to-bed eyes, which are only afforded such adjectives in the absence of visible and/or visual impairment.

The movement from the conception of eyes as unconscious symbols of sexual organs to the conception of blindness as castration may be found in numerous literary representations. For instance, whether we think of Freudian or Sophoclean renditions of the Oedipus myth, it would be difficult to read Green's *Blindness* without noting the use of eye symbolism. The modernist novel resonates with Blank's interpretation of the castration complex when, for example, the nurse informs John that he has had his eyes removed: "Oh, so his eyes were gone. Now that was irritating, a personal loss. Dore had been furious because his appendix had been removed the term before last, he said it was a blemish on his personal beauty, but eyes were much more personal" (51). Of course there is nothing remarkable about the implication that John's loss is greater than Dore's, that the eyes are far more useful than the appendix and their absence more noticeable to others. But the psychosocial nature of this personal loss becomes more apparent when John endeavors to further his relationship with Joan Entwhistle by paying her compliments about the presumed beauty of her eyes:

> "Yes, they are so calm, so quiet. Such a lovely blue."
> "But they are dark brown."
> "Oh. Then your dress does not match?"
> "No, I suppose not."
> "But what does that matter? They are such lovely brown eyes. And sometimes they light up and burn, perhaps?"
> "How do you mean?"
> "Well . . . But have you ever been in love?"
> "I don't know."
> "Maybe they are burning now?"
> "N-no, I don't think so."
> "How sad. And mine, if they had not been removed, would have burned so ardently."
>
> (153–54)

John has been made aware that Joan is wearing blue and extrapolates from this detail in order to flatter her in ophthalmocentric terms. He has never seen her eyes but nonetheless uses what Kleege calls the "conventional language of love" in which "the eyes are always the focal point" (*Sight Unseen* 76). Consequently, he is deemed deficient. Ophthalmocentric discourse renders eyes the means of expressing desire, as well as its cause, meaning that John is excluded on two counts. He cannot see the beauty of Joan's eyes nor express desire through his own. The deficiency is emphasized when Joan subsequently thinks of "poor John who had no eyes," in contrast with a wonderful dream about "a young man who had made love to her, with blue eyes" (175). The manifest content of this dream would require little in the way of Freudian interpretation, for the latent meaning is barely hidden, the phallic eye symbolism quite evident: corresponding with Freud's, Ferenczi's, and Blank's studies, the dream man seems to make love using his eyes, the very organ that is unavailable to John.[7]

A similarly ophthalmocentric episode can be found in Sontag's *Death Kit,* a close reading of which reveals a portrayal of blindness that accords with the definition of castration as a consequence of masturbation. Soon after their initial meeting on a train, the protagonist, Diddy, tells the blind character, Hester, that he wants to make love to her, and they go into the washroom together. But this encounter does not proceed as we might expect insofar as Diddy is more interested in the unveiling of Hester's eyes than in any other part of her body. True, as Hester stands in only her shoes, stockings, garter belt, and bra, Diddy is "astonished and excited by her sudden virtual nakedness," and, yes, when she removes her bra he "feels his body weaken again, his sex cringe" (32), but the sight of neither her genitalia nor her breasts is articulated. I stress this point only because, contrarily, when Hester removes her glasses the narrative lapses into something of a monologue about eyes:

> Bleached eyes.
> Tiffany glass eyes.
> Eyes like teeth.
> Eyes like cooked white of egg.
> Eyes like a specimen of dried white of egg, prepared for the microscope.
> Eyes like tulip bulbs.
> Eyes like an electric drill.
> Prehensile eyes.
> Guilty eyes.
> Metal eyes.
> Meteor eyes.
> Lima-bean eyes.
> Paper eyes.
> Carrion eyes.

Annealed eyes.
Damp eyes.
Wet eyes: the intricate vial of liquid.
Crisp eyes, soggy eyes.
Tattered eyes, elegant eyes.
Stained eyes, clean eyes.
Creased eyes, smooth eyes.
Rotten eyes, fresh eyes.
Sharp-focus eyes, soft-focus eyes.
Concave eyes, convex eyes.
Bespoke eyes, ready-to-wear eyes.
Stiff eyes, flexible eyes.
Univalve eyes, bivalve eyes.
Single eyes, multiple eyes.
Eyes with and without their outer shell.
Empty eye sockets.
The white hymen of the eyeball.

(Sontag 30–31)

Even when this monologue is over, Diddy remains similarly preoccupied. On the basis that eyes are not only organs of vision, that, like the mouth and hands, they are also organs of suffering, he repeatedly asks Hester if she ever cries. Given that she is undressing at the time, Hester understandably wants to know why Diddy is so interested in her eyes. He retorts that his interest is in her, rather than in her eyes, a claim that we know is disingenuous. But although Diddy's desire is manifestly ophthalmocentric, a symbolic meaning is indicated by the reference to the hymen of the eyeball. This metaphor is reminiscent of the case study in which Ferenczi interprets a woman's frequent eye injuries as manifestations of her fear of rupturing her hymen. In these terms, eyes symbolize genitalia, from which we may gather that tears pertain to sexual satisfaction, as is confirmed when Diddy "drives his last sightless thrust deep" into Hester and "surrenders to his body's need to weep" (33). Thus, when Hester says, "Are you asking me if I've worn out my eyes weeping?" (32), and we are informed that this may well be what Diddy has in mind, the implication is that on a deeper level he is more interested in her sexuality, or rather her castration. Specifically, given the use of the personal pronoun in Hester's question ("Are you asking me if I've worn out my eyes weeping?"), Diddy reveals his suspicion of her excessive masturbation.[8]

Infantilization, Dependency, and Psychosocial Castration

As well as to ophthalmocentrism, the portrayal of blindness-castration synonymy in Sontag's *Death Kit* pertains to manifestly ocularcentric—and, by extension, ocularnormative—discourse. In respect of the gender roles delineated in Garland-Thomson's *Staring*, for example, Hester's deficiency is suggested thus: "Is it so easy for her to be naked with a stranger because she can't see herself being seen? Because exposure of her body to the eyes of a stranger seems no different than exposure of her face to all invisible strangers?" (Sontag 32). As she cannot see that she is the object of the look, stare, and/or gaze, and therefore cannot fulfill the feminine role, Hester is ascribed innocence that verges on the infantile. Granted, as found in chapter 2, Hester differs from many of her predecessors in terms of sexual awareness, yet the scene of passion is not entirely at odds with the asexualizing infantilization motif. There is something "cool and experienced about Hester's undressing," says Sontag's narrator, only to pose the contradictory question: "But does the girl really know what she's doing?" (32). The sexual passion of the scene is repeatedly interrupted by such opposing propositions: first, Diddy asks Hester to remove her glasses, a request that is sexually charged in ophthalmocentric terms, to which she silently agrees but "holds them out, for him to put somewhere safe"; second, Hester unzips the back of her dress, but Diddy "helps her pull it over her head"; third, she pulls down her slip but "extends it to Diddy to take from her"; and fourth, she stands naked, in eager anticipation, but he "piles their clothes on the sink" (30–32). In other words, again and again the suggestion of Hester's sexual prowess is contradicted by her infantilization. Moreover, while the act in which the scene culminates is mercifully free of infantilization, the postcoital activity involves Diddy handing Hester her clothing "item by item, helping with her dressing when he can," setting "her glasses on her face," and asking her if she wants to wash her hands (33–34). Indeed, when later wondering if a "blind person" can be the "best judge of her own safety," Diddy realizes he sounds "much more like an anxious parent than a lover" (235–36). Despite the historical context of the sexual revolution, then, the implication is that Hester and Diddy accept ocularcentric gender roles, meaning that as a woman she is deemed deficient and infantilized as a consequence.

Arguably, in accordance with the dynamic outlined earlier, while Hester is infantilized because she cannot see that she is the object of the look, stare, and/or gaze, Green's John is infantilized because he cannot look, stare, and/or gaze.[9] A dramatic illustration is provided when he needs to be fed by his childhood nanny:

> "What is there for tea, Nan?"
>
> "Well, I thought you might like buttered toast and bread and butter, you always was that fond of at nursery teas, and the Easter cake . . ."
>
> "I'll break the rules and have a bit of that first, Nan, please."
>
> She cuts a slice and begins to feed him bit by bit, at intervals putting the teacup into his hands. She loves doing it. For years she has watched him getting more and more independent, and now she is feeding him again. It is nice. [. . .]
>
> "Would you like a sip of tea again, Master John?"
>
> "Thanks, and some buttered toast."
>
> "I do so love feeding ye, Master John, like I used to with the bottle. I remember . . ." (46)

For many years Nanny has watched John becoming increasingly independent, only to be reduced to an infantilized state in which she is feeding him again, as though his blindness has brought about a second childhood.[10] In psychoanalytic terms, we might say that he regresses to the oral phase of development, as buttered toast, bread and butter, Easter cake, and tea substitute for the bottle, which is in itself a substitute for the breast. Like Diddy, Nanny effectively takes on a parental role, and like Hester, John becomes childlike in a scenario that illustrates the way in which social roles are infused with issues of dependency. As an emasculated man, John comes to occupy the dependent position that is stereotypically occupied by women and children, for in binary terms one must be either independent or dependent.

Taken as a whole, though, Green's novel may be thought of as a "reimagining of blindness," what Kleege calls a "radical departure from the Oedipal tradition in which blindness must be a life sentence of despair and dependency with no hope of respite or parole" (*Sight Unseen* 78). In these terms, while inconsistent with the facts of visual impairment, John's need to be fed serves to bolster the novel's prevailing theme; it marks an early point in the progression toward independence. The "loss of sight" represents, as Kleege puts it, a "change in life that evolves through stages," the titles of the narrative's three sections ("Caterpillar," "Chrysalis," and "Butterfly") implying that the result of the "evolution is a fully matured life-form, natural, independent, even beautiful" (*Sight Unseen* 74). But I would complicate any praise for the state of independence, including that found in Sontag's *Death Kit,* where Diddy, a "chronic if erratic connoisseur of spiritual independence" (78), knows independence of character is "far more potent than physical strength" (8) and has faith in Hester's "independence of spirit" (185). My concern is that implicit in many such assertions of independence there are psychosocially castrating notions of parasitic dependency. To draw a parallel with a point made earlier, we might think of the way in which ophthalmocentric and ocularcentric notions of desire ultimately direct us to blindness-castration synonymy. I would go so far as to say the state of independence is no less extreme nor unlikely than parasitic dependency, the one concept being based on the other and, yes, vice versa. The perpetuation of the naturalness of independence links Green's *Blindness* to the Modernist context from which it hails, the pejorative implication being that dependency is unnatural, avoidable, and undesirable.

In their most extreme, both independence and dependence may be considered psychosocially castrating, for in relation to society the independent person theoretically is situated beyond and the dependent beneath. In practice, however, psychosocial castration tends to involve one party regarding her, his, or their role in such high esteem that the other becomes unacknowledged, the former being perceived as independent, the latter as dependent. Indeed, during the first half of the twentieth century it was precisely the belief that people with impairments were bound to be parasitic that provided an attitudinal basis for eugenics—and, by extension, the policy of institutional segregation in the United Kingdom, the extensive sterilization program in the United States, and the extermination of hundreds of thousands of people in Nazi Germany.[11] When probing the characterization of blindness as psychosocial castration, then, more significant than claims of independence are representational departures from the independent-dependent binary. There is, as Albert Memmi's *Dependence* (1984) recognizes, "in almost every dependency, even if it is apparently parasitic, some sort of symbiotic relationship" (66). With this in mind we might note that Green's John is not the only one to gain in the feeding episode. Given that Nanny uses the verb *love* to express just how "nice" she finds the experience, it is clear that she is benefiting profoundly. Others, too, may be said to profit from the dependency, for his stepmother, according to Kleege's reading, "sees an advantage in keeping John dependent and isolated," because if he "stays single, she could stay on as the mistress of the estate she loves" (*Sight Unseen* 75). Comparable interdependence can be found in Sontag's *Death Kit,* for although Diddy devotes himself entirely to taking care of Hester (228), he feels as if he is "the blind one, utterly dependent on another's good will" (279). These and other acknowledgments of symbiosis point to the middle ground, to the continuum of dependency, to the fact that the extremes of parasitic dependency and independence are both myths. As noted in chapter 1, Tom Shakespeare and Lennard Davis (among others), assert the universality of the experience of the body's limitations, the natural consequence being that everyone is dependent to some extent, that symbiotic dependency is universal.

When deemed parasitic, though, dependency becomes burdensome from one side and suffocating from the other. That is to say, dependency, from the most objectifying of normate positions, is burdensome and thus likely to appear suffocating if and when considered with allusion to the position of the apparent dependent. Accordingly, John's dependency counters the Modernist ideal of the independent subject, defining a state from which to escape. In next to no time he realizes that Nanny is "remembering him when he had hardly been alive," gloating that he is weak and helpless again: "He would have to have her near him day after day, while she bombarded him with her sickening sentimentality" (Green 47).[12] The same sense of suffocation can be found in Sontag's *Death Kit,* when we are informed that attached to Diddy's pledge of devotion there is one stipulation: "Hester is to depend on him, and on no one else. To see the world through him only, not through the eyes of any other. That much is fixed. Diddy won't share Hester with anyone" (228). There is no denying that the subjectivity of the overt dependents is acknowledged in these two novels, but psychosocial castration remains evident because the very idea of dependency is deemed parasitic. To accept this premise would be to conceive of as suffocating for one if not burdensome for the other the arrangements between, say, a runner who has a visual impairment and her guide, a teacher who has a visual impairment and his reader, a piano technician who has a visual impairment and her driver, a shopper who has a visual impairment and the shop assistant, indeed, any person who has a visual impairment and the persons on whom he or she may depend from time to time. This erroneous exemplar may be deliberately or unwittingly applied to all relationships between people who have and people who do not have visual impairments.[13] The inference, as mentioned earlier, may then be that people who have visual impairments do not have sexual partners, that masturbation is the only available means of expressing erotic desires. Although in this respect Hester's character does temporarily depart from the metanarrative of blindness, notably, neither she nor John has a sexual partner when their respective novels end.

Conclusion

Be it feminine or masculine, romantic or erotic, pornographic or psychoanalytic, eye symbolism is frequently sexual. In the cultural imagination eyes are sexy in their appearance, especially in women, and sexy in their function, especially in men. So ubiquitous is the ocularnormative construct that it permeates what is often accepted as common sense. All that said, I am in no way denying that eyes can be beautiful. Nor am I necessarily refuting that eyes may be sexually alluring. Who am I to contend the psychoanalytic proposition of unconscious associations between eyes and erotogenic zones? But as eyes become the fundamental focus of the look, stare, and/or gaze, there is a tacit wink from the normate position that both implicates and excludes people who have visual impairments. Ophthalmocentric renderings of sexual attractiveness are problematic in their implicit exclusion of, for instance, women who have no eyes or whose eyes are visibly impaired. This ophthalmocentrism, moreover, is underpinned by ocularcentric renderings of desire, the psychocultural prominence of the look, stare, and/or gaze that may exclude, for example, men who have visual impairments. The gender divide is explored most famously by Laura Mulvey, work I begin to follow in this chapter by exploring how the masculine/feminine, ocularcentric/ophthalmocentric, and independent/dependent binaries correspond with each other, combining, as they do, in a multifaceted symbolic castration that is central to the metanarrative of blindness. In a deconstructive vein, the chapter shows that cultural notions of sexy eyes are predicated by those of blindness-castration synonymy, and vice versa, and so on, and so forth, meaning that both notions become diminished as a result of exposure to informed criticism and theory. The disruption of binary oppositions continues as I now pick up on the point made at the start of this chapter that, despite the assumption that people who had visual impairments would not have sexual partners, an institutional policy of strict sex segregation was deemed necessary. The implication is that beneath the multifaceted construct of blindness-castration synonymy there is a fear of hypersexuality.

"A Hand of the Blind Ventures Forth"

The Grope, the Grip, and Haptic Perception

If we wish to be unprejudiced in our actions and attitudes, then we do our utmost to resist metanarratives that perpetuate negative stereotypes. That is an undeniable fact. Yet so-called positive stereotyping too frequently remains unchallenged or unnoticed. Extraordinary senses constitute the most obvious example of ostensibly positive stereotyping that, even in our own century, is often aimed at people who have visual impairments. That these lingering stereotypes appear as tropes in twentieth-century literary representation is illustrated in, for instance, James Joyce's exemplary Modernist novel, *Ulysses* (1922), when Leopold Bloom ponders the blind stripling's lack of visual perception: "Of course the other senses are more" (173).[1] But despite the representational frequency of this assumption, as noted in Berthold Lowenfeld's mid-twentieth-century investigation, "The Case for the Exceptional" (1946), not one of the studies that compare the sensory acuities of people who have visual impairments and people who do not have visual impairments reveals any superiority of the former (207). People who have visual impairments may well "learn to use such capacities more effectively," states a later twentieth-century study, but "compensation is not automatic; rather, it is the product of persistent practice" (Kirtley 141). What the present book brings to this conversation is the contention that, more than being inaccurate, cultural representations of extraordinary senses serve, at best, to render magical the talent and achievements of people who have visual impairments and, at worst, to justify the ascription of various animallike characteristics.

Drawing on notions of extraordinary senses in a way that parallels the stereotype of the piano tuner mentioned at the start of the book, another career-based assumption that illustrates the metanarrative of blindness is that those of us who have visual impairments will necessarily make good physiotherapists. Of course some people who have visual impairments might choose, or may have chosen, to follow this particular occupational path, and that is all well and good. But there is a real problem in the assumption that visual impairment is a necessary or indeed sufficient condition of the physiotherapist. Any such assumption is predicated on the stereotypical notion of extraordinary touch, tropological manifestations of which are far from subtle. I make this assertion because blind characters are often ascribed a sense of touch that is grotesque, a grope or even a monstrous grip, rather than simply a means of perception. Owing to the consequential connotations of lecherousness and fear, the implication is that more than being symbolically castrated, as Jacques Derrida points out, the blind have come to present "a sort of phalloid image, an unveiled sex from head to toe, vaguely obscene and disturbing" (*Memoirs of the Blind* 106). This cultural construct resonates with concerns considered in chapter 3—namely, masturbation mania and the eugenic anxieties that were manifest in the strict policy of sex segregation in early twentieth-century institutes for the blind. The thing is that lurking behind the symbolic castration is a specter of hypersexuality, an animalistic lack of control that sometimes becomes manifest in extraordinary senses.

In exploring the bizarreness of extraordinary senses, especially notions around haptic perception, this chapter returns repeatedly to *Ulysses* but also draws on James Kelman's more recent stream of consciousness, the vernacular variant found in *How Late It Was, How Late* (1994). Kelman provides a portrayal of blindness that is told from the perspective of the newly blinded protagonist, Sammy Samuels, and as such contrasts harshly with Joyce's rendering of the blind stripling, a purely peripheral character framed in the internal monologue of Leopold Bloom. But common to both novels is the Modernist myth of independence: Joyce's blind stripling is covertly slated for the kind of dependence from which Kelman's Sammy strives to escape. This myth is entangled with the pseudo-science of eugenics, for the Sterilisation Law was developed by Harry Laughlin in 1922 and targeted, among others, the blind and economically dependent (Kühl 39). As the findings of the chapter become more malevolent, therefore, I also turn to a couple of classic science fiction texts, the famous eugenicist H. G. Wells's short story "The Country of the Blind" (1904) and, what must be its best-known successor, John Wyndham's novel *The Day of the Triffids* (1951). Both works envisage societies in which the vast majority of the population is blind. For Wyndham the result is absolute chaos, a state only worsened by the proliferation of the three-legged, ambulant, malevolent, venomous, and apparently communicative eponymous plants,[2] while Wells imagines a utopian valley where all is well until the arrival of the one sighted character, Nunez.

The starting point in the chapter is something that recurs in all four texts, the idea that people who have visual impairments will also have extraordinary powers of perception, ranging from the magical sixth sense to the overtly sinister monstrous grip. When analyzing the material, however, it soon becomes evident that, while the ascribed powers may well be ostensibly positive, they are underpinned by ocularcentric assumptions and give rise to ocularnormative implications. A counterillustration of what I mean can be found in *The Two-In-One* (1999), where Rod Michalko refers to an interview in which Mark, a three-year-old boy who has a visual impairment, loses a ball but gives up the search after a short while, saying that it can be found more easily by his sighted mother, because "she's got really, really, really long arms" (27). In other words, because touch is paramount for Mark, he assumes it to be likewise in his mother's search for the ball. The fact is that, while quite striking, this scenario is no more erroneous than the ocularnormative antithesis portrayed by Joyce, Kelman, Wells, and Wyndham, the recurrent implication that normalcy depends on visual perception, that any deviation from the primacy of vision is abnormal.

The Fifth-Sixth Sense

Even from an ocularcentric perspective, among representations of people who have visual impairments the only sense that can be deemed extraordinary is sight. After all, as noted in chapter 1, the vast majority of people who are legally blind have residual vision, so the sense of sight should not or at least need not be an extraneous factor. Only 5 or 10 percent of people who are registered as blind will be "unable to make out anything more than changes in light levels," according to one late twentieth-century study, and an "even smaller percentage will be totally unable to perceive even bright sunshine" (Dodds 1–2). But this vast and varied category of visual impairment is seldom represented in twentieth-century writing, the general rule being that characters are either sighted or blind.[3] In other words, unlike the majority of people who have visual impairments, literary representations accord with the binary logic that is emblematic of Modernism.

Rather than considering the complex sight of people who have visual impairments, authors have tended to displace it in favor of what becomes the fifth-sixth sense. Kelman's *How Late It Was, How Late* tells a story that begins with Sammy waking in a lane after a drinking binge. He gets into a fight with some plainclothes policemen, known in the novel as sodjers, and sustains injuries that result in his complete loss of sight. In a rich Glaswegian dialect the narrative furnishes us with a detailed account of blindness that considers social, psychological, and cultural factors. We are informed, for instance, that Sammy "once read this book about bats; they have this incredible sense of hearing, it's sonic or somefuckingthing like they've developed their own radar, compensating the blindness" (100). This memory is noteworthy for us because it is articulated immediately before that of a "blind guy" who could "stand on one side of a wall and know what was happening on the other," who could "actually pick up what was going on in a different room, whereabouts people were standing and all that" (101). Indeed, more than alluding to the blind-as-a-bat simile, the narrative goes so far as to state that it was like the blind guy "had developed some sort of different sense-organ" (101). The fact of the matter is, of course, that someone who has a visual impairment may learn to concentrate on faintly audible clues to her or his environment, as pointed out by several social scientists: "These clues include echoes from nearby objects and structures, echoes which anyone can detect if he [or she] listens closely, but which if never noticed would lead to the belief that there is some sixth sense that enables blind people to avoid obstacles" (Monbeck 17). That is to say, for many people who have visual impairments the task of getting from one place to another does not accord with ocularnormative notions, involving, as it often does, a varied combination of the available senses—not to mention the all-important environmental knowledge.

More than covertly animalizing people who have visual impairments by invoking an honorary membership in the order Chiroptera (or, put differently, by alluding to the blind-as-a-bat simile), the fifth-sixth sense often reaches far beyond logistical matters.[4] Those who confront people who have visual impairments, according to Erving Goffman's *Stigma* (1963), "may have a whole range of belief that is anchored in the stereotype," assuming "the blinded individual draws on special channels of information," that he or she is "subject to unique judgement" (16). This visionary aspect of the fifth-sixth sense ties in with a blurring of the line between dreaming and the waking state, a constructed link that is illustrated in John Hull's autobiographical work, *Touching the Rock* (1990):

> Is there any more to this than metaphor? Am I becoming a creature of the night? Am I not close to dreams? Does not blindness give me an affinity with darkness? If the sun is the symbol of consciousness then the moon represents the magical sources of our deeper life. (122)

As though toying with whether or not to key himself to the metanarrative of blindness, Hull poses a chain of rhetorical questions with a tropological underpinning of what I term nocturnalism, blindness-darkness synonymy, the fifth-sixth sense, and blindness-dream confusion.

What I mean by blindness-dream confusion is illustrated in Joyce's *Ulysses,* when Bloom refers to the blind stripling by pondering, "What dreams would he have, not seeing? Life a dream for him" (174). The relation of "visual impairment to dreaming" is a "topic that has long interested psychologists, as well as curious laymen, both blind and sighted" (Kirtley 169).[5] For example, in Robert Scott's *The Making of Blind Men* (1969), we are told of an instance in which a curious layperson asks a man who has a visual impairment how he knows when he is awake (29). Though far from being profound, this question has been raised *by* (if not *in*) many philosophical works. Indeed, blindness-dream confusion may well be thought of as an exaggeration of the Cartesian philosophy to which Jonathan Rée's *I See a Voice* (1999) alludes: "When we dream of tastes or smells or bodily sensations, we experience them as if they were really affecting us physically" (47).[6] The full significance of Rée's philosophical enquiry becomes a little clearer when, setting aside the sense of sight, he says that dreamed smells, tastes, and touch are genuine, that they form "a kind of bridge into the waking world" (47). If we fall asleep in an uncomfortable chair, for example, we might well end up dreaming of physical discomfort, a consequence of haptic information that becomes a component in the dream state. As is illustrated in what Freud terms alarm-clock dreams, moreover, a comparable bridge between dreams and the waking world may be formed by the sense of hearing:

> I used to make use of an alarm clock [says Hildebrandt] in order to be up regularly at a fixed hour. It must have happened hundreds of times that the noise produced by this instrument fitted into an osten-

> sibly lengthy and connected dream as though the whole dream had been leading up to that one event and had reached its appointed end in what was a logically indispensable climax. (*Interpretation of Dreams* 86–87)

The notion that I am probing with these philosophical points is that because touch, smell, taste, and hearing can all bridge the dream and waking states, while sight apparently cannot, people who have visual impairments are beyond reality.[7] That is to say, in the cultural imagination the blind seem closer to the dream state than are their sighted counterparts. Hence, Derrida recalls effectively keying himself to the metanarrative of blindness so as to sustain (and thus more accurately record) a dreamed experience: "Without turning on the light, barely awake, still passive but careful not to chase away an interrupted dream, I felt around with a groping hand beside my bed for a pencil, then a notebook" (*Memoirs of the Blind* 16). The cultural function of the groping blind figure is considered later in the chapter, so the thing for us to note here is the implication that the manifest dream can only be disrupted by the sense of sight: in fact, as Freud and Rée have shown, this is not even the case before the dreamer awakes. Like the related fifth-sixth sense, blindness-dream confusion is based on ocularcentric sophistry, a charge that, as we now find, may also be made of the less metaphysical senses that are just as mysterious and magical in their cultural construction.

Extraordinary Senses

Though frequently extraordinary, the senses of the blind oscillate between being superhuman and subhuman. When thinking about this claim it is worth us remembering that the five senses, according to Aristotelian doctrine, fall into two categories, of which the first pertains to contact, the second to distance. The contact senses of smell, taste, and touch have objects that impinge on the body before perception, while the distance senses of sight and hearing have objects that are spatially separate from the perceiver. However, as Rée explains, in some situations the perception of sound is virtually indistinguishable from that of touch: "You can pick up the thunder of an avalanche in the mountains, or the hooves of galloping horses, the beat of a rock band, or the slamming of a door, by feeling them through your feet as much as hearing them with your ears" (36). This being so, sight is the only truly legitimate member in the second of the Aristotelian groupings, a point that becomes noteworthy if consideration is given to the idea that the distance senses are "epistemologically and ethically more respectable," that they are "nobler, purer" and "more detached" than the contact senses (Rée 34). In these ocularnormative terms, the senses available to the culturally constructed group of the blind are lowly, corrupt, and detached; they are epistemologically and ethically inconsequential. But when the senses are considered one by one, as I now illustrate, the essentially subhuman rendering is not always apparent.

In the case of "the blind man," writes Derrida, "hearing goes farther than the hand, which goes farther than the eye" (*Memoirs of the Blind* 16). In accordance with this maxim, of all the senses it is hearing that receives most attention in the metanarrative of blindness on which Wells draws when envisaging his isolated mountain valley.[8] The inhabitants have been blind for generations but have senses that have become marvelously acute: "they could hear and judge the slightest gesture of a man a dozen paces away—could hear the very beating of his heart" (135).[9] The apparently logical result is that the people sleep through the day, when it is warm, and work in the lower temperatures of the night. It is in this inverted community that Nunez finds himself living, having fallen from the mountains in an avalanche. He initially comforts himself with the maxim that in the land of the blind the one-eyed man is king but comes to learn that sight is not advantageous in a society that, for generations, has been organized on the basis of the other four senses. "It was marvellous," says the narrator, "with what confidence and precision they went about their ordered world. Everything, you see, had been made to fit their needs" (135). This observation reveals that there are subhuman assumptions beneath the superhuman allusions, for efficiency in such adapted surroundings can hardly be deemed marvelous—a point on which proponents of the radical British social model of disability would come to maximize critically decades later, as noted in chapter 1.

Most awkwardly placed in the contact category is the sense of smell, for although an odor impinges on the body before perception, the impingement can occur from quite a distance. It is this anticipatory quality that makes the sense of smell particularly important in the animal kingdom, providing, as it does, a fairly reliable signifier of potential pleasure or pain. But a problem arises when, for example, the blind inhabitants of Wells's mountain valley are ascribed a sense of smell that is evocative of animalization. "Their sense of smell was extraordinarily fine," says the narrator, "they could distinguish individual differences as readily as a dog can" (135).[10] The animalizing aspect of this simile is echoed when, a couple of pages on, the same characters are said to "halt and sniff the air" before one "struck" Nunez's "trail in the meadow grass, and came stooping and feeling his way along it" (137). The animalizing and thus dehumanizing implication of such renderings of extraordinary senses is that the blind belong to a lower evolutionary order than do the sighted—a eugenic notion further explored later in the chapter.

Frequently coupled with the sense of smell, second in the contact category is the sense of taste. Accordingly, the animalizing sense of smell is implicit in Joyce's *Ulysses*. Having "watched curiously, kindly the lithe black form" of a cat that "blinked" her "shameclosing eyes," the "dark eyeslits" that narrowed until "green stones," Bloom turns his attention to the blind stripling: "Sense of smell must be stronger too. Smells on all sides bunched together. Each person too. Then the spring, the summer: smells" (53–54, 173). But again illustrating the oscillation of extraordinary senses, the blind stripling's taste is assumed inferior to that of his sighted counterparts. He is infantilized by notions of needs and care that are inconsistent with visual impairment: "Slobbers his food, I suppose. Tastes all different for him. Have to be spoon fed first" (173). The ocularnormative implication is that visual impairment brings about significant alterations in the bearer's sense of taste, a notion that is bolstered as Bloom's thoughts continue: "Tastes. They say you can't taste wines with your eyes shut or a cold in the head. Also smoke in the dark they say get no pleasure" (232). It seems that alcohol and tobacco are somehow too sophisticated for the taste of the blind. This ocularnormative implication, though certainly found elsewhere in twentieth-century writing, is contradicted by the provision of more than fifteen references to Sammy's smoking in Kelman's *How Late It Was, How Late*.[11] Unlike Joyce, then, Kelman evidently considers the blind every bit as susceptible to nicotine as are their sighted counterparts. A historical factor must be acknowledged, however, for Kelman was writing since nicotine was linked with heart disease and various forms of cancer, since, we might say, it largely ceased to be thought sophisticated.

Of the three contact senses, touch is most commonly the focus in literary representations of the blind. If the senses available to this culturally constructed group are deemed lowly and corrupt, as sometimes suggested, touch is by far the most extreme. Indeed, according to Constance Classen's *The Book of Touch* (2005), it is the customary Western emphasis on the brute physicality of touch that often deters us from exploring its cultural representation: "The sense of touch, like the body in general, has been positioned in opposition to the intellect, and assumed to be merely the subject of mindless pleasures and pains" (5). This binary opposition corresponds with the seeing-knowing synonymy considered in chapter 1 and similarly deconstructs when examined from a less ocularcentric perspective. For instance, Hull asserts that subsequent to the onset of his visual impairment he comes to appreciate the "illumination" and sense of "real knowledge" gained through haptic perception (133). Yet, as Classen points out, touch has often passed under the academic radar: "Like the air we breathe, it has been taken for granted as a fundamental fact of life, a medium for the production of meaningful acts, rather than meaningful in itself" (2). We are therefore covering relatively new ground when investigating the histories, politics, and revelations of touch that, according to Classen, have "animated social life" (2). How do we communicate via touch? What are the cultural dimensions of the pleasure-pain binary? Do women and men somehow inhabit distinct tactile worlds? These are some of the important questions for Classen, concerns that, as we discover, take on an ideologically profound significance when applied to the metanarrative of blindness.

Returning to Joyce's *Ulysses*, then, we can find an oscillating but nonetheless ocularnormative representation of touch in Bloom's thoughts about the blind stripling's hands: "Like a child's hand his hand. Like Milly's was. Sensitive. Sizing me up I daresay from my hand" (173). The thing for us to note is that despite this infantilization, this apparent immaturity, the blind stripling has a sense of touch that is extraordinarily acute, a point that is further illustrated in thoughts of how he might experience a woman's beauty: "His hands on her hair, for instance. Say it was black for instance. Good. We call it black. Then passing over her white skin. Different feel perhaps. Feeling of white" (173). As well as excluding people who have visual impairments from the implied readership, the pronoun *we* indicates that, for Bloom, a division exists between the blind and their sighted counterparts. This division is bolstered in Bloom's suggestion that the blind might refer to the color black by another name, as well as in the evocation of synesthesia—that is, the reference to the feeling of color. This evocation is noteworthy for us because, as illustrated in the blind stripling's ascription of fingers that "must almost see" (173), not to mention *How Late It Was, How Late,* wherein Sammy is informed that "persons who entertain sight loss come to feel bodily materials with such perfect exactness that one is tempted to suggest they see with their hands" (Kelman 222), the sense of touch, according to Classen, "overflows its own boundaries and merges with other sensory phenomena" (3). The trouble is that synesthetic notions may predicate ophthalmocentric renderings of haptic perception.[12] It is "as if a lidless eye had opened at the tip of the fingers," remarks Derrida, "as if one eye too many had just grown right next to the nail, a single eye, the eye of a cyclops or one-eyed man" (*Memoirs of the Blind* 3). Given the findings of chapter 3, any such ophthalmocentric depictions of touch can be identified as emblematic of ocularcentric assumptions about perception. The ocularnormative implication is that, in relation to the visual, haptic means are at best a substitute and at worst a variant.[13] What is more, the sexualization of eye symbolism renders ophthalmocentric depictions of touch problematic, raising, as they do, the specter of the groping blind figure.

The Groping Blind Figure

In the context of disability, the sense of touch "*frustrates* hierarchy," because it "crosses boundaries rather than creates distance" (Price and Shildrick 69). A critical concern in the present book, this distance is integral to the binary system on which the metanarrative of blindness rests. Indeed, it is cultural anxieties about this very distance being encroached by the act and sense of touch that underpin the construct of the groping blind figure. Like the labels *blind man* and *blind girl* discussed in chapter 2, the verb *grope* is recurrent in the discourse that invokes the metanarrative of blindness, having meanings that pertain not only to synaesthesia and lecherousness but also to the gait and disempowerment of the blind.[14] A detailed illustration can be found in Wyndham's *The Day of the Triffids,* when the hospitalized protagonist William Masen recovers from a work-based eye injury. We are made aware that the accident has happened during a study of the poisonous plants on which Masen is an expert. But the irony is that having his eyes bandaged deters him from watching a blinding display of shooting stars. Thus, on removing the bandages he finds that, while he can see, the vast majority of the population is without sight. The thing for us to note is that in the resulting collapse of civilization, London is rendered "The Groping City" (36), a place where crowds stand in front of broken shop windows, "groping for any recognizable object" (42). Collisions "were taking place every now and then," says Masen, the most significant being one in which the subjects were "groping along a shop front from opposite directions until they met with a bump" (39).[15] Insofar as these characters cannot escape their predicament, the act of groping has no useful function; it merely signifies the tragic helplessness with which blindness is sometimes associated. Indeed, we are informed from the outset that it would have been the end of the world if Masen had lost his sight.

More frequently the verb *grope* is used to differentiate the gait of the blind from that of the sighted. The repeated suggestion in twentieth-century writing is that, rather than walking, people who have visual impairments grope their way around.[16] Accordingly, prior to removing his bandages, Masen remembers that he "groped" his "way back to bed" (11) and later that the landlord of the Alamein Arms "groped his way to the stairs" (19), much as numerous blind persons were seen "groping their ways to safer parts" (67). Similarly, though free from the threat of triffids and the overtly nightmarish rendering of blindness, Sammy, in Kelman's *How Late It Was, How Late,* is said to have "groped his way around" (11), "groped his way to the end wall" (24), and "groped his way to the counter" (215). With a variant of this usage the alterity becomes still more profound, as is illustrated when Sammy is "groping about" (100) and "groping forwards" (315), much as when Wyndham's Masen remembers a man "groping towards" Josella (46) and Dennis "groping right across" a familiar lane (140). In these and other such instances the blind do not grope their way around; they do not grope while walking; on a discursive level they do not walk at all.[17]

In keying characters to the metanarrative of blindness the grope may well signify disempowerment, may affect or indeed displace the assumed normal act of walking; yet common to all applications is implicit lecherousness. The denotative meaning pertains to haptic perception, as is illustrated in Kelman's *How Late It Was, How Late,* for as well as "groping" for his jeans (333), Sammy "groped" for a chair (32), the shop window (55), the door (226), and his drink (278), much as in *The Day of the Triffids* Masen "groped around a bit to find the bell-push" (10), and Doctor Soames "groped about" until he found the telephone rest (16).[18] But attached to the verb *grope* are colloquial connotations of molestation. Accordingly, in Wells's "The Country of the Blind," a crowd is said to come about Nunez, "holding on to him, touching him with soft sensitive hands" (131), the dramatic effect of which is compounded in a subsequent violation: "They were moving in upon him quickly, groping, yet moving rapidly. It was like playing blind man's buff, with everyone blindfolded except one" (138). This implicitly hypersexual portrayal is particularly notable because, as Ruth Hubbard's "Abortion and Disability" (1990) points out, eugenics was partly in response to the notion that so-called "genetically inferior people were reproducing faster than superior people and would eventually displace them" (190). Thus, the hypersexual connotations of the grope must be recognized as ideological and, as they consolidate the normate subject position of the sighted, more specifically, ocularnormative.

Given the previous chapter's discussion of the look, stare, and/or gaze, we might be tempted to invoke a parallel with the touch, feel, and/or grope, for in both triads the last actions are more explicitly sexualized than the first. Like the gaze in relation to the look, moreover, the grope presents more of a violation than does the touch. But in accordance with ocularnormativism, the haptic triad is far more sinister than its visual counterpart, culminating, as it sometimes does, in the monstrous grip.[19] This motif is illustrated in "The Country of the Blind" when Nunez is said to have "struggled against a number of hands that clutched him," "gripped him firmly," "holding on to him, touching him" (130–32). The illustration is more dramatic in *The Day of the Triffids* when a blind man ostensibly asks one of the few sighted characters for directions:

> The outstretched hand sought and touched her sleeve. He lunged forward, and caught both her arms in a painful grip.
>
> "So you can see, can you!" he said. "Why the hell should you be able to see when I can'tnor anyone else?"
>
> Before she could realize what was happening he had turned her and tripped her, and she was lying in the road with his knee in her back. He caught both her wrists in the grasp of one large hand, and proceeded to tie them together with a piece of string from his pocket. Then he stood up, and pulled her on to her feet again.
>
> "All right," he said. "From now on you can do your seeing for me." (46)

This episode contains something of a eugenic warning as the blind man attacks the sighted woman, thereby invoking notions of sexual violation and the associated spread of so-called impurity and disease.[20] Ultimately, then, the monstrous grip and other variants of the groping blind figure are ocularnormative because they advance pejorative notions of relationships between people who have visual impairments and people who do not. Indeed, at one point in the novel, having been attracted by a light in the unusual urban darkness, Josella and Masen discover a group of fellow sighted survivors whose plan it is to establish a postapocalyptic community. The proposed rural colony would rebuild the human population, a social project that, importantly, is only open to sighted men, sighted women, and some blind women. The exclusion of blind men from this demographic is especially noteworthy for us because it reveals an anxiety that resonates with the male bias considered in the previous chapters (the blind man's prominence over the blind girl, as well as the fact that blindness-castration synonymy and masturbation mania are more commonly male in their construction).

Conclusion

So starting with a general exploration of extraordinary senses, including the fifth-sixth sense and the associated blindness-dream confusion, as well as sight, smell, taste, and hearing, this chapter focuses on the sense of touch. While the senses in general are found to oscillate between ostensibly positive and overtly negative renderings, particular attention is paid to haptic perception because its portrayal frequently invokes the groping blind figure. Usually used in one way or another to differentiate and distance the blind from their sighted counterparts, this ocularnormative trope raises connotations of lecherousness that are monstrous on a couple of levels. First, in the cultural imagination, when the hand of the blind ventures forth it seems almost disembodied, inducing fear as it gropes, grasps, grips in ways that must surely contradict any supposed extraordinary sensitivity. Second, on an ideological level, the trope embodies the essence of negative eugenics, implying, as it does, that the blind are out to violate and infect their sighted counterparts. The underpinning anxiety is that to connect with is to become as one with the blind, a divisive concern that becomes all the more evident as consideration is given to the notion of contagious blindness on which I now focus. But there is an irony that must not be missed, for although an attitudinal basis for eugenics is provided by the belief that people who have impairments are bound to be parasitic, the groping blind figure, at its simplest, is a grotesque representation of independence. Someone who has a visual impairment may endeavor to reach for, say, a door handle in order to enter or leave a room unassisted, but when consciously or unconsciously keyed to the metanarrative of blindness he or she may be seen groping around, posing a supposed lecherous threat to people who do not have visual impairments.

Social Friction and Science Fiction

Alterity, Avoidance, and Constructs of Contagiousness

The link between contagiousness and avoidance is obvious, for many if not most of us endeavor or at least wish to avoid anyone who has pretty much anything deemed contagious. But avoidance is also a common act of prejudice, as noted in the introduction to the present book, positioned, as it is, in Gordon Allport's list of worsening behaviors that ranges from antilocution to extermination. This list, in its explication of negative eugenics, raises the point that avoidance, as a prejudicial act against people who have visual impairments, may be explained with reference to the notion of contagious blindness. After all, there are people, as illustrated by a conversation in Stephen Kuusisto's late twentieth-century autobiographical work, who do everything they can to get out of the way when encountering someone who has a visual impairment: "You know, those people who see you coming with the white cane and they flatten themselves against the walls of buildings or jump into the gutter" (*Planet of the Blind* 161–62). Of course few of us who have visual impairments are likely to hold anything against someone who helpfully steps out of our way, but there is a problem in the frequently adopted melodramatic approach. Some people step back and prepare to run, as though escaping a monster, the underlying fear being one of contagiousness: "Yeah, well, they're afraid that you'll bump them, and then they'll be blind too—everyone knows that blindness is like a game of freeze tag" (Kuusisto, *Planet of the Blind* 162).[1]

The social sciences inform us that such notions of contagiousness may be explained as the result of psychosocial barriers. These barriers are said to be symbolic yet frequently impenetrable, producing, as they do, an action like that of two magnets whose similar poles have been matched. The "avoidance reactions" are "often induced by a fear that direct contact with a blind person may be contaminating, or that the stigmatized person will somehow inflict physical or psychic damage" (Scott 24). Signposted by Kuusisto's memoirs and these references to physical and psychic damage is the fact that constructs of contagious blindness may fall into several categories, a number of which are considered in this chapter.

Also pondered here is the fact that the contagiousness motif contains an element of monstrosity. There should be a "book of etiquette" for those of us who find ourselves in the "predicament of the monster," asserts Kuusisto, raising, as he does, the fearsome aspect of contagious blindness (*Planet of the Blind* 212). This aspect is explored when a taxi driver ostensibly describes the onset of his aunt's visual impairment, but Kuusisto recognizes it as a navigation of what he terms the land of dark spells.[2] The aunt is described as a beautiful girl who loses her sight when she gets involved with a so-called voodoo man: "One day when the voodoo man's wife is gone, she goes to his house and tells him that she's going to clean up. She opens the door to the voodoo man's closet. She could feel a wind blow right through her head, and then she was *blind*!" (185). The motif of contagious blindness is further invoked as the taxi driver refers to his aunt by adding that "no one will go near her—she has the voodoo now" (185). The episode shows us how notions of malevolence, such as dark spells, may emerge from the blindness-darkness synonymy and fifth-sixth sense considered in previous chapters. Illustrated, too, is the way in which these dark spells result in avoidance. At best, as G. Thomas Couser writes in "Conflicting Paradigms" (2001), the "rhetoric of horror" encourages pity, at worst, revulsion (80). Indeed, the motif of contagious blindness is entangled with the monstrous grip that chapter 4 illustrates with reference to H. G. Wells's "The Country of the Blind" (1904) and John Wyndham's *The Day of the Triffids* (1951). This being so, the focus of the book stays on science fiction but now moves to John Varley's short story "The Persistence of Vision" (1978) and José Saramago's novel *Blindness* (1995). These late twentieth-century texts, along with their early and mid-twentieth-century antecedents, form a science fiction quartet that portrays the blind as a social majority that, in many ways, imposes blindness on the sighted minority.

Vision and the Commune

Varley's "The Persistence of Vision" is narrated by a forty-seven-year-old man who travels from one commune to another until he comes across a segregated community of deaf-blind people. This commune, which the unnamed narrator calls Keller, is said, in passing, to be an eventual consequence of numerous pregnant women catching rubella before abortion was readily available, meaning that five thousand deaf-blind children were born in one year. So many "potential Helen Kellers" could not be "sent" to a small number of "special" institutions, as may have previously been possible, and this was supposedly a problem for many parents who could not cope (235). Some of the children were said to be "badly retarded," "virtually impossible to reach, even if anyone had been trying," and "ended up, for the most part, warehoused in the hundreds of anonymous nursing homes and institutes for 'special' children" (235). In addition, children with "undamaged brains" were "shuffled in among the retarded because they were unable to tell anyone that they were in there behind the sightless eyes" (235). But the pivotal point in this story is that hundreds of the deaf-blind children were soon found to be of so-called normal intelligence, and a suitable education was developed. Before too long, largely (and thus notably) as a result of the educators' patience, love, and dedication, all graduates of the emergent schools could communicate with their hands; some could talk; and a few could write. The majority went on to live with relatives; others were helped to fit into society; most were reasonably happy; and some "achieved the almost saintly peace of their role model, Helen Keller" (235). In time, though, a select few decided to create an alternative community. This is the history of the commune that the narrator initially visits and ultimately joins.

If we apply Allport's model to "The Persistence of Vision," the deaf-blind children to whom Varley's narrator initially refers are deemed special and as such legitimately placed in segregated institutions or, put differently, designated Other and thus accommodated where they are most easily avoided. We might say that, in the terms of the present book, the label *special* keys the children to a metanarrative that perpetuates their avoidance. But something similar may be said of the alternative, Keller, too, for though endorsed as a utopian community *of* (rather than an institution *for*) deaf-blind people, it is nonetheless initially approached by the narrator with avoidance in mind: "Most of me said to turn around, go back to the wall by way of the pasture and head back into the hills.

These people probably wouldn't want me around. I doubted that I'd be able to talk to them, and they might even resent me" (238–39). Not only this ambivalent approach but also the fact that the narrator proves unusual in his subsequent attachment to the place may be thought of in terms of avoidance: "I was the only visitor, the only one in seven years to stay at Keller for longer than a few days" (265). As a rule, then, akin to the Wellsian country of the blind, Varley's Keller evidently has limited appeal to sighted characters; it is somewhere to pass through, to visit as a tourist, a sightseer, not somewhere to reside or remain.

Entangled with avoidance is a need for division, which may involve conscious and/or unconscious, explicit and/or implicit, intentional and/or unintentional distinctions between them and us, Other and Self, out-group and in-group, abnormal and normal, and so on. Varley's "The Persistence of Vision" explores division from a perspective that is not overtly ocularcentric, as is illustrated when the narrator questions the level of his own inclusion in the community: "I was not part of the organism, no matter how nice the organism was to me. I had no hopes of ever becoming a part, either. Pink had said it in the first week. She felt it herself, to a lesser degree" (267). Pink is a thirteen-year-old girl who has been born into the deaf-blind community, but like the narrator, she can see and hear. In fact this is true of all the children at Keller; only the adults are deaf and blind. Indeed, though generally implicit, it is undoubtedly the case that a profound division between the minority and the deaf-blind majority is indicated recurrently.

Again following the Wellsian example, "The Persistence of Vision" employs the strategy of role reversal, exploring, as it does, issues of prejudice and division. Because deafness and blindness are common to most of the Kellerites, and certainly to the most dominant among them, Varley's narrator comes to infer a fundamental hierarchy: "Unless I was willing to put out my eyes and ears, I would always be on the outside. I would be the blind and deaf one. I would be the freak. I didn't want to be a freak" (267). The story, then, subverts the dynamics of prejudice that are often experienced by those of us who have impairments. This state of affairs would have obviously been much worse when Varley was writing, during what he calls the time of the growth of the disability rights movement, the time before parking places and special restroom stalls for "the handicapped" (231). For this reason he concludes his introduction to the story by claiming a community of spirit, asserting that many of the people who thanked him for writing it were disabled.

Given that most of the Kellerites are deaf as well as blind, Varley's role reversal may be said to extend and emphasize what is often considered the key point of its closest antecedent. "The Persistence of Vision," according to Lennard Davis, shows that our "construction of the normal world is based on a radical repression of disability, and that given certain power structures, a society of people with disabilities can and does easily survive and render 'normal' people outsiders" (*Enforcing Normalcy* 22). Along similar lines, Wells's "The Country of the Blind" is praised by several disability scholars as a radical portrayal of a land in which all the inhabitants are unsighted and order their lives on the basis of their four senses, meaning that the one sighted character, Nunez, is at a disadvantage. For example, Rod Michalko's *The Mystery of the Eye and the Shadow of Blindness* (1998) argues that the story is revealing because it "reverses" the way in which blindness is immersed in a sighted world: "Blindness is always experienced in the midst of sightedness. People are either born blind into a world organized by sight or lose their sight in the same world. Most people are not blind, and the meaning of blindness is understood within the social context of its rare occurrence" (8).[3] In brief, informed by the narrator's assertion that "the blind call their day night" (133), many scholars defend the Wellsian classic on the grounds that it reverses the tradition of a blind person in a sighted world. In this respect Varley's story goes further insofar as it may be said to reverse the tradition of a deaf-blind person in a hearing-sighted world.

It is, however, in this very notion of reversal that a representational problem lies. The trouble is that, in the science fiction quartet, people who have visual impairments and people who do not have visual impairments are often represented as though antithetical to one another. This method of representation raises the issue that, while constructs of the blind and the sighted may well be antithetical, people who have visual impairments are not so to people who do not have visual impairments. Humanity is obviously fundamental to people who have and people who do not have visual impairments alike, but the ocularnormative endeavor to construct a counterpoint for the sighted often results in dehumanizing depictions of the blind. Humanity "will manage to live without eyes," says the narrator of Saramago's *Blindness*, "but then it will cease to be humanity" (241). The essence of the representational problem, then, is that any strategy of role reversal is predicated on the binary system critiqued throughout the present book.

The main problem with this system is the psychosocial (and, indeed, psychocultural) process of Othering. For a "secure definition of self," according to Sander Gilman's *Difference and Pathology* (1985), "sexuality and the loss of control associated with it must be projected onto the Other" (24). In relation to sexuality and the loss of control (hypersexuality, we might say), Varley's story goes much further than do those by Wells and Wyndham. As noted in chapter 4, "The Country of the Blind" and *The Day of the Triffids* represent hypersexuality implicitly, in the form of the groping blind figure. But there is no such subtlety when Varley's narrator describes social gatherings at which the Kellerites are generally naked and frequently engaging in casual sex. Granted, there may seem to be momentary departures from ocularcentrism when Keller is considered in terms of haptic perception: "Everybody touched everybody else, as routinely as glancing" (244).[4] Indeed, the various suggestions of a haptic culture may be read as a challenge to, or at least a comment on, ocularnormativism. However, any such counterhegemonic interpretation is problematized by the unmistakable hypersexualization of the deaf-blind characters: "Everyone touched my face first, then went on with what seemed like total innocence to touch me everywhere else. As usual, it was not quite what it seemed. It was *not* innocent" (244). In other words, the motive of the tactility is, in fact, sexual rather than social. Indeed, the hypersexualization becomes still more evident when the narrator goes on to say that he "could not think of the Kellerites as bisexual, though clinically they were. It was much deeper than that. [. . .] They were pansexual; they could not separate sex from the rest of their lives" (261). This is sexual alterity, the sexuality of the Other as defined by Gilman (among others), a complete lack of control.

Given the generalized hypersexuality of the Kellerites, the nature of the narrator's relationship with Pink is perplexing if not perverse. With reference to her giving him a lesson in "bodytalk," for example, he asserts that they were "making love," that she understood talking to his penis with her hands as a sort of conversation (258). The trouble is that, while there is passing reference to him having sexual encounters with adults, the narrator's only real desire is for this thirteen-year-old girl. Granted, he asserts that it took him a few weeks to think of her as a sexual being, that although still in the middle flush of puberty she was regarded in the commune as an adult, and he came to accept her as such. Accordingly, he renders this essentially pedophilic relationship as a departure from cultural conditioning, a defense to which I return in a moment. But the claim that Pink is regarded as an adult is not always shown to be true. When the narrator first meets her, for instance, she defines herself as "one of the children" who "all hear and see quite well" (243), a distinction that is sustained when the adults leave her and engage in a mysterious activity referred to as ***ing: "Why can't I join them? Why can't I (smell-taste-touch-hear-see) sense with them?" (259). That is to say, Pink openly laments the very distinction that the narrator denies, for her sight and hearing are embedded with the fact that she is a child. We should also note that there is no suggestion of the narrator entering into pedophilic relationships at any of the nondisabled communes. Returning to the defense, then, I would argue that the narrator's relationship with Pink is in itself a manifestation of cultural conditioning. Underpinned by eugenics, it is cultural conditioning of the ableist kind. The disturbing implication is that the sighted hearing child makes a far more likely and/or perhaps appropriate love interest than do any of the many deaf-blind adults.

Blindness and the Asylum

A commune for Varley—about which I have more to say in a moment—the Wellsian country of the blind becomes an asylum in Saramago's *Blindness.* Starting with a man who spontaneously loses his sight as he waits in his car for the traffic lights to change, an unexplained epidemic of blindness ensues. The novel, according to Michael Davidson's *Concerto for the Left Hand* (2008), "imagines a world no longer dependent on sight," where people "begin to rely on other senses for communication, location, locomotion, and survival" (17). The initial response of the government to this scenario is to quarantine all newly blinded people in an unused mental asylum:

> A loud, gruff voice was raised, by someone whose tone suggested he was used to giving orders. It came from a loudspeaker fixed above the door by which they had entered. The word Attention was uttered three times, then the voice began, the Government regrets having been forced to exercise with all urgency what it considers to be its rightful duty, to protect the population by all possible means in this present crisis, when something with all the appearance of an epidemic of blindness has broken out, provisionally known as the white sickness, and we are relying on the public spirit and cooperation of all citizens to stem any further contagion, assuming that we are dealing with a contagious disease and that we are not simply witnessing a series of as yet inexplicable coincidences. The decision to gather together in one place all those infected, and, in adjacent but separate

> quarters all those who have had any kind of contact with them, was not taken without careful consideration. (41)

But this assertion of careful consideration is somewhat dubious because only six people are affected when blindness is first classed as an epidemic—that is, when the blind are banished from society. The resonance with negative eugenics is illustrated further by the idea that segregation of the blind will protect the population. Moreover, chiming with *The Day of the Triffids,* rather than "The Country of the Blind" or "The Persistence of Vision," the resultant community is essentially dystopian: starvation, squalor, rape, and other violence soon become commonplace. There are, however, a few people who manage to function as a group, and it is largely on their experiences that Saramago's narrator focuses.

The doctor, the secretly sighted doctor's wife, and a few others eventually break free from the horrors of the asylum only to find that blindness and the associated inhumanity seem to have struck the whole population of the unnamed city. This inhumanity becomes manifest in many ways, one of which is a blurring of the human-animal distinction. Accordingly, it is argued in Kevin Cole's "Saramago's *Blindness*" (2006) that the dog of tears "becomes a full-fledged character" (109). Indeed, expanding on the narrator's remark that the character is an "animal of the human type" (253), Cole goes so far as to assert that the dog is humane. The logic is that the dog of tears and the doctor's wife can be categorized together because both are sighted figures who act as heroic guides for their blind counterparts. The trouble is that this canine anthropomorphism is coupled with a converse animalization of blind humans. That is to say, on the level of connotation, the sighted dog becomes human, and the blind humans become dogs.

Underpinned by the human-animal binary, animalization is a recurrent motif in the metanarrative of blindness. Honorary membership of the order Chiroptera is considered in chapter 4 of the present book, but still more pejorative are recurrent allusions and references to the family Canidae.[5] Allusion can be found in Wells's "The Country of the Blind," for instance, where an unnamed blind boy is said to have "nipped" the hand of Nunez (131), but the trope is quite explicit in Saramago's *Blindness.* No dog "recognises another dog or knows the others by the names they have been given," says the doctor's wife; "a dog is identified by its scent and that is how it identifies others, here we are like another breed of dogs, we know each other's bark or speech, as for the rest, features, colour of eyes or hair, they are of no importance" (55). This notion is bolstered within the novel by several instances in which blind characters are depicted "on all fours," by the fact that some are referred to as thieving dogs (102), not to mention the old blind woman's assertion about survival: "I kill a rabbit or chicken, And eat them raw" (233). As examples of animalization, allusions and references to the family Canidae are particularly revealing because of their multilayered pejorative connotations. After all, to refer to someone as a dog may be taken as a comment on her or his appearance, morality, and/or personal hygiene.

Bearing in mind that, just prior to the turn of the twentieth century, what Anglo-American scientists called eugenics became known as racial hygiene in Germany, that the "people who designed these policies and the later policies of euthanasia and mass extermination as well as those who oversaw their execution looked on them as sanitary measures" (Hubbard 192), it is notable that whether the unkemptness of the blind be regarded as animalistic or simply untidy, an evocation of uncleanness is assured.[6] This uncleanness is epitomized by the state of the asylum in which Saramago's blind characters initially reside:

> No imagination, however fertile and creative in making comparisons, images and metaphors, could aptly describe the filth here. It is not just the state to which the lavatories were soon reduced, [. . .] but also the lack of respect shown by some of the inmates or the sudden urgency of others that turned the corridors and other passageways into latrines at first, only occasionally but now as a matter of habit. The careless or impatient thought, It doesn't matter, no one can see me, and they went no further. When it became impossible in any sense, to reach the lavatories, the blind internees began using the yard as a place to relieve themselves and clear their bowels. (125–26)

The dehumanizing nature of this image is bolstered by the notion that the doctor "was dirty, dirtier than he could ever remember having been in his life. There are many ways of becoming an animal, he thought, this is just the first of them" (89). If there are many ways of becoming an animal, then there are many more of representing someone as such. These methods include sublimation into a general appearance of unkemptness, one recurrent example being the growth of a beard.[7] Hence, the newly blind doctor feels the "roughness of his beard after three days without shaving, It's preferable like this, I hope they won't have the unfortunate idea of sending us razor blades and scissors" (66). Though evidently something of an issue according to the metanarrative of blindness, there is, in fact, nothing in any degree of visual impairment that necessarily alters a person's ability to shave. Nevertheless, Saramago's narrator explains that although the doctor "had everything necessary for shaving in his suitcase," he "was conscious of the fact that it would be a mistake to try" (66). Of course the ascription is not necessarily pejorative, but a problem resides in the homogenizing assumption that, for men, a beard is a consequence of blindness.

Notwithstanding the sophistry of their origin, the unkemptness and uncleanness of the blind predicate the seemingly obligatory construct of disease. The Other is, as Gilman puts it, "both ill and infectious, both damaged and damaging," for the idea of disease as a "corporeal invasion of the self, a 'thing' lying outside the self that enters to corrupt it," has not been "shaken off by modern medicine" (24). Though central to Saramago's *Blindness,* the disease motif is not always played out on the most obvious, physical level. For example, the doctor warns his wife against the exposure of her solitary vision: "Think of the consequences, they will almost certainly try to turn you into their slave, a general dogsbody, you will be at the beck and call of everyone, they will expect you to feed them, wash them, put them to bed and get them up in the morning and have you take them from here to there" (127). This suggestion of a more metaphysical contagiousness is bolstered when the doctor's wife subsequently addresses the girl with the dark glasses by saying, "I am blind with your blindness" (281).[8] As the initial medical concern takes on a social, indeed, psychosocial aspect, it becomes clear that the blind Other may be thought to infect the sighted Self in a multitude of ways that are explored in the social sciences.

But before we briefly turn away from literary representation it must be stressed that even the physical aspect of the contagious-blindness motif is far from straightforward, for not only the eyes are affected. This aspect of the contagiousness motif occurs when Saramago's doctor's wife envisages rabbits "waiting for that blind hand to bring them cabbage leaves then grab them by the ears and put them out kicking, while the other hand prepares the blind blow that will break the vertebrae near the skull" (234). In other words, blindness spreads through and potentially beyond the body as the blind character is ascribed a blind hand that casts a blind blow. The social sciences can deepen our understanding of this aspect of the metanarrative of blindness greatly, for visual impairment is conceptualized in Berthold Lowenfeld's "What Is Blindness?" (1974) as an "injury, not only to the eyes, but to the human being as a whole" (223). With reference to Erving Goffman's work on stigma, we might say that people who have visual impairments are keyed to the metanarrative of blindness when the "perceived failure to see" becomes generalized into a "gestalt of disability, so that the [sighted] individual shouts at the blind as if they were deaf or attempts to lift them as if they were crippled" (16). Indeed, I am sure it is the case that most of us who have visual impairments can "recount innumerable instances of being addressed in terms that might normally be used for talking with a child—or in a near shout," thereby indicating that the impairment is "even equated with loss of intelligence or diminution of one or more of the other senses" (Dobree and Boulter 113). This claim certainly resonates with the encounter in the resource center considered at the start of the present book.

The psychological and physical factors may be said to come together in the form of stigma, a phenomenon that is in itself somewhat contagious. People, according to Goffman, are "obliged to share some of the discredit of the stigmatized person to whom they are related," one response being to embrace this fate and "live within the world of one's stigmatized connexion" (43). These connotations of contagiousness are bolstered when people who "acquire a degree of stigma in this way can themselves have connexions who acquire a little of the disease twice-removed" (Goffman 43). A late twentieth-century slant on this notion of contagiousness is demonstrable in Allan Dodds's consideration of the exhaustion from which rehabilitation workers are said to suffer: "The term 'burn-out' is itself a metaphor. It conjures up a picture of something which was once very much ablaze being dead, with no possibility of revitalization. Psychologically, it covers aspects of mood such as depression, states of mind such as cynicism, and avoidant coping behaviour" (174). Picturing the death of something that was once very much ablaze, Dodds's explanation of the burnout metaphor is evocative of darkness, revealing that, in accordance with blindness-darkness synonymy, a sense of contamination is implicit in the idea that rehabilitation workers suffer from burnout as a result of prolonged contact with people who have visual impairments. This implication is sustained by the fact that also cited as symptomatic of burnout is depression, a psychological element of the metanarrative of blindness with which people who have visual impairments are frequently associated, as illustrated in chapter 7. It is as though not only visual impairment but also other aspects of the complex construct of blindness may be passed from person to person, as though there is a kind of second-order contagiousness that need not be predicated on the first, meaning that the assumed depression may be contracted without the underpinning visual impairment.[9] Hence, according to one late twentieth-century study, many people would "avoid looking" at people who had visual impairments "because the mere sight of them" brought on depression (Kirtley 24).[10] It is even suggested that burnout itself may be spread from one person to another, although in this respect Dodds's study acknowledges that the disease metaphor is misplaced. Nevertheless, he claims, "it does suggest that burn-out can be experienced by a number of people who may have to cope with the same stresses from which they cannot escape" (Dodds 174). The point for us to note is that Dodds challenges the disease metaphor's application to people who have burnout but not to those who have visual impairments: the contagiousness of the sighted is repudiated, while that of the blind is confirmed. Of course it cannot be denied that exhaustion may be an issue for rehabilitation workers, as for anyone, but the notion of specificity is indicative of Otherness that only serves to consolidate an ocularcentric subject position.

Blind Fear

So in representing the blind as a group that is largely, for Varley and Saramago respectively, hypersexual and malevolent, "The Persistence of Vision" and *Blindness* may seem indicative of one fear: the fear of the blind that is embodied in the groping blind figure considered in chapter 4. But this fear is a rather slippery idea that may well amount to a fear of contacting and contracting blindness. Given the ocularcentrism and ocularnormativism considered in previous chapters, it is perhaps not too surprising that even in our own century it may be asserted that there are "few fears more terrible than that of losing our sight" (James and Harvey Wood vii). Far more concerning is the late twentieth-century suggestion that the person who is "consciously or unconsciously fearful" may "identify blindness itself with the horrible thing that they think is responsible for it" (Monbeck 100). Accordingly, John Hull remembers his faith-healing friend's expostulation that "sin" is the "cause of blindness" (67), from which notions of malevolence seem to follow.[11] It is as if the fearsome cause and effect become interchangeable, meaning that evil causes blindness, blindness becomes evil, and so on.

Given the anxiety around such pejorative notions, it is probably fair for us to say that in keying others some people fear simultaneously keying themselves to the metanarrative of blindness. Certainly, some relatively subtle examples of what I mean by *blind fear* pertain to such notions of identification. It is sometimes argued, for example, that implicit evidence of the fear of blindness by identification may be noticed when some parents teach their children not to stare at people who have visual impairments. Consciously, this is "done out of politeness," but according to Kirtley's late twentieth-century psychological study, on the "level of the irrational unconscious, the critical motive may be fear of an ensuing identification with the person stared at" (24). The fear is "based on identification," which as Lowenfeld's "A Psychological Approach to Blindness" (1949) puts it, can be "expressed by such a thought as 'How frightful it would be if I were blind'" (85). This scenario is explored in the characterization of Saramago's doctor insofar as he is at home consulting reference books on ophthalmology when he goes blind. Similarly, the old man with the black eye patch loses his sight when looking at his blind eye. Feeling as if the inside of the "empty orbit" is inflamed, he removes the patch to satisfy his curiosity but at that moment goes blind (121).[12] To see unseeing eyes, then, is to risk infection, a notion that constitutes an inherent component of the evil-eye superstition: "In horror stories, those who see the evil eye frequently become evil themselves" (Kirtley 23). In the cultural imagination the evil blind eye is evidently a multiple source of anxiety: it represents malevolence and the danger of becoming malevolent, blindness and the danger of becoming blind.

Because the nyctophobia—that is, fear of the dark—"inherent in most young children can leave a lasting impression" (Dobree and Boulter 113), the fearsome motif is at the very least perpetuated by blindness-darkness synonymy, as implied at the start of this chapter in Kuusisto's reference to the land of dark spells. The synonymy is recurrent in science fiction, epitomized, as it is, in Wells's description of "elders who sat in darkness in the Country of the Blind," beneath a "roof of rock and stone and darkness" (132, 143), as well as in the way that Wyndham's William Mason has to decide if he is more scared of endangering his sight by prematurely removing the bandages from his eyes or "staying in the dark with the willies growing every minute," thereby foreshadowing the clergyman's prayer for "those who still wander alone in darkness" (14, 107). Though arguably less pejorative, Varley's "The Persistence of Vision" is nonetheless relevant, for it makes reference to the Kellerites "being in the quiet and dark all the time" (264). Saramago's *Blindness* may seem like an exception to this rule, of course, but although the blind man, among others, is "plunged into a whiteness so luminous, so total, that it swallowed up rather than absorbed, not just the colours, but the very things and beings, thus making them twice as invisible," a passing reference is made to "the darkness in which the blind live" (8). That is to say, Saramago's construct of blindness is one of whiteness, as opposed to the more traditional blackness, but the incidental detail is no less revealing. As a point of reference in all four works, blindness-darkness synonymy offers us a clue to the malevolence in Saramago's *Blindness* and the hypersexuality in Varley's "The Persistence of Vision": such things are often confined to darkness, so from an ocularcentric perspective they are indeed predicated by the synonymy. A parallel may be drawn with the way in which men who rely on mirrors to shave assume that those of us who perceive little or nothing visually will necessarily grow beards. In other words, those of us who perceive visually may express our hypersexual and malevolent feelings in the darkness with which blindness is associated and infer accordingly.

A fundamental point emerges when we consider that in some applications of the fearsome motif the white cane, as an obvious and, indeed, official symbol of blindness, metamorphoses into a stick, a sword, or some other elongated hand-held weapon.[13] This recurrent scenario is illustrated when Saramago's blind guard is "wielding" his "stick" in "slow motion, to one side then the next, as if blocking the passage of anyone who might try to approach" (149).[14] Such representations arguably give the impression of an assumed jealousy.[15] Hence, one of Saramago's blind internees addresses a sighted soldier by saying, "I'll gouge your eyes out" (105). The supposed malevolence is medicalized in Wells's "The Country of the Blind," where Nunez's love for Medina-Sarote results in him agreeing to have his eyes removed. In order to "cure him completely," says the blind doctor, "all that we need do is a simple and easy surgical operation—namely, to remove these irritant bodies" (143). These and other such characterizations chime with the ocularcentric notion that those of us who have visual impairments will be enraged by the thing that is bound to be sought: sightedness.

We find this jealousy echoed and extended when turning back to Varley's "The Persistence of Vision," where the contagiousness motif provides a sense of narrative closure. The unnamed narrator eventually leaves Keller and seeks happiness beyond it, essentially retreating to what he has left behind. Somewhat predictably, then, he cannot find anyone with whom to share his life: "There was only Pink for that, Pink and all her family, and we were separated by a gulf I didn't dare cross" (268). This separation, indeed this gulf, underpins the metanarrative of blindness, whose presence can hardly be denied when Varley's narrator returns to Keller and finds that in the interim Pink has been made a fully fledged member of the community: "Her eyes were stones in her head. She was blind. She was deaf" (269). What is more, the story ends with Pink gently touching the narrator's eyes and ears, the result being that light and sound are permanently shut out, so the two of them live "in the lovely quiet and dark" (270). That is to say, blindness and deafness are passed from the Kellerite adults to Pink, when she comes of age, and then from her to the narrator in order to bridge the supposed gulf between them, a sense of closure that seems to contrast sharply with ocularnormativism and the way in which Saramago's characters regain their sight at the end of *Blindness*. But it should be stressed that Varley's ending does not contain a so-called mixed relationship, that the fundamental distance between the blind and the sighted remains intact.

Conclusion

The texts on which this chapter focuses are indicative of a science fiction quartet that depicts alterity in terms of a distinction between the sighted and the blind. In relation to the idea of a blind majority, Varley's "The Persistence of Vision" (like Wells's "The Country of the Blind") takes a manifestly laudatory approach, whereas Saramago's *Blindness* (like Wyndham's *The Day of the Triffids*) is overtly pejorative. Be it via sexual, psychological, or physical means, a common factor is the motif of contagious blindness and the associated fear. Fear of blindness becomes fear of the blind. The idea is that the blind Other poses a threat to the ocularcentric subject position and as such should be avoided. Sublimation of this logic can be found in the suggestion that people who have visual impairments belong together, away from those of us who do not have visual impairments. As an endorsement of institutionalism, this is consistent with what social scientists refer to as the "accommodative approach," advocates of which believe that people who have visual impairments are "incapable of true independence," that "most of them prefer their own company" (Scott 93). Such twentieth-century endorsements of avoidance, however, only reveal part of the story, as illustrated recurrently in literary representation. For example, when Varley's narrator first approaches Keller, knowing only that it is a commune for deaf-blind people, avoidance may well be the initial compulsion, but he soon succumbs to curiosity: "I was fascinated, as who wouldn't be? I wanted to see how they managed it" (239). It is to this relationship between avoidance and fascination that I now turn, to the objectifying implications of the unseen look, stare, and/or gaze.

Visual Violation

Staring, Panopticism, and the Unseen Gazer

Be it via the look, the stare, or the gaze, uninvited scrutiny is unwelcome for many reasons and on many levels. Indeed, there can be no denying the ubiquity ofocularcentric notions, behaviors, and practices, yet the rendering of vision as the supreme means of perception has profound implications for us all. For example, in identifying members of social out-groups, according to various works of psychology and sociology, it is often the case that prejudiced persons are far more accurate than are their nonprejudiced counterparts. This can be explained as a result of the look, stare, and/or gaze in which victims of prejudice are so often caught, the means by which some people learn what Gordon Allport calls the "cues" that identify their "enemy" (133). It is "through our sense of sight," agrees Erving Goffman, that "the stigma of others most frequently becomes evident" (65). The information may be purely optical, purely superficial, but by "focusing on differences" we "actively create stigmas," for "any attribute or difference is potentially stigmatizable" (Coleman 219). The look becomes a stare, or a gaze, and the looker assumes a normate subject position from which alterity is confirmed if not constructed. The Other is framed as such and evaluated accordingly.

But staring, according to Rosemarie Garland-Thomson's now-definitive work on the subject, is far more benevolent than this; it "strives toward knowing by reducing unfamiliarity" (*Staring* 194) and is therefore distinct from gazing, an "oppressive act of disciplinary looking that subordinates its victim" (9). We "may gaze at what we desire," she adds, but we "stare at what astonishes us" (13). These definitions are indicative of a distinction that predicates a radical interpretation of the stare, but one whose pertinence to visual impairment is complicated in the present book. I say this because I am bound to argue that, explicitly ocularcentric, the idea of striving toward knowing via the stare is implicitly ocularnormative. It invokes the ubiquitous notion that seeing is synonymous with knowing, from which we may infer that visual perception is the normal means of acquiring knowledge. Indeed, according to an earlier study, Roland Barthes's "Right in the Eyes" (1982), there are three combinable ways in which the gaze can be scientifically interpreted, information, possession, and relation, meaning that gazes are exchanged in a manner that may be described as linguistic. The trouble, for me, is that if and when only one party has access to this language the other is necessarily unable to contribute, to refute or confirm accusation and admiration alike. So whether we think of the language of the gaze or learning via the stare, the gains are exclusive to those of us who perceive by visual means.

Distinct from the stare, the unseen stare has far more in common with the male gaze, a concept that, as Garland-Thomson acknowledges, feminism has explored fruitfully: it is a "position of privilege in social relations which entitles men to look at women and positions women as objects of that look" (*Staring* 41). Indeed, I would say that privilege, entitlement, and objectification are some of the defining factors of the male gaze. But the fact is that the unseen stare constitutes a comparable position of privilege that certainly seems to entitle some people to look at, and objectify, those of us who have visual impairments. If the male gaze is men doing something to women, then the unseen stare involves those of us who do not have visual impairments doing something to those of us who do. Both dynamics are similarly illustrative of a fundamental point made by Garland-Thomson: cultural Othering depends on looking as an "act of domination" (*Staring* 42). In general, then, it might well be the case that the stare is elicited by astonishment and the gaze by desire, but—given the ocularcentric, ophthalmocentric, and ocularnormative notions of sexuality considered in previous chapters—the distinction is disrupted by the unseen stare. The astonishment of the unseen starer is, after all, elicited by asymmetry that itself raises issues of desire, as this chapter reveals. It is for these and other such reasons that the terms *unseen gaze, unseen gazer,* and *gazee* are adopted.

But something more about asymmetry should be stressed from the outset. Visual perception is a form of power that, like any other, may be compared, abused, and thus utilized as a means of control. The unseen gaze, by definition, is asymmetrical, as Jean-Paul Sartre philosophizes in *Being and Nothingness* (1943): "What I apprehend immediately when I hear the branches crackling behind me is not that there is someone there; it is that I am vulnerable, that I have a body which can be hurt, that I occupy a place and that I cannot in any case escape from the space in which I am without defence—in short, that I am seen" (259). Importantly, a state of uncertainty about the duration of such vulnerability is also induced, for withdrawal of the unseen gaze reaches the gazee no more clearly than does the gaze itself. [1] The effect of this uncertainty may be deemed Orwellian,[2] evocative of what Michel Foucault's *Discipline and Punish* (1975) refers to as panopticism.[3] After all, the panopticon is a machine for "dissociating the see/being seen dyad," for in the "peripheric ring, one is totally seen, without ever seeing," while in the "central tower, one sees everything without ever being seen"; it induces a "state of conscious and permanent visibility," ensuring that, even if discontinuous in its action, surveillance is continuous in its effect (Foucault 201–2). Such dissociation is fundamental to the unseen gaze that occurs in many twentieth-century representations of blindness, which this chapter illustrates with reference to Brian Friel's play *Molly Sweeney* (1994), as well as a couple of works already introduced—namely, Rupert Thomson's novel *The Insult* (1996) and Mary Norton's short story "The Girl in the Corner" (1951). If, as Garland-Thomson observes, Foucault's panopticism constitutes a revision of the Freudian superego, then here the dynamic is rendered ocularnormative in the extreme.

Spectacles of Blindness

Before exploring literary illustrations of what I mean by spectacles of blindness it is important that we have some appreciation of experiential knowledge. A vivid illustration is provided in the childhood memories articulated by Stephen Kuusisto:

> A boy I think of as a friend steals my glasses and my panic brings me alive like a tree filled with birds: I navigate with my hands.
>
> "Hey, Blindo, over here!"
>
> He laughs along with several others, then they run.
>
> I lunge with my arms straight following the sounds of sneakers. I'm determined not to cry: steel keys revolve and lock in my brain. Then I trip on a curb and cut my hands on a storm drain.

> To this day I picture that boy clutching my glasses at a safe distance and watching me drift about. (*Planet of the Blind* 21)

Of course it might be argued that these memories merely illustrate the maxim that children can be cruel, that Kuusisto, like many of us, may have been bullied irrespective of his visual impairment. For this reason it is helpful to consider a second example in which John Hull remembers an incident that involves not schoolchildren, but the very personification of maturity and sensitivity, namely, academics:

> I was in the middle of a group of people who greeted me with cries of, "Now here's a surprise for you. Can you tell who this is?" Another voice broke through the noise saying, "Do you recognize my voice, John?" I could not tell how many people there were, possibly four or five, maybe as many as seven or eight. Amongst the various voices, I recognized someone I knew and greeted him by name; someone else was still asking me if I knew him, so I then turned towards him. With a laugh I said, "No, I am ever so sorry, old chap. I'm afraid that I have no idea who you are. As far as I know, I have never met you before in my life. Now if you'll excuse me, I am going to the bar with my friend to get a drink." I began to shoulder my way through them. This reply was met with howls of laughter, which was, I think, sympathetic towards me. The voice continued, now more urgently, "No, no. Come on John. You know me. You must know my voice, surely. We've been at conferences together." Again, with a smile, I cheerfully replied, "I really am sorry. It must be a terrible blow to your ego but I'm afraid that if we did happen to meet in the past, your impact upon me has been negligible. [. . .] Now, whoever you are, Goodbye." With this, I resumed my path towards the bar. Once again there were guffaws and hoots of laughter around the circle. (127–28)

Like Kuusisto's school friends watching him "drift about," Hull finds himself "in the middle" of a "circle," turning from one unseen gazer to another. Reminiscent of the popular game of blind man's buff, moreover, the spectacle involves failed attempts at nonvisual recognition, but in Hull's case it is via aural rather than haptic means—"Can you tell who this is?" asks one person, "Do you recognize my voice, John?" says another. Each failed attempt, when caught in the unseen gaze, serves to demonstrate the supremacy of visual perception: the premise is ocularcentric and the effect, unsurprisingly, ocularnormative. Accordingly, as question turns to statement, there is clear evidence of assumed authority—"Come on John. You know me. You must know my voice, surely." The epistemological inferiority associated with blindness is accepted to the extent that, on account of his sight, this virtual stranger presumes to know Hull's mind better than does the man himself. From the perspective of this normate subject position the result is a pleasurable sense of epistemological superiority. But from the perspective of the gazee Hull says, "I have never had such a sharp sense of being the centre of a game of Blind Man's Buff as I did in the foyer of Staff House" (128), a sentiment with which Kuusisto agrees in memories of belonging "so thoroughly to other people," of being "in effect, their possession," of being "put on display" (*Planet of the Blind* 21). In short, both of these autobiographical texts demonstrate that pleasure is derived from the asymmetry of the unseen gaze, from the very fact that the gazers can see but the gazees cannot.

Some of the many issues raised by Kuusisto and Hull find dramatic expression if not exploration in Friel's *Molly Sweeney*. Set in Ballybeg, this late twentieth-century play tells the story of the eponymous protagonist Molly; her overzealous husband, Frank; and her ophthalmologist, Mr. Rice. As a massage therapist who has been classed as blind since she was a baby, Molly leads a relatively full and happy life. However, largely at Frank's behest, Mr. Rice performs an operation on Molly that has bittersweet consequences. Though restoring her sight after forty years of blindness, the apparently miraculous medical intervention ultimately leaves the central character institutionalized and gravely ill.

The supremacy of visual perception is challenged recurrently in the play as we are furnished with Molly's version of events. On the night before the pivotal operation, for example, there is an impromptu party for Molly, but far from being excited at the prospect of visual restoration, she nurses major epistemological concerns. Why should she have to learn a new way of knowing? Will she ever again experience community in a profound way? These and other such worries about exile and homesickness challenge ocularcentrism and become animated when Molly moves to the center of the room and asks the fiddler to play what she calls a "mad, fast hornpipe":

> And the moment he began to play, I shouted—screamed, "Now watch me! Just you watch me!" And in a rage of anger and defiance I danced a wild and furious dance round and round that room; then out to the hall; then round the kitchen; then back to the room again and round it a third time. Mad and wild and frenzied. But so adroit, so efficient.

> No timidity, no hesitations, no falterings. Not a glass overturned, not a shoulder brushed. (24)

Buffed by neither sighted counterparts nor the usual array of strategically placed obstacles, Molly weaves through a crowd, "darting between chairs and stools and cushions and bottles and glasses with complete assurance, with absolute confidence" (24). What is more, she demonstrates an element of choice when addressing her counterparts with the exclamation "Now watch me!" However, a loss of control is conveyed through the way in which the nouns *rage* and *anger* are coupled with the adjectives *wild, furious, mad,* and *frenzied.* In fact, more than being lost, the noun *defiance* indicates that control is passed over to the sighted characters, a hypothesis on which the chapter later expands. But the thing for us to note now is that in Molly's performance blindness is constructed as a spectacle, a site where astonishment and pleasure merge.[4]

Yet the focus of the spectacle of blindness need not be in any way spectacular; it may involve the most routine of activities and behaviors.[5] So while Molly's performance at the party may be said to demand attention, no such claim can be made about a far more intimate moment in which Frank covertly watches her through the bedroom door:

> She was sitting at her dressing table, in front of the mirror, trying her hair in different ways. When she would have it in a certain way, she'd lean close to the mirror and peer into it and turn her head from side to side. But you knew she couldn't read her reflection, could scarcely even see it. Then she would try the hair in a different style and she'd lean into the mirror again until her face was almost touching it and again she'd turn first to one side and then the other. And you knew that all she saw was a blur. (51)

Given the ocularcentric rendering of sexuality considered at length in chapter 3, it is notable that Frank remembers the ease with which he "watched" through the bedroom door, while Molly saw only "a blur," "couldn't read her reflection, could scarcely even see it," had to "peer," had to "lean into" the mirror until "her face was almost touching it." In other words, Frank focuses on a contrast between his gaze and Molly's: he implicitly, perhaps unconsciously, measures the two, and the latter is found wanting. Thus, his pleasure is derived from the psychosexual sense of generative power that results from her symbolic castration.

More than merging astonishment and pleasure in ways that result in neither closure nor exposure, the spectacle of blindness may be explicitly climactic. Jacques Derrida describes the experience of looking at people who have visual impairments by asserting, "The living signification of their gaze dissimulates for me, in some way and up to a certain point, this body of the eye, which, on the contrary, I can easily stare at in a blind man, and right up to the point of indecency" (*Memoirs of the Blind* 106). On this level the spectacle of blindness may be thought of in terms of *jouissance,* which Bruce Fink's *The Lacanian Subject* (1995) defines as "pleasure that is excessive, leading to a sense of being overwhelmed or disgusted, yet simultaneously providing a source of fascination" (xi).[6] This means moving beyond the pleasure principle to a point where Eros becomes Thanatos, where joy is effectively extinguished by its own intensity. Frank's unseen gaze hints at this concept in Friel's *Molly Sweeney,* but a more vivid literary illustration can be found if we return to a novel considered in chapter 2—namely, Thomson's *The Insult.* During one of his many nocturnal strolls, the protagonist Martin Blom finds himself in the hospital washroom at the same time as Smulders, a character labeled fat as well as blind:

> Peering round the edge of the partition, I watched intently as he stripped his nightshirt off and let it fall to the stone floor. He stood stark naked for a moment, listening. Then he reached out with both hands. He looked like a ghost—his arms horizontal, his fingers tickling the air. At last he found a tap. He turned it on, began to soap himself. His hands sucked and belched in the fleshy pockets of his armpits. The hair that grew there was matted, long and lank, identical to the hair you might pull from the plughole of a bath. It was like seeing a human being for the first time. We're ugly, aren't we? It's extraordinary how ugly we are. For a moment I was afraid I might vomit. (I hoped I wouldn't; apart from anything else, I didn't want Smulders knowing I was there.) I sank down, behind the partition. As I fought the nausea I had a curious thought: what a blessing blindness could be, what a respite from the frightful squalor of the world!
>
> At last I turned back.
>
> There he was, still soaping himself, his breath issuing in ragged gusts and the occasional grunt of satisfaction. I let my eyes course his ample contours. It looked as though handfuls of fat had been attached to him at random. There were creases and folds all over his body, places where one parcel of obesity had collided with another. And what would happen if you opened out those creases? You'd find

> a sort of melted butter there, mottled and rancid. The smell would be enough to burn out whole banks of olfactory cells. And then there was the ultimate crease, the most elaborate of folds: his foreskin. (20)

First, in the terms of Fink's definition of *jouissance,* disgust is evident in the references to nausea, ugliness, hands that "sucked and belched," "fleshy" armpits, hair that grew "matted, long and lank," "handfuls of fat," "creases and folds," colliding parcels of obesity, the notion that Smulders would perspire a "sort of melted butter," "mottled and rancid," the smell of which would be "enough to burn out whole banks of olfactory cells"; second, overwhelmingness becomes apparent when Martin says, "I sank down, behind the partition"; and, third, fascination drives him to watch "intently." All in all, despite the overwhelming sense of disgust, Martin's eyes "course" the object of his unseen gaze until they encounter "the ultimate crease, the most elaborate of folds"; as though seeking Aristotelian structure (a start, middle, and end), he is driven to gaze until the sight of Smulders's foreskin. In other words, Martin proves unable to relinquish the unseen gaze prior to the moment of climax.

Though different in terms of *jouissance,* Thomson and Friel correspond on some important aspects of the unseen gaze. Yes, watching Smulders in the washroom, Thomson's Martin reaches an optimum level of pleasure, which is not the case when Friel's Frank peers through the bedroom door at Molly. But both characters depend on asymmetry; both gazes are rewarding precisely because of their covertness. Like Molly before him, Smulders is tending to mundane aspects of personal hygiene that bring pleasure to the gazer largely, if not only, because of the unseeing and unseen elements of the scenario. Indeed, like Frank in relation to Molly, Martin could easily halt Smulders's humiliation: he could break the silence or simply look away. In choosing to do neither the unseen gazer may seem passive but, in fact, actively contributes to the condemnation of the gazee.

It is sometimes so that the spectacle of blindness becomes sublimated in the form of a topic, that as Kenneth Jernigan's "To Man the Barricades" (1971) puts it (in language even more assonant than my own), quizzed, queried, and quantified, diagnosed, defined, and dissected, people who have visual impairments are reduced to objects of research, subjects of demonstration. This type of objectification is illustrated in Georgina Kleege's memory of visits to a teaching hospital:

> The teacher-doctor says, "Note the pigment clumping throughout. There are some beautifully deformed blood vessels around the nerve

> head." My damaged retinas are beautiful, a textbook example, but better than a textbook. One of the students gasps when she sees them. Anyone else listening to this might be disturbed. I'm used to it. They stare into my eyes, losing themselves in the contemplation. It's an act of extreme intimacy, but they speak of me as if I am not there. (*Sight Unseen* 155)

Damaged retinas will be of obvious interest to a group of ophthalmologists, but the "gasps" that accompany this "act of extreme intimacy" are illustrative of nullified if not negated ontology, a degree of objectification. Such medical diagnosis is referred to by Garland-Thomson as "one form of person-to-person staring that is highly impersonal, scripted, and asymmetrical" (*Staring* 28). This is the Foucauldian rendering of the clinical gaze, a kind of religious confession that exposes the body for judgment. The "invasive stare of the medical expert," as Garland-Thomson explains, "probes the patient's body and pronounces its fate," scrutiny that "seldom encompasses the whole person but rather focuses on the aspects that are suspected of revealing pathology" (*Staring* 28–29). The sublimation of the spectacle of blindness, therefore, constitutes a scientific version of normate reductionism, be the science in question medical or social.[7]

The clinical variant of the unseen gaze is explored a little in *The Insult,* when Thomson's "obsessive, almost pathological" ophthalmologist Bruno Visser appears "deep in thought" over Martin's file, even though it is the middle of the night (196, 33). But a more detailed example can be found in Friel's *Molly Sweeney,* when Mr. Rice remembers what he calls Frank's "essential" folder:

> Across it he had written, typically, Researched and Compiled by Frank C. Sweeney. [. . .] And it did have some interest, the folder. Photographs of her cycling by herself across a deserted beach. Results of tests she had undergone years ago. A certificate for coming first in her physiotherapy exams. Pictures of them on their honeymoon in Stratford-on-Avon—his idea of self-improvement, no doubt. Letters from two specialists she had been to in her late teens. An article he had cut out of a magazine about miraculous ophthalmological techniques once practised in Tibet—or was it Mongolia? Diplomas she had won in provincial swimming championships. And remarkably—in his own furious handwriting—remarkably, extracts from essays by various philosophers on the relationship between vision and knowledge, between seeing and understanding. (6–7)

In effect, Frank presents a medical, educational, sociological, and philosophical study of his wife's life. Particularly revealing is the fact that it is not Molly's name that takes pride of place, that the folder's cover reads only "Researched and Compiled by Frank C. Sweeney." This nominal displacement is indicative of the unseen gazer's assumed authority over the gazee. The implication is that, as well as the folder, Frank has compiled Molly's very life experience. It is also worth us noting that, for ophthalmologist Mr. Rice, the photographs of Molly "cycling by herself across a deserted beach" are of more "interest" than are the results of medical "tests she had undergone years ago" or the letters from specialists "she had been to in her late teens." Indeed, more than prioritizing the spectacle of blindness over ophthalmology in this way, and despite recognizing blindness as Frank's "latest cause," Mr. Rice remembers capturing Molly in his gaze:

> No, not a thought; a phantom desire, a fantasy in my head; absurd, bizarre, because I knew only the barest outlines of her case, hadn't even examined her yet; the thought, the bizarre thought that perhaps, perhaps up here in Donegal—not in Paris or Dallas or Vienna or Milan—but perhaps up here in remote Ballybeg was I about to be given—what is the vulgar parlance?—the chance of a lifetime, the one-in-a-thousand Opportunity that can rescue a career—no, no, transform a career—dare I say it, restore a reputation? And if that opportunity were being offered to me and if after all these years I could pull myself together and measure up to it, and if, oh my God if by some miracle pull it off perhaps . . . (7–8)

Sitting there, "erect in her seat and staring straight ahead," Molly is neither performing nor even engaged in mundane activity, yet her blindness predicates pleasure in the shape of "phantom desire." She is keyed to the metanarrative of blindness that features an element of cure that is potentially beneficial to Rice. Indeed, his reference to a miracle implies a notable divine sense of elevated status to which we later return.

From the normate subject position of the unseen gazer, then, the gazee may be reduced to the point of virtual inanimation (Molly's animated performance notwithstanding), to the extent that he or she is regarded quite literally as an object, not of fun or desire, but the paradoxical figure of a being without ontology.[8] Someone who has an impairment is "turned into a disabled person by the Medusa-like gaze of the observer" (Davis, *Enforcing Normalcy* 12), and this is an "attempt to control the other" (Garland-Thomson, *Staring* 43). The thing is that in such a mindset the gazee may seem amorphous, meaning that he or she can be far more easily manipulated, more effectively controlled.

Overshadowed by the Panopticon

From the perspective of the gazee, awareness of the objectifying dynamic of the unseen gaze may predicate self-consciousness, or what I call the potential for internalizing the key to the metanarrative of blindness.[9] This complex and profound form of manipulation via the unseen gaze is portrayed in another work introduced in chapter 2, Norton's "The Girl in the Corner," as the title character is observed during her train journey:

> There was a certain self-consciousness about her movements; the swift, nervous smoothing of her skirt over her knees; the quick glance round the compartment—a defensive, independent glance which flickered swiftly, seeming to see without deigning to look; and, with the glance, went a secret little smile, as though what she saw had caused her amusement. (5)

The profundity of this self-consciousness is implicit when Norton's narrator subsequently refers to Ivy by saying, "She seemed, without once having glanced at her, to be conscious of Pippa's far from obvious scrutiny" (6). After all, without invoking the fifth-sixth sense discussed in chapter 4, the accuracy of detection is rendered moot by the "far from obvious" nature of Pippa's scrutiny, so it follows that Ivy may come to feel watched, to appear self-conscious, irrespective of the gazer's physical presence. The reading becomes more convincing if we consider a contemporaneously published study, Berthold Lowenfeld's "Effects of Blindness on the Cognitive Functions of Children" (1948), which finds that "inability" to "control" the "environment by sight" renders people who have visual impairments "frequently disturbed by a fear of being observed" and, because unable to "determine" when this observation "begins or ends," compelled to "control" all "movements" and "behaviour," the result being a "state of tension and self-consciousness" (77). It is this consciousness of scrutiny where there is no scrutiny that may be interpreted as imaginary surveillance.

Indeed, when issues around the psychosocial implications of the unseen gaze are discussed, the charge of paranoia is often made. It is my contention that this response amounts to a medicalization of the social encounter, but it is certainly fair to say that self-consciousness reaches the level of persecutory anxiety in the literary imagination. There is some sense of this thinking in Norton's "The Girl in the Corner," to which I return in a moment, but the paranoia becomes quite explicit in Thomson's *The Insult.* After all, having admitted to feeling "paranoid sometimes" (143), to believing that he is followed by Visser, Martin refers to his apparent residual vision by saying: "My secret power, I thought. What if it wasn't a secret at all? Or rather, what if it was a secret everybody knew about except me? What if it was actually a secret I'd been excluded from? And what if it was being monitored? What if it had been monitored all along?" (196). Such inducement of self-consciousness that may be said to verge on paranoia is evocative of the panopticon, for although the "prisoners are not really always under surveillance," they "think or imagine that they are" (Bozovic 16). In these terms, a state of mind is inflicted on the gazee by the unseen gazer.

But more than believing they may be observed at any given time, a key point about the Foucauldian rendering of panopticism is that the prisoners come to adjust their behavior accordingly. The way in which the omnipresence of the unseen gaze might have an impact on behavior is explored when Thomson's Martin refers to his sighted counterparts by saying, "I sat up. Smiled. Dusted my left sleeve, even though it didn't need it. You have to do normal things or they don't go away. You have to reassure them. Or they just stand there staring at you, as if you're a car-crash, or pornography" (65). This depiction illustrates how the objectifying asymmetry of the unseen gaze induces self-consciousness that relates to various assumptions contained in the metanarrative of blindness. As a blind man, what is expected of me? What must I do to challenge those expectations? What must I do to appear normal? This is the implied line of thinking, the operative word being *must,* for the objectifying unseen gaze evidently initiates an external locus of control.[10] Thomson's Martin unnecessarily dusts his sleeve, much as Norton's Ivy glances round and looks at a magazine, and this is to say nothing of Molly's spontaneous performance at her leaving party, scenarios that are essentially ocularnormative, for the behavior of the blind is induced by that of the sighted, meaning the former are effectively controlled by the latter.

It is as if ability to deliver the unseen gaze suffices as a condition of authority; as if the gazee has no subjectivity to express. Accordingly, Kuusisto writes of being "watched everywhere you go," of feeling "buried beneath the graffiti of other people's superstitions" (*Planet of the Blind* 185). This reference to graffiti is particularly pertinent because, due to the way in which objectification facilitates authority, the relationship between the unseen gazer and the gazee is comparable to that between author and text.[11] In terms of panopticism, moreover, the assumption of authority, authorship, indeed ontological elevation extends still further, as is suggested when Miran Bozovic's introduction to *The Panopticon Writings* (1995) refers to the construction of God by saying, "A gaze and a voice that cannot be pinned down to any particular bearer tend to acquire exceptional powers, and by themselves, as it were, constitute divine attributes" (11). In other words, as depicted when Friel's Rice fantasizes about his miraculous treatment of Molly, the ontological status of the gazee is reduced, but quite the contrary is true of the unseen gazer.

If visual perception becomes sufficient as a condition of this ontological elevation, it follows that, irrespective of immorality, criminality, and so on, people who do not have visual impairments can assume authority over those of us who do. Again the panopticon is invoked, for it "does not matter what motive animates" the inspector, writes Foucault; it might be "the curiosity of the indiscreet, the malice of a child, the thirst for knowledge of a philosopher who wishes to visit this museum of human nature, or the perversity of those who take pleasure in spying and punishing" (202). Taking these points in turn, we may recognize the curiosity of the indiscreet in the gaze of which Norton's Ivy is so aware, the malice of a child in Kuusisto's childhood memories, the thirst for knowledge of a philosopher in the essential folder compiled by Friel's Frank Sweeney, and the perversity of those who derive pleasure from spying in the washroom gaze of Thomson's Martin Blom. The malice of a child is particularly noteworthy because of the infantilization discussed in previous chapters, for rather than an ontological hierarchy in which the blind are posited alongside children, the latter become necessarily dominant in accordance with panopticism.[12]

For such panopticism to apply, though, the child must have some awareness of the metanarrative of blindness. Without this factor the unseen gaze does indeed become far more like Garland-Thomson's rendering of the stare. This striving for knowledge via a reduction of unfamiliarity is illustrated in Kuusisto's memory of a shopping trip:

> In the supermarket we're spotted by a small child.
>
> "Look, Mommy, there's a dog in the store!"
>
> "Shhhh! Be quiet, dear!"

"But Mommy, that man has a dog!"

"That's a blind man! The dog helps him."

"Is the dog blind too?"

"No, the dog sees for the man!"

"What happens if the dog is blind?"

"The dog isn't blind, honey, the dog can see. It's the man who can't see!"

"The man can't see?"

"That's right, blind people can't see."

"If he can't see, how does he know when it's morning?"

"Shhhh! Be quiet! The man gets up because he has to have breakfast!"

The woman hurries her little boy down the cleaning products aisle. I hear his thin voice from some distance.

"How does he eat?"

(*Planet of the Blind* 179–80)

Importantly, it is not the sight of a blind man but that of a dog in the store that initially captivates the child.[13] Indeed, revealing no sign of the blind fear discussed in chapter 5, the boy appears quite unaware of the metanarrative from which it derives. But the extract illustrates how the metanarrative can inform common-sense discourse. First, avoiding the masculine pronoun *he,* the woman opts for a more objectifying alternative by asserting *that's* a blind man. Second, although the woman has never even spoken to Kuusisto, she deems him a "man who can't see," the logic being that all guide-dog owners are legally blind, and all legally blind people cannot see—in fact, as mentioned in chapter 1, of all the people registered as blind, few are without visual perception. Third, appropriating the myth, the boy accepts that Kuusisto cannot see daylight, and the enquiry proceeds on this basis: "If he can't see, how does he know when it's morning?" The response alludes not to time, which ought to be the case, given that clocks and watches are available in large, tactile, or talking formats, but to the most basic of instincts, hunger: "The man gets up because he has to have breakfast." This misplaced use of the conjunction *because* implies that the woman is considering *why* Kuusisto would rise, rather than how he might know when to do so. In other words, the boy's question pertains to epistemology, but his mother's response—that is, the answer provided by a significant pedagogue—constitutes a disparaging statement about the ontology of the blind.

Extrinsic to the idea of a positive correlation between ontological status and visual acuity is the likelihood of eye-to-eye complicity, which in its simplest form involves two or more unseen gazers silently uniting to link someone who has a visual impairment with the metanarrative of blindness—as the woman in Kuusisto's example may have wished, if only her child had understood the rules. To express this with allusion to the Barthesian, linguistic rendering of the gaze, we might say that unseen gazes communicate exclusion. At this juncture it must be acknowledged that staring encounters, for Garland-Thomson, are "pliable interventions that respond to the immediate needs and aims of both starers and starees"; stares can be "broken off, turned away, continued, softened, or hardened"; and an experienced staree "often can take the lead, but a starer must be willing to follow, to stay with the staree if the interaction is to generate any mutual recognition" (*Staring* 194). Staring encounters, then, must involve at least two participants, the starer and the staree. However, the very essence of what I mean by eye-to-eye complicity is that the gazee does not, may not, and indeed cannot participate. This social dynamic is portrayed in Norton's "The Girl in the Corner," for when Ivy is asked if she would like to "see" some pictures, her husband's eyes "swivelled round to Pippa—and he smiled apologetically, as though to say: "We have to put it like that—we have to play her game"" (11). When Ivy asks if she may buy a kitten, moreover, the narrator describes her husband's hesitation by saying, "Another helpless one to care for, his eyes seemed to say, another tie" (14).[14] The paradox of this dynamic is that, while being of great curiosity value, the blind become ontologically insignificant, effectively vanish in the language and identification of their sighted counterparts, in the identification of unseen gazers. It is as though comparable visual acuity constitutes a stronger connection than even the closest of relationships.[15] Norton's Ivy, for example, is betrayed by her husband. This state of affairs is worsened by the fact that she is betrayed to complete strangers, the implication being that elevated ontology and epistemology can be not only appropriated by but also taken for granted among unseen gazers.

Conclusion

As a controlling presence, the unseen gazer may be said to personify ocularnormativism. He or she regards the gazee as something of a spectacle, an object of not only astonishment but also pleasure, both of which are derived from asymmetry. Deemed asexual, the gazee becomes a safe object for the unseen gaze. This objectification is a form of normate reductionism and as such makes the gazee all the easier to influence. After all, from the ocularcentric subject position of the unseen gazer, the gazee appears stripped of her or his subjectivity. What is more, according to the concept of panopticism, the gazee is likely to internalize this reductionism and thus the norms that grow from ocularcentric assumptions. That is to say, in endeavoring to deflect the unseen gaze by mimicking visual perception, the gazee falls under ocularnormative control. The influence may seem relatively benign in the examples explored in this chapter, but there are also deeply disturbing manifestations in the form of internalized notions of pointlessness, the suicidal tendencies to which I now turn.

Culturally Assisted Suicide

The Mourning and Melancholia of Blindness Deconstructed

Many self-help books are written to explain how people can "endure" or "triumph over" impairments, observes Michael Davidson, and several figures are deemed exemplary in this respect—as illustrated in chapter 5 with reference to the fictional community named after Mary Keller. This ableist ideology serves both to shape a "fragile sense of embodiment" and to erase the work of those of us who have impairments from birth, not to mention those of us who struggle for "changes in public policy and social attitudes"; it also reinforces the binary system that "divides the world into lives worth living and those that are not," a division that provokes much debate about physician-assisted suicide (Davidson xvii). The focus in this chapter is the same damning division, but the aspect of ableism under consideration is more specifically ocularnormative. The metanarrative of blindness is underpinned by a binary system that divides the world into lives worth living and those of people who do not perceive by visual means. Implicit in this division is, to employ the terms of Gordon Allport's model of prejudicial behavior, a kind of extermination, the idea that death is the best way forward for people who have severe visual impairments. Thus, in accordance with Davidson's definition of a critical disability aesthetics as one that defamiliarizes the entrenched binary system, I deconstruct the tragic suicidal figure who lurks beneath explanations of how people "endure" or "triumph over" impairments.

The coinage of the critical term *culturally assisted suicide* is grounded in a multidisciplinary array of sources including autobiography, psychosocial research, and literary representation. For the purpose of this chapter, the traditionally tragic rendering of blindness can be illustrated sufficiently with reference to Joseph Conrad's *The End of the Tether* (1902), a seafaring novel that takes Captain Whalley's struggle with blindness to the extreme. Yet the suicidal mode of depiction is disrupted by J. M. Synge's contemporaneous play, *The Well of the Saints* (1905), which renders not blindness but visual restoration unbearable for the central characters, Martin and Mary Doul. Though explicitly very different, when compared and contrasted, these literary texts both serve to illustrate the complexities of culturally assisted suicide. The outcome is grave not only when Captain Whalley journeys into blindness but also when Martin and Mary escape from sightedness. Such representations illustrate how a chasm is constructed between the blind and the sighted that suggests those of us who have visual impairments are fundamentally distinct from those of us who do not.

The Mourning and Melancholia of Blindness

As we might say of pretty much any narrative, a transitional phase is included in the metanarrative of blindness, the noteworthy implication being that people end up mourning the loss of vision. There are, according to Freud's "Mourning and Melancholia" (1917), four "distinguishing mental features" of mourning: an end of interest in the "outside world," a loss of the "capacity to love," a general "inhibition" of "activity," and "profoundly painful dejection" (252). The trope of blindness-castration synonymy alone would be enough to align these features with the metanarrative of blindness, as illustrated in chapter 3, so the idea to which we now attend, profoundly painful dejection, only underscores that relevance.

An autobiographical rendering of painful dejection can be found when John Hull remembers mourning his loss of vision for four and a half years, "like a long, slow and lingering death" (114). Even after the proposed phase has passed, Hull is "sometimes still afflicted by a sharp sense of grief and loss," especially in the presence of his children, and anticipates that "many of these feelings will recur," that he "shall lapse into mourning again and again" (113–14). Such feelings are also documented in the work of a number of twentieth-century social scientists.[1] For example, mourning is implicit in the way that some people who have visual impairments are said to refer to their "dead eyes" (Blank 11). Indeed, the state is sometimes likened to grieving for the death of a loved one: "We may always miss the deceased, but nevertheless we go on living, eventually to regain a reasonable degree of happiness" (Kirtley 35). We might think of the contagiousness motif considered in chapter 5 when reading that, as part of an adjustment process, the mourning is for the "generalized global loss of vision," that there is a "generalized global awareness" of being "different" (Tuttle 54). But judging by these and other such studies, some people who have visual impairments (and/or some people with particular interests in visual impairment) do accept the cultural notion of dead eyes, meaning that mourning becomes an entirely appropriate response.

The idea of mourning the loss of sight is embedded with the assumption that people who have visual impairments must, and/or should, long to see.[2] Such ocularnormative thinking, however, is challenged by Georgina Kleege's experiential knowledge: "If I lost the sight I have, I would miss it. But to mourn that loss as I mourn the loss of loved ones would be to buy the assertion that human experience is always, first and foremost, visual. I see through that now" (*Sight Unseen* 119). In the terms of the present book we might say that there is an ocularnormative logic that equates life with light and sight, from which it follows that sightlessness may be equated with darkness and death—a tragic extension of the blindness-darkness synonymy considered in chapter 1.

This mournful line of thought is captured in a number of literary characterizations, one of which can be found in Conrad's *The End of the Tether.* An experienced seaman, Captain Whalley is blind but carefully conceals this fact in order that he may continue working and thus financially supporting his estranged daughter, Ivy. The narrative moves forward, in part, as a result of the gradual revelation of Whalley's blindness.[3] This sense of movement proves particularly important later in the chapter, but the thing for us to note here is that it is in no way positive. He describes his blindness by saying, "It is as if the light were ebbing out of the world. Have you ever watched the ebbing sea on an open stretch of sands withdrawing farther and farther away from you? It is like this—only there will be no flood to follow. Never. It is as if the sun were growing smaller, the stars going out one by one" (269). In the ocularcentric terms of Conrad's novel, blindness and the associated darkness are indicative of old age and misery, a departure from the light and life that Whalley is leaving behind. In losing his sight he loses his life, and blindness becomes as one with death.

But more than depicting someone in mourning, it might be said that Captain Whalley's great sadness becomes pathological, that his character is defined in terms of melancholia. The difference between mourning and melancholia is, for Freud, a "lowering of the self-regarding feelings to a degree that finds utterance in self-reproaches and self-revilings, and culminates in a delusional expectation of punishment" ("Mourning and Melancholia," 252). This punishment takes the form of death in several literary representations.[4] Indeed, Conrad's Captain Whalley is said to experience "the darkness of the living grave" (289), as though life with blindness were a metaphorical death that could only be relieved by literal death. The darkness of this state is significant because, as well as connotations of malevolence, attached to the word *darkness* are those of depression. To denote blindness with the word or derivatives of the word *darkness* is simultaneously to connote melancholia.[5] Like the mental features of mourning, then, the additional feature of melancholia is clearly relevant to the metanarrative of blindness.[6]

Embedded with the mourning and melancholia of blindness is the platitude that death is preferable to life with a visual impairment. If we accept this profoundly pejorative proposition, the specter of suicide is likely to be raised. In literary representation the motif takes the form of not only the suicidal act, which is considered later, but also invocation.[7] For example, Conrad's Captain Whalley says, "It seems to me that, like the blinded Samson, I would find the strength to shake down a temple upon my head. [. . .] I've been praying for death since" (266). Bearing in mind the underpinning notion that blindness constitutes an end of life, it is something of a paradox that Whalley's prayers are for death. After all, is his state not supposed to be a variant of that very desired outcome? But for us the salient point about any such invocation of suicide is that it reveals, or at least suggests, the internalized key to the most disturbing element of the metanarrative of blindness. It is as though Whalley regards suicide as if it were the obvious way forward.[8]

That suicide may seem like an obvious option not only for blind characters but also for people who have visual impairments is illustrated as Hull remembers a social encounter comparable to those considered in the introduction to the present book. Hull and his daughter go out for a meal during which he begins to feel strangely remote. The waiters do not address any remark to him, the consequence being that he reluctantly makes his requests for service through his daughter. That she is sitting opposite rather than next to him only deepens the feeling that she is "not really there," his "sense of abstraction and isolation" (Hull 127). He feels emotionally drained by the time he gets home and succumbs to an overwhelming desire to lie down. From the warmth and comfort of his bed he begins to wonder what it would be like to lie under a blanket of snow:

> I have read that people caught in snowstorms find that, if they give in to the temptation to lie down and rest, they often feel perfectly cosy, but they never wake up. I found myself wondering what it would be like if that were to happen to me now. When I woke up after a couple of hours sleep, the thought occurred to me that what I have been experiencing was not so much depression, since I felt rather happy, at least physically. My body felt relaxed. Had it been a sort of desire to die? Do people die in their sleep during such conditions? Can the psyche simply renounce life? Can the spirit simply not return? Can one commit suicide by mere desire? (127)

Hull explains this episode by asserting that the most profound feelings go beyond feeling, for they leave us numb. He infers that beneath the conscious desire to escape, he is "in the grip of a profound melancholy" caused by the impoverishment of his relationship with his daughter (127). For me, however, the relational impoverishment on which we should really focus is the one between Hull and the restaurateurs. The ocularcentrism of the scenario is not surprising, given that most customers are likely to have access to often useful visible cues, but the ocularnormative shift is highly problematic. Visual perception becomes not simply sufficient but a necessary condition of subjectivity, meaning that Hull is effectively excluded from his own conversation with the restaurateurs. He internalizes this thinking on two levels: implicitly, when he questions the very presence of his daughter, and explicitly, when he comes to invoke suicide.

Much twentieth-century research considers this supposed link between visual impairment and suicidal contemplations. For example, Blank provides a psychoanalytic case study of a thirty-five-year-old woman who, having previously cherished an ideal of "independence," becomes profoundly depressed, apparently unable to tolerate the "inevitability" of remaining "hopelessly dependent" (15). She angrily refuses to learn braille or to associate with other people who have visual impairments. Her time is spent on inactive hatred of herself and others. She is said to become useless at her job, in spite of the assistance offered by colleagues. Finally she is persuaded to seek psychiatric support but prior to her appointment attempts suicide by taking a large number of barbiturates. A late twentieth-century work of psychology agrees that some people cannot "bear" to face the fact that they are "stuck with their blindness for the rest of their lives," the immediate conclusion being that life is not worth living: "They will either retreat into a world of passivity and self-pity from which they may never emerge, or they may even initially panic and try to take their own lives" (Dodds 2). Thus, notwithstanding a point made in our own century by the psychologist Trevor Hine, that actual attempts at suicide among people who have visual impairments are very rare, there are several documented cases that resonate with the invocation of suicide in literary representations.

Like Hull's autobiographical account, many fictional representations of blindness go no further than the invocation or contemplation of suicide, but this is not the case in Conrad's *The End of the Tether*.[9] "God seems to have forgotten me," writes Captain Whalley in a letter ultimately read by Ivy. "I want to see you—and yet death would be a greater favor. If you ever read these words, I charge you to begin by thanking a God merciful at last, for I shall be dead then, and it will be well. My dear, I am at the end of my tether" (298). What causes this eponymous state of mind is expressed without ambiguity, for Whalley goes on to assert that his "sight is going" (298). In effect the letter becomes a suicide note, for Whalley decides to drown himself and puts pieces of iron into his pockets in order that the chances of survival are negligible (294). This episode illustrates the least subtle form of the suicide motif—namely, the act. In relation to invocation the suicidal act is, by definition, more extreme, but that is not to say that it is always explicit, that it is never ambiguous—a point illustrated later with reference to the end of Synge's *The Well of the Saints*.

Resonant with Conrad's novel, the consequence of visual impairment can indeed be grave according to a number of late twentieth-century case studies, such as the one provided by Lloyd Caplan in which a thirty-year-old man has two unsuccessful eye operations and commits suicide while awaiting a third (169). The man is out with a friend in an unfamiliar area when he attempts to navigate a dimly lit hallway. But he trips over a low obstacle, falls down a flight of stairs, and cuts his face in several places. Two days later he takes his own life. This suicidal act corresponds with no fewer than twelve case studies gathered at the end of the twentieth century by Diego de Leo, Portia Hickey, Gaia Meneghel, and Christopher Cantor. One of the studies also involves hearing loss, but it is stressed that the deceased begins to lose his eyesight shortly before committing suicide, a point bolstered by another example in which an eighty-one-year-old woman with "no known psychopathology or recent traumatic life stressors" kills herself the day she is told that "the prognosis of her condition" is "blindness" (de Leo et al. 341–42). Like the invocation of suicide, then, the act is explored in the medical and social sciences as well as literary representations.

Of course these and other such case studies are interpreted in many ways. The psychological autopsy findings are said to indicate that "those with worsening sight and the prognosis of eventual blindness are at comparatively high risk of suicide" (de Leo et al. 343). It is also said to be "crucial" to "assure the person about to undergo eye surgery" that there are "methods to assist" her or him into a "productive and gratifying life regardless of the outcome" (Caplan 165). But as we might expect, these and other such conclusions do not take into account the significance of cultural representations. In the terms of the present book it might be postulated that the hegemonic force of ocularnormativism plays a part, that the grave results are indicative of the internalization of the metanarrative of blindness. As Allport puts it, one's "reputation, whether false or true, cannot be hammered, hammered, hammered" into one's "head without doing something to one's character" (142). With this point in mind we can easily illustrate the notion of culturally assisted suicide, for in Blank's study the woman's anger is not based on the reality but on the very idea of learning braille and associating with the blind; in Caplan's study the man fantasizes about blindness, about "being led helplessly through a dark maze of dangerous streets and alleys" (169); and in de Leo et al.'s study the man commits suicide as he begins to lose his eyesight, the woman on the day she is given the prognosis of blindness. That is to say, in each case the suicidal act is explicitly based on beliefs rather than experience, notions that reflect the metanarrative of blindness invoked by the characterization of Conrad's Captain Whalley, among many others, rather than the lives of people who have visual impairments.

The Poisonous Cure

Though evidently a cardinal component in the metanarrative of blindness, misery is not always so straightforward in twentieth-century representations, as illustrated in Synge's *The Well of the Saints.* The play opens with a conversation between Martin and Mary Doul. That they are both blind is implicitly linked to the topic of the conversation, Mary's supposedly striking beauty, for the stage directions furnish us with a very different account of a weather-beaten, ugly woman:

> MARY DOUL: Who wouldn't have a cracked voice sitting out all the year in the rain falling? It's a bad life for the voice, Martin Doul, though I've heard tell there isn't anything like the wet south wind does be blowing upon us for keeping a white beautiful skin—the like of my skin—on your neck and on your brows, and there isn't anything at all like a fine skin for putting splendour on a woman.
>
> MARTIN DOUL: [teasingly, but with good humour] I do be thinking odd times we don't know rightly what way you have your splendour, or asking myself, maybe, if you have it at all, for the time I was a young lad, and had fine sight, it was the ones with sweet voices were the best in face.
>
> MARY DOUL: Let you not be making the like of that talk when you've heard Timmy the smith, and Mat Simon, and Patch Ruadh, and a power besides saying fine things of my face, and you know rightly it was "the beautiful dark woman" they did call me in Ballinatone.
>
> MARTIN DOUL: [as before] If it was itself I heard Molly Byrne saying at the fall of night it was little more than a fright you were.
>
> MARY DOUL: [sharply] She was jealous, God forgive her, because Timmy the smith was after praising my hair -
>
> MARTIN DOUL: [with mock irony] Jealous!
>
> MARY DOUL: Ay, jealous, Martin Doul; and if she wasn't itself, the young and silly do be always making game of them that's dark, and they'd think it a fine thing if they had us deceived, the way we wouldn't know we were so fine-looking at all. (67–68)

The implication from the outset is that the Douls are oblivious to the reality experienced by the sighted characters—and, by extension, the reader and audience of the play. This ocularcentric deceit contributes to an implied contentment. Indeed, many literary critics go further in stressing that Martin likens blindness to dreaming dreams in the night (Synge 90), that the "tension between dream and actuality" is thematic in the play (Price 139), that the Douls "build up their sense of identity by means of conversation and daydream rather than by action" (Skelton 92), and that they find "comfort in the truth of dreams" (Upton 356). In these terms, when blind, the Douls lead a dreamlike existence that contrasts harshly with the nightmare endured by Conrad's Captain Whalley.

So as to avoid giving the simplistic impression that *The Well of the Saints* is an iconoclastic text, it should be acknowledged that discourse in and around the play frequently rests on aspects of the metanarrative of blindness—such as the blindness-dream confusion considered in chapter 4—but the thing for us to note here is that, for the Douls, blindness does not mean misery. On the contrary, it is visual restoration that causes multiple levels of upset. For example, we are presented with a radical variation of the theme considered in chapter 6, the spectacle of blindness, for it is when cured that Martin becomes the source of much amusement. With the benefit of visual perception he finds himself no longer able to recognize his own wife:

> MOLLY BYRNE: Let you keep away from me, and not be soiling my chin. [People laugh loudly.]
>
> MARTIN DOUL: [bewildered] It's Molly's voice you have.
>
> MOLLY BYRNE: Why wouldn't I have my own voice? Do you think I'm a ghost?
>
> MARTIN DOUL: Which of you all is herself? [He goes up to Bride.] Is it you is Mary Doul? I'm thinking you're more the like of what they said. [peering at her] For you've yellow hair, and white skin, and it's the smell of my own turf is rising from your shawl. [He catches her shawl.]
>
> BRIDE: [pulling away her shawl] I'm not your wife and let you get out of my way. [The people laugh again.]
>
> MARTIN DOUL: [with misgiving, to another girl] Is it yourself it is? You're not so fine-looking, but I'm thinking you'd do, with the grand nose you have, and your nice hands and your feet.
>
> GIRL: [scornfully] I never seen any person that took me for blind, and a seeing woman, I'm thinking, would never wed the like of you. (Synge 79)

Something of the beauty Martin has been led to expect is observed in other women whom, as a consequence, he mistakes for Mary, confusion found hilarious by the villagers who jeeringly and repeatedly ask him to try again. The timing is crucial because, rather than being elicited by Martin's bewilderment alone, in each case the laughter is held back until the very point of his rejection: Molly says to Martin, "Let you keep away from me," and "People laugh loudly"; Bride says, "Get out of my way," and "The people laugh again"; and the girl "turns away, and the people laugh once more." The thing for us to keep in mind is that part of the so-called entertainment value of blind man's buff is derived from the blows received by the person to whom the task of mimicking blindness falls. In Synge's inversion of the game, therefore, the sighted villagers hold back their laughter to sustain their deception and thus ensure that Martin feels the metaphorical blows of rejection.

The play also departs a little from the metanarrative of blindness insofar as it is more representative in terms of gender. Most obviously, the dramatis personae include a blind woman as well as the more common blind man, meaning that, nominally at least, the ideas are explored from both female and male perspectives. For example, albeit after Martin, Mary is similarly cured and teased about her spouse's appearance, as illustrated when Molly asks, "What is it you think of himself, with the fat legs on him, and the little neck like a ram?" (80).[10] But there surely can be no doubting that Martin is the main character in the play. His retort to the jeering of the sighted villagers is bold and impassioned: "Isn't it a black shame for a drove of pitiful beasts the like of you to be making game of me, and putting a fool's head on me the grand day of my life? Ah, you're thinking you're a fine lot, with your giggling, weeping eyes, a fine lot to be making game of myself and the woman I've heard called the great wonder of the west" (79). The dominance of the blind man is furthered, in terms of the metanarrative of blindness, for although even conventional beauty may be perceived by other than visual means (especially in intimate relationships), Martin bears the full brunt of the supposed aesthetic unawareness as he recalls the "bad black day" when he was "roused up" and found he was the "like of the little children do be listening to the stories of an old woman, and do be dreaming after in the dark night that it's in grand houses of gold they are, with speckled horses to ride, and do be waking again, in a short while, and they destroyed with the cold, and the thatch dripping, maybe, and the starved ass braying in the yard?" (87). That is to say, in accordance with the social roles considered in chapter 3, the most dramatic points of the play pertain to the fact that Martin gets to look, stare, and/or gaze at Mary, roles disturbing for both of the newly sighted characters.

So with allusion to Plato's Pharmakon, which will "always be apprehended as both antidote and poison" (Derrida, "Rhetoric of Drugs" 235), we might say that *The Well of the Saints* complicates the glorious, life-enhancing restoration of sight that is implied by tragic modes of representation.[11] Though a pivotal point in *The Well of the Saints,* Martin and Mary Doul's cure by a wandering friar becomes complex in a way that differs greatly from, say, Conrad's application of blindness. After all, in *The Well of the Saints,* the first instance of cure is temporary, as indicated when Timmy tells Martin that those cured by the saint "lose their sight after a while" and that Mary is "dimming again" (84), but when something permanent is offered the response may seem a little surprising. Martin defends himself and Mary by saying, "We're not asking our sight, holy father, and let you walk on your own way, and be fasting, or praying, or doing anything that you will, but, leave us here in our peace, at the crossing of the roads, for it's best we are this way, and we're not asking to see" (100). The role of the blind beggar is posited as a challenge to the ocularnormativism exemplified when the saint asks, "Is his mind gone that he's no wish to be cured this day, or to be living or working, or looking on the wonders of the world?" (100). Mary, it must be said, is half persuaded by the saint and the villagers that sightedness could be beneficial for her, but Martin remains resolute as the second, supposedly permanent cure is offered. The saint begins the procedure with reference to the power of the water from "the grave of the four beauties of God," but Martin knocks the can to the ground (103), meaning that the Douls ultimately remain blind.

The metanarrative of blindness continues to deconstruct if, as Synge is set against Conrad, *The Well of the Saints* against *The End of the Tether,* psychosocial research about depression in sight restoration is invoked to counter the ocularnormative position. For instance, David Lester's collection of case studies includes a woman who has a forty-five-year history of deteriorating vision. She is found to have dislocated lenses and, after having her vision partially restored by glasses, becomes "distraught and depressed" (678), as though moving beyond her comfort zone. Along similar lines, a "large proportion" of senile patients who have had cataract operations are said to have become "psychiatrically disturbed" (Lester 679). In a second gathering of examples, Lester includes a man whose occipital lobe is injured in a car crash, but who denies the fact of his visual impairment until it passes and then becomes "severely depressed," as well as a thirty-three-year-old man who has his sight restored after twenty-seven years of visual impairment but suddenly begins to feel depressed (757). The resonance with *The Well of the Saints* becomes especially clear in the instance of a woman who complains to her father that everything she sees causes her a "disagreeable emotion," saying, "I was much more at ease in my blindness" (Lester 679). The implication for us to note is that blindness constitutes a place, rather than a characteristic.

In thinking about the most extreme response to sight restoration it is worth us pondering the ambiguous ending of *The Well of the Saints.* Sight is rejected by the Douls, who, in return, are rejected by the sighted villagers. The wish to be left in peace at the crossing of the roads is denied, so Martin and Mary set off on the long, stony, and often flooded pathway to the towns of the south. Timmy says, "I'm thinking the two of them will be drowned together in a short while," to which the saint replies, "They have chosen their lot" (105). Given that the Douls reject the place with which they are familiar, in favor of a deadly terrain, it might be argued that their refusal to see culminates in a form of suicide.[12] The likelihood of death by drowning is high but nonetheless preferable to the sighted existence offered by the saint and the villagers.

The implied fate of the Douls corresponds with a number of factual examples. Lester links the restoration of vision not only with depression but also with the act of suicide by citing the cases of a farmer who jumps to his death four days after having cataracts removed, two other people who attempt suicide after similarly successful surgery, and a fifty-two-year-old man who commits suicide within a year of having his vision restored (678). There is also a woman who becomes suicidal subsequent to restoration of an appreciable amount of vision without which she has lived since childhood (Lester 757). The argument ventured by Lester is that, having visual impairments and enduring the associated hardships and frustrations, these and other such people may eagerly seek visual restoration as the change that will lead to a better and happier life. But in practice, asserts Lester, visual restoration gives a person a "difficult rehabilitative task" and removes a "convenient well-defined cause" for any unhappiness. When this crutch is removed the person is forced to realize that the unhappiness has its source in her or his personality (Lester 757). In short, suicide becomes a viable option because the person can, if we iterate Lester's location metaphor, no longer believe the grass is greener on the other side of the hill.

Worlds Apart

What the location metaphor implies is that blindness and sightedness are fundamentally different.[13] A philosophical slant on this differentiation is offered when Jonathan Rée remembers being told that he could damage his eyes by straining or tiring them, the solution being to keep them shut whenever possible: "If I lost my eyesight, I thought, I would never be able to tell what was brushing up against me, or what I was about to tread on or sit in. I would not even know what I was picking up and putting in my mouth" (17). He departs only a little from the ocularnormative epistemology by asserting that, although the "weight and solidity of things, as revealed by touching, pushing or shoving," contribute much to the idea of their "thinghood," it is through the eyes that the vast majority of this knowledge is acquired: "My sense of things seemed to be the natural partner of my sense of sight. What horrified me about the idea of going blind was the thought of being cut off from this visible world of things" (42). The ocularnormative implication is that interactions with the world are not partly but essentially visual.

The location metaphor also connotes the idea that blindness and sightedness are places rather than characteristics. The problematics of this notion begin to emerge if we stay in a philosophical frame of mind but consider the phenomenological approach of Maurice Merleau-Ponty's *The Visible and the Invisible* (1968), which disputes the notion that "the world is what we see" by saying, "if we seek to articulate it into theses or statements, if we ask ourselves what is this we, what seeing is, and what thing or world is, we enter into a labyrinth of difficulties and contradictions" (3). The trouble, for me, is that to accept the notion of a visual world is to predicate that of its nonvisual counterpart, and vice versa, the result being what seems like a natural and necessary division between the inhabitants of each. This thinking resonates in the work of social scientists who find that people who have visual impairments "dwell in a world that is apart from and beyond the one ordinary men [and women] inhabit" (Scott 4), that they "give the impression" of "being in another world" (Dodds 36). This other world is, presumably, the blind world and as such must be not only differentiated but also distanced in relation to the sighted world.[14]

Though hinted at in Conrad's *The End of the Tether* when Captain Whalley conjures up the image of an ebbing sea on an open stretch of sands withdrawing farther and farther away, the differentiated and distanced world of the blind is explored at some length in Synge's *The Well of the Saints*. The Douls constitute an out-group in relation to the sighted villagers, as is implicit when Martin says "the people" are "after passing to the fair" (67), and Mary says, "It's great jokes the people'll be making now" (93), for the noun *people* is successfully employed to denote only the sighted villagers. It is also noteworthy that upon losing their sight the Douls reunite as quickly as they separate when it is initially gained, the implication being that the blind belong together, away from the sighted. Indeed, at the onset of his blindness, Martin himself alludes to the notion of two separate worlds: "And that's the last thing I'm to set my sight on in the life of the world—the villainy of a woman and the bloody strength of a man. Oh, God, pity a poor blind fellow, the way I am this day with no strength in me to do hurt to them at all" (92). Although villainy and bloody strength are in no way related to sight, Martin implies that they are to be left behind when blindness is regained, that he is moving from "the life of the world" to some spectral substitute.

Embedded with the differentiated and distanced world of the blind is the eugenic division between people who have visual impairments and people who do not. Resonating with institutionalism, the division is consistent with the accommodative approach considered in chapter 5. This segregation is explored in one woman's first impressions of a twentieth-century institution called, rather predictably, the Lighthouse:

> We visited the Braille library; the classrooms; the clubrooms where the blind members of the music and dramatic groups meet; the recreation hall where on festive occasion the blind dance with the blind; the bowling alleys where the blind play together; the cafeteria, where all the blind gather to eat together; the huge workshops where the blind earn a subsistence income by making mops and brooms, weaving rugs, caning chairs. As we moved from room to room, I could hear the shuffling of feet, the muted voices, the tap-tap-tapping of canes. Here was the safe, segregated world of the sightless—a completely different world, I was assured by the social worker, from the one I had just left. [. . .] I was expected to join this world. To give up my profession and to earn my living making mops. The Lighthouse would be happy to teach me how to make mops. I was to spend the rest of my life making mops with other blind people, eating with other blind people, dancing with other blind people. I became nauseated with fear, as the picture grew in my mind. Never had I come upon such destructive segregation. (Goffman 51)

Differentiation is explicit in the reference to a completely different world, and distance is implied by the sense that a world is being left behind. Given the point made earlier in the chapter, we must recognize that the woman is new to visual impairment, that her nauseating fear of entering into the blind world is based on the metanarrative of blindness rather than on actual experience. But the thing for us to note here is that the very idea of a safe, segregated world of the sightless is indicative of enforced separation, as is the prospect that the blind only eat, play, work, and dance with the blind. This thinking illustrates what is meant by a "cultural map" that points out "the land of blindness and that of sightedness with a clearly defined border between the two," but without "border crossings" (Titchkosky 102). There is a clear expectation that the woman will no longer interact with people who do not have visual impairments, that she will become as one with the exclusive and homogenous group, the blind.

Conclusion

At its most extreme, the metanarrative of blindness perpetuates the polarity of lives worth living and those of people who do not perceive by visual means. In these ocularnormative terms it follows that some people who have visual impairments will be preoccupied with a longing to see that, if and when unsatisfied, may result in misery, desperation, and/or suicide. This terrible logic is bolstered by the lack of critical engagement with cultural renderings of a null-and-void existence, whereby suicide is flagged up as a viable option for people who have visual impairments. After all, people whose vision is newly impaired will be nonetheless familiar with the metanarrative of blindness, which is therefore likely to contribute to any initial responses. Yet suicidal notions of blindness are countered by those of sightedness in several cultural representations, and according to some social scientists, those of us who have visual impairments may be prone to suicide if faced with visual restoration.[15] It is my contention that this apparent contradiction is indicative of the entrenched binary system that becomes manifest in renderings of a differentiated and distanced world of the blind. The construct of a separate world resonates with the eugenic idea considered in chapter 5, that people who have visual impairments should be kept apart from people who do not have visual impairments. The trouble is that defining the antithetical entities of the blind world and the sighted world—and, by extension, the blind and the sighted—means simultaneously inserting a vast space between the two. Thus, sight loss and sight restoration both come to present the bearer with the same disturbing sense of a chasm to cross, meaning the cause of despair can be more accurately located in the binary system that underpins the metanarrative of blindness.

Epilogue

Though not in a position to make any overarching claims about literature, I can assert that evidence of the metanarrative of blindness is recurrent in twentieth-century writing. If I speculate a little about why this is so, I wonder if it is simply because authors who do not have visual impairments can nonetheless close their eyes and imagine blindness, albeit distinct from the experiential knowledge of people who have visual impairments. Maybe it could have something to do with the fact that such authors can sometimes stare at people who have visual impairments without interruption, that the unseen gaze provides a pleasurable opportunity of and for writing that is not to be missed. Perhaps there is an element of authorial aloofness, of being able to get away with drawing on the metanarrative of blindness rather than exploring experiential knowledge on account of remoteness. This state of affairs is indicative of both avoidance and discrimination, for even in our own century the vast majority of writing is not readily accessible to many of us who have visual impairments. It could be this very remoteness that makes the construction of alterity so tempting for the creators of fiction. It may be that too many authors are just too quick to follow in the direction of their antecedents, too willing to accept problematic tropes, terminology, and etymology. All of these speculations are supported in this book, underpinned by what is known as ocularcentrism, as well as what I call ophthalmocentrism and ocularnormativism. The result is the supposed supremacy of sight that predicates the mystery if not tragedy of blindness, and vice versa, a binary trap to which many twentieth-century writers seem vulnerable.

The metatheory posited in this book is underpinned by Gordon Allport's classic model of prejudicial behavior. Here, however, antilocution, avoidance, discrimination, physical attack, and extermination, Allport's five incremental stages, are extended in accordance with various works in critical theory and disability studies. First, cultural representations are located somewhere alongside antilocution. Second, the act of avoidance is expanded to include institutionalization and other methods of segregation. Third, discrimination is explored in terms of ocularcentrism and ableism. Fourth, visual violation emerges as a subtle illustration of physical attack. Fifth, and most controversially, the category of extermination comes to include culturally assisted suicide, meaning that the model is not only incremental but also circular. We might say that these are some of the ocularnormative outcomes of the metanarrative of blindness, that in keying people who have visual impairments to the metanarrative, we engage in an act of prejudice.

The metatheory to which I refer is a response to the metanarrative of blindness, which is an essentially Modernist construct and as such may be said to render the book postmodern. This being so I must finish by supplementing the sections on irony and appropriation (in chap. 1 and chap. 2) with a brief consideration of experientially informed parodic portrayal, such as that found in Charles Wheeler's *Snakewalk* (1989). Many criticisms can be aimed at Wheeler's novel, but the thing for us to note is how the more informed portrayal differs from those considered thus far. To this end it helps to juxtapose the parodic portrayal with illustrations of the received notion of suicidal blindness, for the contrast with ocularnormative ideas of life worth living underscores the value of progressive representation.

If culturally assisted suicide is aligned with the most extreme of prejudicial acts, then one of the most dramatic representations is found in a novel considered in chapter 4, John Wyndham's *The Day of the Triffids* (1951). I say this because of what happens when protagonist William Masen unbandages his eyes. He ventures beyond his hospital room and discovers the distraught Doctor Soames, a senior member of staff who has evidently lost his eyesight and insists on being shown to his office. The doctor endeavors to make an urgent phone call without success. He takes a moment to find his bearings and then unexpectedly launches himself at the fifth-floor window and crashes through (16). Given the hospital setting, like Brian Friel's *Molly Sweeney* (1994) and the extracts from Rupert Thomson's *The Insult* (1996) considered in chapter 2 and chapter 6, this episode might be read as a comment on the medical model of disability, for the doctor's action instantly eliminates the normative problem posed by incurable impairment. But it is not only medical experts who follow this course of action in Wyndham's novel. Indeed, Doctor Soames sets something of a standard insofar as many other characters follow suit.

Suicide is recurrent and somehow becomes merciful when the perpetrator involves someone else, when he or she maximizes, from a eugenic perspective, on the destructive outcome. Indeed, so obvious is suicide as a response to blindness that we are informed that such things are "happening all around" when the transient character Jimmy takes not only his own life but also that of his unnamed lover:

> She clung to him, and he put one arm round her.
> "We'll be all right, darling. Come along."
> "But Jimmy, that's the wrong way—"
> "You've got it twisted round, dear. It's the right way."
> "Jimmy—I'm so frightened. Let's go back."
> "It's too late, darling."
> By the window he paused. With one hand he felt his position very carefully. Then he put both arms round her, holding her to him.
> "Too wonderful to last, perhaps," he said, softly. "I love you, my sweet. I love you so very, very much."
> She turned her lips up to be kissed.
> As he lifted her he turned, and stepped out of the window. . . . (56)

It is important to stress that this is not a double suicide, for Jimmy makes a decision to which his unnamed lover is oblivious: in a tragic display of patriarchy he takes control of the situation by eliminating life that is not worth living. That is to say, we should recognize that the merciful, romantic, and sexual connotations serve only to obscure the fact that this is a homicidal suicide. Jimmy commits both suicide and murder in the ultimate ocularnormative act.

In another example the patriarchy is disrupted, but the scenario becomes still more disturbing insofar as it involves an infanticidal double suicide. Masen enters a saloon bar and finds the landlord frantically opening bottles and discarding them when he discovers they contain gin rather than whiskey. The landlord is newly blind and concludes, correctly (as we later discover), that his blindness is the result of him watching the green shooting stars that Masen has missed. Albeit a little less accurately, the landlord also infers that Masen is the only person who did not watch the comet and thus the only person who can still see. Masen uses his sight to help the landlord locate the eagerly sought bottle of whiskey from which the courage to act derives:

> Wha's good of living blind's a bat? [. . .] Thash what my wife said. An' she was right—only she's more guts than I have. When she found as the kids was blind too, what did she do? Took 'em into our bed with her, and turned on the gas. Thash what she done. An' I hadn't the guts to stick with 'em. She's got pluck, my wife, more'n I have. But I will have soon. I'm goin' back up there soon—when I'm drunk enough. (19)

The already inebriated landlord drinks the whiskey neat and then, explicitly unhindered by Masen, leaves the scene in order to join his wife and children in the kind of death that contributes directly to the eugenic solution. If anything, therefore, rather than challenging the terrible ocularnormative logic, Masen may be said to assist the landlord in his suicide. The implication is that Masen has a lofty aim of saving humanity, but blind characters, such as the landlord, constitute a legitimate sacrifice: they are presented with an invalid existence.

A very different idea of life worth living and thus a far more informed approach to suicide is found in Wheeler's *Snakewalk*. This novel tells the story of Patrick Todd, a largely contemptuous and manifestly self-centered young man who has a profound disdain for conventionality. The bulk of the novel explicates the fact that Patrick is blinded in a boating accident and enrolls at the California Institute for the Blind. For a while he dedicates much of his time at the institute to casual relationships and the consumption of alcohol but is attracted by the comforts of the conventional life he has always despised when he meets and falls in love with one of the novel's many other blind characters, Geri Ciccone. With her he comes to accept the prospect of a long-term relationship, of having children, and of finding regular employment. However, Geri is compelled to end the relationship when they attend a social gathering and Patrick reverts to type insofar as he gets drunk and starts a fight with one of the other guests. Predictably, he makes no effort to change her mind, and at the end of the novel, although in a manifestly negative framing, we are left with the message that blindness does not alter someone's personality—and, by extension, personhood.

Importantly, or at least notably, Wheeler himself has a visual impairment and is said in the blurb to base *Snakewalk* on his experience of a rehabilitation center for the blind in California. Given that I too spent several months at such an institution in the late 1980s, albeit in the rather less sunny English seaside town of Torquay, I must say that the novel does capture something of the experience. With each read I am reminded of institutionalization, incidents, attitudes, and terminology from my own past. So even before reading around the work I inferred an underpinning authorial appreciation of visual impairment. That is not to say that *Snakewalk* departs from the metanarrative of blindness completely, or even substantially, but rather that it contains much detail that is evidently informed by experiential knowledge.

But where Wheeler's *Snakewalk* certainly does depart from the metanarrative of blindness is on the issue of suicide. A counterhegemonic message is advanced repeatedly as Patrick derides the "very high rate of suicide" (11), jokes with Tania that due to her absence he "contemplated suicide a couple times" (125), and teases a bus driver by overtly keying himself to the metanarrative of blindness:

> "Where you headed, boss?" the driver said.
>
> I turned slowly, a very sober look on my face, and pointed. "Out there," I said.
>
> "There ain't no buses runnin' that way, boss. That's the bridge."
>
> "I know," I said, straight-faced, fucking with him. What the hell. A blink can't walk out on a bridge without blowing skirts up. (266)

That we are referred to the metanarrative of blindness cannot be denied, but the tenor of this parodic rendition of the suicide motif is ridicule. The assumptions are explored from an evidently knowing perspective. In Patrick, Wheeler posits a character who is well aware of the metanarrative of blindness, a blind man who knows what that very designation invokes. What is more, he is ascribed awareness that the invocation of suicide is unfounded, that visual impairment is not a sufficient condition of suicide. We might say, therefore, that the metanarrative employed by Wyndham is troubled by Wheeler or even that the informed portrayal scoffs at the likes of its manifestly ocularnormative predecessor.

When I explore this contextualization of the metanarrative with my students, there are sometimes questions about what literary works we *should* read, as though my continual concern about representation is an incitement to avoid certain books. Should we turn away from all pejorative portrayals such as those provided by Wyndham and seek something aligned with social or affirmative models of disability? Should we put an end to our Barthesian mourning for the death of the author and focus our reading on fiction that is written by people who have experiential knowledge of visual impairment, such as Wheeler, or his eminent predecessors James Joyce, Jorge Luis Borges, and so on? When learning about the construct of blindness, should we displace our works of fiction in favor of autobiography? My students are well aware of the pleas of James Charlton's *Nothing about Us without Us* (1998) and, more recently, Lizzy Clark's "Don't Play Me Pay Me" campaign, which seeks to remove the barriers that disabled actors face in finding work, so perhaps it follows that I might well climb on this activist bandwagon and ask people to *read us rather than write us.*

But of course the real problem is not with the primary works that we read. The metanarrative of blindness is tangible in society, so authors are bound to reflect and construct accordingly, be it on a critical, basic, or regressive level. Rather, the salient point is that we engage with those works from a perspective that is informed by disability studies. After all, the discipline is largely led by people who have impairments. That is to say, the editors of the main book series, anthologies, and journals, the authors of the key texts, and the directors of the related research centers generally have experiential knowledge of disability, be it direct or otherwise. What this means is that, in the academy and beyond, even if our primary texts are uninformed, our analyses may benefit from experiential knowledge. The metatheory developed in this book is driven by my own experience of visual impairment and grounded in key works of disability studies, including autobiographical as well as more obviously academic works. The deconstructive process that I adopt often involves a subversion of ableist, ocularcentric, and ophthalmocentric binaries, the effect being a dismantling of the metanarrative of blindness that was recurrent if not prominent in twentieth-century Anglophone writing. The ultimate aim of the project is disruption of the ocularnormativism in which the metanarrative of blindness results.

Notes

Introduction

1. Kleege's *Sight Unseen* outlines another approach. She asserts at the outset that writing the book made her blind and goes on to describe "a sort of 'coming out' narrative, though one without fanfare or a specific time line" (5). Kleege's approach echoes that found in Garland-Thomson's *Extraordinary Bodies,* a book referred to as "the consequence of a coming-out process" (ix).

2. G. Thomas Couser's name has become synonymous with the study of life writing and disability. In "Signifying Bodies" he asserts that as a "medium perhaps unique in its registration of the nexus of the individual, culture, and the body, autobiographical literature can provide a valuable component to humanities courses on disability" (109). The present book is not an autobiography, of course, but for the uninitiated Couser's point helps to explain the use of my anecdotes and the autobiographical passages of others.

3. *JLCDS* is a constant source of information for those of us who work in the field of cultural disability studies, but of particular relevance, here, is Kleege's special issue, "Blindness and Literature."

4. This point is explained and explored more fully in Michalko's "Blindness Enters the Classroom."

5. DS-Hum is a popular electronic mailing list that caters to scholars who work on disability studies in the humanities.

6. Published contemporaneously with Goffman, Hunt's edited collection about stigma is another important early work in the field.

7. Goffman's *Stigma* is also revisited for a disability studies readership in our own century by Barnes and Mercer.

8. I cannot help thinking, here, of an instance in which one of my colleagues was approached by another with an inquiry about how to talk to me, on account of my visual impairment. Would special training be necessary? On one level this question is ridiculous, easily dismissible. But on reflection it is only fair to point out that when someone speaks to me in a noisy setting I may not pick up on the subtleties of the conversation, given my lack of access to visible cues—the nods, winks, and gestures

that assist many of us in sustaining such contact. I would have been more than happy to explain these things, of course, but the problematic assumption was that training would be necessary before any such conversation could take place.

9. Rewriting (though not disputing) the disability studies truism that if we live long enough we all become disabled, McRuer goes so far as to assert, "sooner or later, if we live long enough, we will all become normate" (198). This assertion is said to reflect the dominant story of the gay movement at the turn of the last century, being met with much resistance in more recent years, as cultures have effectively become privatized.

10. This theorizing teases out another level (that is, the anxiety) of the question about how one might talk to someone who has a visual impairment.

11. These and other such jokes are frequently made in our own century but often seem no more progressive than the nineteenth-century cartoon character Mr. Magoo.

Chapter 1

1. From the outset I must stress that when I refer to the disability community I mean academics, activists, and advocates in the field as well as people who have experiential knowledge of impairment and disability. The unifying factor, for me, is a passive or active resistance to ableist and, more specifically, ocularnormative attitudes and actions.

2. Vidali engages with this trope at length in her article on disability and metaphor.

3. Though fairly representative, this sample of twenty dictionary definitions is by no means definitive. Kirtley provides an extensive study of *Webster's Third New International Dictionary* (1966), finding 155 citations under the word *blind* and its grammatical variants, of which only 14 percent pertain to impaired vision (38–41). The remaining nine categories are summarized as concealment, screening, deception; closed or closed at one end, passing only partially through, filled, empty, plugged up, blocked, covered; defective, abortive, diseased, incapacitated, stupefied, dead, sterile, worthless, poisonous, pestiferous; animals; lacking intensity, luster, coloring, or gilding; ignorance, lacking mental vision, judgment or plausibility, carelessness; unintelligibility, indiscernibility, obscurity; purposeless, fortuitous; and profanity. In brief, the familiar pattern occurs, with only one category pertaining to visual impairment and the rest being largely pejorative.

4. Indeed, in Conan Doyle's *Sir Nigel,* Andreas is said to have "lived for many years in darkness" (287); Green's *Blindness* makes more than thirty-five direct references to darkness; Sontag's *Death Kit* informs us that "the blind" have to "walk in the dark" (25), that Hester is "forced to live consistently in the dark" (43), in "endless darkness" (86); in Shreve's *Eden Close,* Andy wonders if the eponymous protagonist can "remember what he used to look like, after all these years of darkness" (142); and the narrator of King's *The Langoliers* describes the ten-year-old Dinah Bellman as a "little girl forced to live her terror in a darkness which was almost complete" (153). The motif of blindness-darkness synonymy is irrefutably recurrent.

5. It is my suggestion that twentieth-century portrayals of blindness-darkness synonymy draw on the metanarrative of blindness, rather than reflecting the experiences of people who have visual impairments, a misrepresentation that is underpinned by the etymology of the word *blind.*

6. The "first wave of any struggle," agrees Davis in *Bending Over Backwards,*

"involves the establishment of the identity against the societal definitions that were formed largely by oppression"; the identity is "turned positive against the negative descriptions used by the oppressive regime" (10).

7. That Kuusisto came to find these words is demonstrable in the success of his prose and poetry, and that this discovery involved the appropriation of traditional terminology is manifest in the title of his award-winning autobiographical work, *Planet of the Blind.*

8. This process is frequently initiated unintentionally. For example, it is acknowledged by Dodds that the term *the blind* "places a barrier between our ability to empathize with another human being who may just happen to be unable to see, but who is otherwise embedded in the same human condition as ourselves" (5). The paradox is that this use of the pronouns *our* and *ourselves* implies a construct of the sighted, an ocularcentric assumption that the reader of the psychological study must have unimpaired vision. Bearing in mind that Dodds's argument is against the erection of psychosocial barriers, his use of pronouns is paradoxical because it reveals a prejudiced, them-and-us mentality, positing the blind as object in relation to the subject position of not only the Implied Author but also the Implied Reader.

9. There are many literary examples of sweeping statements about the blind: London's *The Sea Wolf* makes passing reference to the "feebleness of the blind" (255); Kipling's "They" states that "the blind sing from the soul" (251); Green's *Blindness* declares that writing is "the only thing in which the blind are not hampered" (161); Sontag's *Death Kit* refers to the "natural mistrust of the blind" (224); Sava's *Happiness Is Blind* refers to the "paradoxical air of peace and power which so often marks the faces of the blind" (162); Shreve's *Eden Close* states that there are a "thousand deceits the sighted can practice on the blind" (144); King's *The Langoliers* claims that "sight-sharing is a frequent fantasy of the blind" (22); Saramago's *Blindness* asserts that "the days of the blind, strictly speaking are never likely to be good" (210); and Thomson's *The Insult* informs us that among "the blind there is no tact, no modesty" (21). All these narratives contain representations of blindness, but their applications of the term *the blind* allude to an external, grand source of understanding about anyone who does not align with the cultural construct of the sighted.

10. White's profile is relevant because he is the BBC's disability affairs correspondent; he has been central to numerous television and radio programs about disability and visual impairment, including *In Touch,* which he has presented for more than thirty years, and he has experiential knowledge of visual impairment.

11. With a focus on language, Rodas's article on blindness provides a provocative and powerful disruption of this binary distinction.

12. Some of my preliminary work on terminology has been published in the *British Journal of Visual Impairment, Disability and Society, Entre dos mundos: Revista de traducción sobre discapacidad visual,* the *Journal of Visual Impairment and Blindness,* and *Language, Bodies, and Health.*

13. The term *persons with a visual inhibition* is suggested in my "Blindness and the Problems of Terminology" (2003), while the terms *visually inhibited individuals* and *persons with inhibited vision* are discussed in my "The Terminology Debate Continues" (2004). While I would be the first to admit that the suggested terminology is wholly inadequate, these articles nonetheless achieved their primary aim of stimulating debate (e.g., the latter imparted both Mary Wilkinson's contention that the alternative terminology is unwieldy and Lennard Davis's observation about the connotations of awkwardness that are attached to the word *inhibit*).

14. Indeed, by the start of the twenty-first century the WHO's own scheme had been revised in the form of the International Classification of Functioning and Disability (2001), recognizing environmental factors and shifting the emphasis from negative descriptions of impairment, disability, and handicap to more neutral descriptions of body functions, body structures, activities, and participation.

15. As well as from assumptions about visual acuity, disability can result from assumptions about visual impairment, from cultural notions of homogeneousness that become manifest in exclusion. For example, the provision of a Braille menu in a pub, restaurant, or café is progressive but useless to most people who have visual impairments. Conversely, large-print and audio formats improve access to literature but may be of little or no interest to fluent Braille users.

16. In a progressive society, according to the radical social model, impairment need not result in disability, which is the conceptual basis for the term *post-disability,* coined in my presentation "A Brief Introduction to Post-Disability Literary Criticism," Keele University, 21 Sept. 2004.

17. I cannot contend this point because my mobility is similarly hindered on a windy day.

18. These and other such approaches accord with my own experience of visual impairment, although I would not go so far as to reject the radical social model completely. I cannot echo Barnes and claim that the problems I encounter as someone who has a visual impairment are all socially created but have to say that this is frequently if not generally the case.

19. Even nonverbal cues are not necessarily read or emitted by visual means—they can be haptic or auditory. It might be, for instance, that a man who has a visual impairment comes to expect a hand on his shoulder when being greeted by a close friend in a noisy bar, or that a woman who has a similar impairment expects to hear a familiar tune being whistled when her partner is approaching in a busy town center.

20. The privileging of eye contact is indicative of not only ocularcentrism but also ophthalmocentrism, a concept that I illustrate at length in chap. 3.

21. The term *people who have visual impairments* is preferable to the term *people who are visually impaired,* for although I have used the latter elsewhere it has problematic implications, as though the designated person *becomes* her or his impairment. These implications are discussed further in chap. 2 with reference to Garland-Thomson's *Extraordinary Bodies.*

22. The term *cultural construct* is used in Michalko's *The Two-In-One* to describe the "common view of blindness" (4), echoing Kent's assertion that "most of the traits possessed by blind characters have no factual basis" (par. 3).

Chapter 2

1. Of course this conceptual clash is not without its practical implications, for a key point about the normate subject position is that it predicates the way in which some people are reduced to impairments during social encounters. This normate reductionism is aided greatly by terminological means, as illustrated when Lee documents the mid-twentieth-century experience of an expert typist, conscientious worker, good student, careful listener, and ardent seeker of employment who, having lost his sight, comes to be labeled a blind man. The dire consequence was that he could not get a job typing telephone orders in a department store: "The personnel man was impatient to get the interview over. 'But you're a blind man,' he kept saying and one could almost feel his silent assumption that somehow the incapacity in one aspect

made the man incapable in every other" (15). In the mindset of the interviewer, visual impairment canceled out the interviewee's other qualities; it reduced him to an objectified status.

2. The issue of nominal omission is brought to our attention in Joyce's *Ulysses* when Leopold Bloom assists the character known as the blind stripling across the road and wonders if he has a name (173). More recently, the unnamed writer in Saramago's *Blindness* declares that blind people "do not need a name" (274), an assertion of superfluousness that the doctor's wife explains by saying that "no dog recognises another dog or knows the others by the names they have been given, a dog is identified by its scent and that is how it identifies others, here we are like another breed of dogs" (55). These assertions betray the correlation between nominal omission and the refutation of personhood.

3. As well as hundreds of instances in Saramago's *Blindness,* other texts that portray a character who is only referred to as the blind man include Strindberg's *A Dream Play,* Yeats's *On Baile's Strand,* Brecht's "The Blind Man," and Amado's *Gabriela, Clove and Cinnamon.*

4. The term *spoiled nominal identity* derives from the title of Goffman's *Stigma: Notes on the Management of Spoiled Identity.*

5. Spoiled nominal identity is illustrated in texts such as Brecht's "A Helping Hand," which refers to "blind Lorge" (27); Thomas's *Under Milk Wood,* which refers to "blind Captain Cat" (25, 40, 87); and Donaldson's "The Lady in White," which refers to "blind Festil" (160). Albeit less explicitly, Synge's naming of Martin and Mary Doul in *The Well of the Saints* is relevant, too, because the surname means "blind" in Gaelic (Upton 353).

6. Conan Doyle's *Sir Nigel* refers to a character as "blind Andreas" (287, 290). Such a designation does not reduce the character to a single attribute (insofar as something of his gender and ethnicity remains), but the emphasis on blindness certainly cancels out other qualities, it is indicative of the normate subject position.

7. In *Sir Nigel,* for example, the name *Andreas* is ascribed, yet the character is repeatedly referred to as the blind man (Conan Doyle 287, 288, 290).

8. I am tempted to italicize the use of labels throughout the chapter, thereby emphasizing the precise nature and sheer abundance of the nominal displacement in question, but this device can prove distracting. Instead I will stress at this juncture that all extracts from primary texts have been included for their use of nominal displacement. It is worth making this point because even in our own century the displacement is so common that it may sometimes go unnoticed.

9. Lawrence's application of nominal displacement accords with Brecht's "A Helping Hand," the contemporaneous tale of a tyrant called Lorge who is blinded in a fight and whose name is used in all but two poignant designations: while living riotously off his property the servants are said to have "left the blind man sitting in his room" (26); and from "a distance" the people from the neighbourhood "looked into this hell where the blind man sat" (27). The word *distance* proves particularly significant as the present book progresses.

10. This image of distance and loneliness also resonates with Lorge's predicament in Brecht's "A Helping Hand."

11. Though peripheral to the focus of this chapter, it must be acknowledged that, in terms of procreation, Lehmann's Timmy and Lawrence's Maurice are set apart from the female blind characters in the survey. Timmy has a daughter, and Maurice's wife is pregnant.

12. A comparable example of nominal displacement (right down to the general-

izing application of the indefinite article and the motif of compensatory powers) can be found in *Night without Stars,* when Giles Gordon asserts, "It's surprisingly hard to cheat a blind man. He comes to hear and identify the slightest sounds, for no one ever stays quite still. He almost always knows when someone is near him and what they are doing" (Graham 75).

13. This distinction between badge and label is made in Shakespeare's *Disability Rights and Wrongs* (chap. 5).

14. This state of affairs echoes *Sir Nigel,* wherein the name of Andreas is displaced to bolster the incitement of fear as the eponymous character elicits information from a priest by saying, "Where is the blind man?" (Conan Doyle 290). The implication is that the character's name is discarded because the label has more clout, that it is not the revengeful Andreas but the mythology of blindness to which he is keyed that elicits fear. Nominal displacement also evokes malign empowerment in Green's *Blindness:* "BLIND MAN MURDERS CHILD—no, TORTURES CHILD TO DEATH" (52). The important difference to note, however, is that, even within the realms of fiction, John's vengeance is pure fantasy.

15. The similarities between Lawrence's "The Blind Man" and Carver's "Cathedral" have also been documented in the work of Keith Cushman and Samantha Gillison.

16. It is in the portion of Carver's "Cathedral" that pertains to the period prior to the narrator getting to know Robert that the label *blind man* is applied most frequently. When Robert arrives, for example, the narrator watches through the window with growing animosity—and, following Quayson, we might say aesthetic nervousness—as his wife parks the car: "She went around to the other side of the car to where the blind man was already starting to get out. This blind man, feature this, he was wearing a full beard! A beard on a blind man! Too much, I say. The blind man reached into the backseat and dragged out a suitcase" (296). While nominal displacement occurs throughout the story, it becomes less frequent as the narrator and Robert become acquainted, as the initial sense of friction diminishes. That is to say, Robert is referred to as the blind man seventy times, half of which occur in the first third of the story, before the two men are introduced to each other. This state of affairs is noteworthy because the narrator is familiar with Robert's name throughout the story, meaning that the nominal displacement is strategic.

17. What I mean by nocturnalism is illustrated in *The Insult,* when Martin goes to the restaurant at midnight to eat his lunch (Thomson 68), and in *Eden Close,* when the eponymous protagonist loses the "common distinction between night and day," often "getting up to prepare herself a meal at three in the morning" (Shreve 261). But while sometimes departing from ocularnormativism, there is often a malevolent aspect of such representations. Nocturnal existence involves "increased susceptibility to peril"; engenders a "multitude of infantile projections concerning monsters, demons, death"; and often results in people who have visual impairments being portrayed as "creatures of the night" (Kirtley 85). Accordingly, in *You Can't Go Home Again,* George remembers how the "sight" of Judge Bland, "frequently to be seen prowling the empty streets of the night when all other life was sleeping and the town was dead, had struck a nameless terror into his boy's heart" (Wolfe 55).

18. In *The Insult,* the identity of the blind man provides a cover for Martin's surreptitious, or perhaps imagined, night-sightedness and can be removed as easily as donned, as is illustrated when he decides to leave home: "When I bought my ticket I disguised myself, replacing my white cane and my dark glasses with one of my father's

gardening hats and a pair of his half-moon spectacles. I didn't want anyone in the station to remember seeing a blind man board the 9.03" (Thomson 56).

19. A similarly explicit illustration of nominal displacement is provided when Thomson's policeman asks, "Are you the blind man, sir?" at which Martin nods wearily, saying, "I'm the blind man" (404). A comparable scenario can be found in Graham's *Night without Stars,* when Giles Gordon is greeted by Madame Colloni: "Oh, it is the blind man, isn't it? You were here last year in the spring" (174). Giles is left pondering, "Was I the blind man?" (174), and in response to the suggestion that Alix "took pity on a blind man," he subsequently refers to himself by asserting that she "saved the blind man" (248). Like Thomson's Martin, then, Graham's Giles is addressed by means of the label that he reluctantly accepts.

20. In *The Insult,* Martin's character is also openly keyed to the metanarrative of blindness when he is approached by a reporter and a cameraman who are working on a program about the missing invisible man. Martin protests that his friend Mr. Loots would be a more appropriate guest, being far better informed about the search, but the program makers remain unconvinced: "'No, no,' they said. 'You don't understand. It's you we want.' They explained that a blind man was a more potent image, a more poignant symbol of the quest" (Thomson 129). The program makers endeavor to ascribe, appropriate, and indeed hide behind the blind man, an identity that is quite evidently extrinsic to Martin's character.

21. Irony is a crude but critical possibility that must be considered about texts deriving from the postmodern context. For example, in *How Late It Was, How Late,* Sammy's nominal identity is displaced as he thinks of himself as a "fucking blind blind blind fucking blind man blind a fucking blind bastard, a walking fucking a walking fucking fuck knows what" (Kelman 173). If we read this example as ironic we must nonetheless recognize that the label *blind man* provides the key to the metanarrative that is being challenged.

22. In Thomson's *The Insult,* the trouble with Martin's ironic allusions to the tacit inadequacy of the blind man is emphasized when the same specter is raised by the sighted character Edith Hekmann. "Not bad for a blind man," she says, as Martin draws a picture in the dust with his white cane (234); "Oh, that was clever," she says, accusing him of working for the police. "They knew it would catch me unawares, arouse my sympathy. Send in the blind man" (380); and "Mazey didn't know what a blind man was," she says, recounting her son's murderous story. "He'd never seen one before" (396). The only significant difference between Martin's and Edith's reference to the blind man is that the former is, and the latter is not, meant to be grounded in experiential knowledge. It follows, therefore, that if Martin's unreliability deems this factor uncertain, his remarks will seem as pejorative as those made by Edith.

23. Another war-blinded character—namely, Giles Gordon—can be found in Graham's *Night without Stars,* which was first published as a novel in 1950.

24. In the United States a number of reports were published during the late 1950s and early 1960s that found between 51 and 69 percent of people whose visual acuity measured 20/200 or less were women (Scott 52–53), much as in the United Kingdom, while forming 52 percent of the general population in 1986–87, women comprised 72 percent of the visually impaired population (Bruce et al. 2).

25. Here I use the adjective *flat* in the Forsterian sense: a flat character, in its purest form, is based on a single idea or quality, the increased number of which introduces a curve toward round characterization.

Chapter 3

1. Far from being exclusive to the institutions of early twentieth-century Britain, the mania remained an issue in the 1990s when people were said to sometimes perceive their visual impairments as a punishment, the misbehavior often being sexual transgression—usually masturbation in the case of males (Wagner-Lampl and Oliver 268). Indeed, Humphries and Gordon are in agreement with Wagner-Lampl and Oliver about a tacit link between blindness and excessive masturbation to which males in particular are frequently keyed.

2. This hackneyed warning premises the logic that people who have no vision have nothing to lose from masturbating compulsively, but what does it say about the early twentieth-century clergy and medical professions by whom the mania was perpetuated? After all, the implication is that only the fear of impaired vision deters people from compulsive masturbation, a pleasure that, in these terms, must be continually (rather than occasionally) denied.

3. In the first half of the twentieth century uninstitutionalized counterparts also experienced problems when forming intimate relationships, the source of which, according to Humphries and Gordon, was the "sneering attitudes of the able-bodied and patronising representations of disabled people in popular culture" (143). As with masturbation mania, moreover, the loss of the capacity for erotic pleasure was still felt in the 1990s, for a number of both women and men who had visual impairments reported feeling "generally impotent and castrated," being "treated by others as though they were asexual" (Wagner-Lampl and Oliver 269).

4. Another aspect of the masculine role pertains to physical strength. Castration in this respect is frequently portrayed as though deriving from a female character. For instance, in Block's "Hot Eyes, Cold Eyes," the strength of a man's eyes is correlated positively with that of his physique: "He was strong, he was direct and he was dangerous. She [the unnamed protagonist] could tell all this in a few seconds, merely by meeting his relentless gaze" (301). Accordingly, in Lawrence's "The Blind Man," Maurice appears "strong-blooded and healthy, and, at the same time, cancelled" (357). Here the construct is of a castrating woman, for it is the view of Maurice's wife, Isabel, that is being articulated, much as in Lehmann's *Invitation to the Waltz* it is in the view of the only woman with whom Timmy dances that he lacks "vitality" (247). A point to note about such representation is that it serves the cause of both negative and positive eugenics, given that, as potential partners for heterosexual women, men who have visual impairments are disparaged, and those who do not have visual impairments are praised.

5. I use the term *ophthalmocentrism* in the paper "A Brief Introduction to Post-Disability Literary Criticism." The term is also used in the article "From Blindness to Visual Impairment."

6. Though somewhat less graphic, an explicitly ophthalmocentric portrayal of desire may also be found in Block's "Hot Eyes, Cold Eyes," for the unnamed protagonist is rarely "untouched by the stares of men" (295). While waiting for the morning bus, a man's red-rimmed, glassy eyes drift insolently down the length of her body. She feels their heat. She feels the embrace of his eyes, like "hot hands upon her buttocks and the backs of her thighs." When the bus arrives, the eyes of the driver are an "innocent watery blue," yet she feels them on her breasts, feels too her "nipples hardening in response to their palpable touch" (296). It is stressed that nothing is done with the intention of provoking male lust, that even at work she feels eyes brushing

her body, that she could cloak herself in a nun's habit and men's eyes would "lift the black skirts and strip away the veil" (296–97). In the evening, however, she relishes those glances, feeds on the "heat in those eyes" (298). Small eyes become cool, calculating, and passionless (299–300), large eyes burn with passionate intensity (301), and it is the possessor of the latter by whom the protagonist allows herself to be seduced.

7. A similarly ophthalmocentric example of castration can be found in Thomas's *Under Milk Wood,* for Captain Cat remembers "long ago when his eyes were blue and bright," when he knew a "herd of short and good time cows" (71). To use the words *blue* and *bright* in this context is to emphasize that Captain Cat's eyes are no longer attractive, but the implied dullness also posits blindness as the condition that banishes sexual prowess to the past.

8. Other literary manifestations of masturbation mania can be found in Kelman's *How Late It Was, How Late,* when we are informed that, lying in bed, the newly blinded Sammy thought about "having a wank; but he couldnay" (79); and in Thomson's *The Insult,* when newly blinded Martin Blom lies awake at midnight, masturbating and fantasizing about Nurse Janssen (30). In both examples the onset of blindness is correlated with masturbation.

9. The apparent necessity of the male look, stare, and/or gaze is portrayed in relation to everything from meeting to falling in love with someone. There is "nay point wandering if ye cannay see fuck all," asserts the narrator of Kelman's *How Late It Was, How Late,* and "Sammy liked looking about, watching the office lassies and the shop lassies, these yins that worked in the style-shops; fucking beautiful man" (126). At the other extreme, in Graham's *Night without Stars,* when asked if he is in love with Alix Delaisse, Giles Gordon says, "I don't know, [. . .] I've never seen her" (172). Indeed, in ocularnormative terms, vision is similarly requisite for meeting and loving someone romantically, as though the latter is no more profound than the former.

10. Consequently, the symbolically castrating conclusion considered in chap. 2, that Green's John could never marry, seems quite logical, his infantilization implicitly deeming potential partners pedophilic.

11. In case we forget, Friedlander, Snyder and Mitchell, and others remind us that the systematic murder of people who were impaired was integral to that of the millions who were Jewish, Romany, and homosexual.

12. The same sense of suffocation can be found in *The Insult* when newly blinded Martin says, "Claudia offered to come and live with me. She'd cook, she'd clean. She'd see to my every need. Her face tilted eagerly. I tried to conceal my horror" (Thomson 26). This horror reveals that Martin's take on dependency is no different from that of his forebear John Haye, that independence remains the rule.

13. A relevant rendering of relationships between the sighted and the blind may be found in Gide's *La Symphonie Pastorale* when the pastor infantilizes Gertrude by saying, "I persuaded myself I loved her as one loves an afflicted child. I tended her as one tends a sick person—and so I made a moral obligation, a duty of what was really a passionate inclination" (50). Similarly, in Lehmann's *Invitation to the Waltz,* having expressed concerns that he has no "frothing and frisking in his life," Marigold explains why Timmy marries his nurse: "I mean loving wouldn't be enough. He wants somebody to take him for granted and make him feel ordinary and safe and practical, and she does that" (289–90). These descriptions of dependency suggest relationships that are more medical than passionate, thereby providing an implicit endorsement of the independent subject, as the blind characters effectively become foils for their

sighted counterparts (the parasitic dependency of the former serves partly, if not largely, to emphasize the independence of the latter).

Chapter 4

1. Similar invocations of extraordinary senses can be found in both *Sir Nigel,* when Black Simon refers to Andreas by saying, "it often happens that when a man has lost a sense the good God will strengthen those that remain" (Conan Doyle 287), and *The Insult,* when Martin Blom goes so far as to say, "Your eyes go, and the efficiency of your nose and ears and all the rest instantly increases by hundreds of per cent" (Thomson 247). Though published in the first and last decades of the twentieth century respectively, the two novels clearly refer to a universal assumption about people who have visual impairments and extraordinary senses.

2. It is worth noting that Wyndham's triffids are said to have "moved rather like a man on crutches" (29), a simile that unnecessarily invokes impairment in order to bolster the sense of monstrosity.

3. Something of an exception can be found in "The Other" when the narrator addresses his younger self by saying, "When you reach my age, you'll have almost totally lost your eyesight. You'll be able to see the color yellow, and light and shadow. But don't worry. Gradual blindness is not tragic" (Borges 10). This depiction departs from the blind-sighted binary, although the implication remains that visual impairment is necessarily progressive.

4. A mundane literary illustration can be found in Carver's "Cathedral" when Robert challenges the assumption that he has no interest in television by saying, "I have a color set and a black-and-white thing, an old relic. It's funny, but if I turn the TV on, and I'm always turning it on, I turn on the color set" (299–300). The fifth-sixth sense is evoked when Robert subsequently refers to a television with which he is unfamiliar by saying, "This is a color TV[. . . .] Don't ask me how, but I can tell" (300). But for a more traditional take on the theme, consideration might be given to *Happiness Is Blind,* where Helen Bourne argues that persons who cannot "see the physical world" can nonetheless "see deeper into the soul and the underlying reality," that they have the "inner vision that the philosophers and mystics talk about" (Sava 192). Similarly, in *The Langoliers,* Dinah has senses, "including that odd, vague one we call the sixth sense," that are "more developed than ours" (King 187).

5. Blindness-dream confusion is illustrated in many twentieth-century literary texts. For instance, the sighted narrator of Kipling's "They" asserts, "I have never seen the faces of my dead in any dream," to which Miss Florence responds by saying, "Then it must be as bad as being blind" (242). But in some instances a counterhegemonic reading is available, for rather than implying that people who have visual impairments are unaware of the difference between dreaming and the waking state, this is portrayed as the belief of people who do not have visual impairments. For example, in *La Symphonie Pastorale,* it is the pastor who refers to Gertrude by asking, "in what way do her waking hours differ from her sleeping?" (Gide 12–13). *Happiness Is Blind* places a still more complex slant on the scenario. On beholding the blind character Helen Bourne, Tony confuses his own reality with dreaming: "The plans for burglary, his war against the world, the very climb itself, had receded into some dim world that was akin to the universe of dreams. Yet this, too, had a dream-like quality. Reality was nowhere in it" (Sava 153). Thus, as well as blindness-dream confusion, Sava illustrates a more explicitly eugenic message of contamination, the contagious blindness that is discussed at length in chap. 5.

6. Descartes blurs the distinction between dreaming and the waking state by suggesting that certainty can be attached to neither: "How many times have I dreamt at night that I was in this place, dressed, by the fire, although I was quite naked in my bed?" (96). In contrast, Merleau-Ponty responds to what he calls the "age-old argument from dreams, delirium, or illusions" by pointing out that it "makes use of that faith in the world it seems to be unsettling" (5). After all, falsity cannot be defined without a reference point that is provided by truth.

7. Is it not the case that, just like touch, taste, smell, and hearing, the sense of sight may bridge the dream and waking states? If we are caught in sunlight when sleeping, for example, is it not the case that some of us may dream of bright lights as a consequence?

8. A late twentieth-century illustration of extraordinary hearing can be found when the eponymous protagonist of *Eden Close* says, "My window is always open. My world is what I hear. I can tell you exactly what time of day it is just by the sounds outside the window" (Shreve 79). Similarly, in *The Insult,* Martin Blom confronts—or at least imagines that he is confronting—his neurosurgeon Bruno Visser by saying, "I can hear the outlines of your body," "I can hear where your body ends and the air begins," "I can hear your heart beating," "I can hear your liver purifying what you drank last night," and "I can hear your bowels" (Thomson 247–48). In these instances the hearing ascribed to the blind characters is superhuman rather than subhuman (i.e., rather than animalistic). The apparent fascination with the hearing of people who have visual impairments is captured graphically in *The Langoliers,* when the sighted characters are said to have turned toward Dinah "curiously," before she "dropped Laurel's hand and raised both of her own. She cupped the thumbs behind her ears and splayed her fingers out like fans. Then she simply stood there, still as a post, in this odd and rather weird listening posture" (King 150). In other words, the hearing of the blind character is rendered explicitly extraordinary with visible signifiers to clarify the point.

9. Implicitly animalized hearing is ascribed in *Sir Nigel,* when Black Simon says that Andreas has "such ears that he can hear the sap in the trees or the cheep of the mouse in its burrow" (Conan Doyle 287), and in *Under Milk Wood,* where the blind character who "hears all the morning of the town" is called Captain Cat (Thomas 40).

10. The species of animal evoked by the extraordinary sense of smell is more vague in Saramago's *Blindness,* for the doctor's wife is said to have "watched" the blind internees "twitching, tense, their necks craned as if they were sniffing at something, yet curiously, their expressions were all the same" (40); another group is said to have "stopped, sniffed in the doorways of the shops in the hope of catching the smell of food" (214); and an old blind woman is said to have appeared "on the landing of the fire escape to sniff out the sounds that were coming into her flat" (244).

11. That the taste of tobacco is too sophisticated for the blind becomes apparent in several twentieth-century literary representations. In *Invitation to the Waltz,* Lehmann's narrator refers to Timmy Douglas by noting, "He didn't smoke his cigarette, but let it burn away between his long fingers" (258). Nearly two decades on, in *Night without Stars,* Giles Gordon says, "I drew at the cigarette but didn't get much fun out of it. Half the enjoyment goes when you can't see the smoke" (Graham 53). Apparently along similar lines, Carver's "Cathedral" contains a narrator who says, "I remembered having read somewhere that the blind didn't smoke because, as speculation had it, they couldn't see the smoke they exhaled. I thought I knew that much and that much only about blind people" (299). However, as we found in chap. 2, the view of Carver's narrator is explicitly bigoted. It would seem that Carver only represents the stereotype

in order to do likewise with its disruption, an inference that is supported when Robert is said to have "smoked his cigarette down to the nubbin and then lit another one" (299). Thus, when Carver's text is juxtaposed with those of Lehmann and Graham, there is an ironic sense of representational progress.

12. As in Joyce's *Ulysses,* an extraordinary sense of touch is portrayed in *Invitation to the Waltz,* when Lehmann's narrator refers to Timmy Douglas and Olivia Curtis by saying, "His hand, holding hers, vibrated as if it had a separate, infinitely sensitive life-long fingers, exquisite nails. He'll guess what I'm like from my voice, from touching me" (248). Like Joyce, Lehmann converts touch into sight, for Timmy "seems to see with his fingers" (290). Similarly, in Saramago's *Blindness* the doctor's wife declares that "thc hands are the eyes of the blind" (301). The ocularnormative implication is that a functional means of perception must be explained in terms of sight.

13. A departure from the metanarrative of blindness can be found in Sava's *Happiness Is Blind,* where the sense of touch is portrayed without reference or allusion to animalization, infantilization, or synesthesia. The protagonist Helen Bourne says, "Music and poetry bring me beauty, and so does the touch of silk and fur and things like that. Normal people know little of the beauty of touch, but it is there for those who can appreciate it" (157). This portrayal reflects not only that beauty is beheld in tactility but also that the perceiver may or may not have a visual impairment (although, of course, the use of the word *normal* is highly problematic).

14. That the verb *grope* keys characters to the metanarrative of blindness is demonstrable in Conrad's *The End of the Tether,* when Captain Whalley "fell on his knees, with groping hands extended in a frank gesture of blindness" (290). But a challenge to this aspect of the metanarrative of blindness is provided in the stage directions of Friel's *Molly Sweeney,* which state that most people who have visual impairments "look and behave like" those who do not have visual impairments: "The only evidence of their disability is usually a certain vacancy in the eyes or the way the head is held. MOLLY should indicate her disability in some such subtle way. No canes, no groping, no dark glasses" (1). Despite this apparent disdain for images of the groping blind figure, however, Molly says, "I stumbled, groped my way" (24). In other words, Friel portrays the internalization of the groping blind figure.

15. Similarly disempowered, in Saramago's *Blindness,* a group of blind characters "advanced very slowly, as if mistrustful of the person guiding them, groping in vain with their free hand, searching for the support of something solid" (48).

16. That the blind grope their way around is illustrated in many twentieth-century portrayals. Brecht's "A Helping Hand" contains a scene in which Lorge is said to have "groped his way home" and "groped his way into the house" (27). The narrator goes on to say that Lorge has to "grope his way along the roads" (28) and in so doing invokes a link with a second Brechtian tale, "The Blind Man," where the protagonist is said to have "groped his way laboriously through the streets" (25). This usage of the verb *grope* continued into the late twentieth century, for in "The Lady in White" Festil "groped his blind way" to Mardik (Donaldson 139). The same meaning is illustrated in Saramago's *Blindness* when, stretching out his hands, the blind man "groped his way along the corridor" (7); when the blind men "approached groping their way" (180); and when "the blind moved as one would expect of the blind, groping their way, stumbling, dragging their feet" (83), "groping their way along" (250).

17. The way in which walking is displaced in favor of groping is exemplified in Synge's *The Well of the Saints.* Of more than thirty direct references to the act of walking, only one ascribes actual movement to the central protagonists—that being when

Molly Byrne asks Martin, "Would you think well to be all your life walking round the like of that[?]" (75). Instead, each of the play's three acts defines the gait of the Douls as a grope. In the first act, rather than walking in, Martin and Mary "grope in" (67); rather than walking up to Timmy, Mary "gropes" up to him (72). In the second act, rather than turning to walk out, Martin "turns to grope out" (92). In the third act, rather than walking in, Martin "gropes in" (93), and rather than walking toward his stone, he "gropes towards" it (104). Other examples can be found in Green's *Blindness,* where John Haye is said to have "groped into the room" (126), to be "groping about," "groping forward," "groping towards the window" (203–5).

18. How the verb *grope* is used to denote haptic perception is illustrated in a number of representations from the second half of the twentieth century. In Beckett's *Endgame,* for example, Hamm is portrayed "groping for wall" (23) and, on a couple of occasions, "groping for the dog" (31, 39). In Saramago's *Blindness,* the first blind man "picked up his suitcase and, shuffling his feet so as not to trip and groping with his free hand, he went along the aisle separating the two rows of beds" (45), before he "groped under the bed to see if there was a chamber pot" (47). When a group of characters is dining, their "blind hands" are said to have "groped and found the glasses" (262).

19. This motif, the monstrous grip, is recurrent in twentieth-century writing. In *The Sea Wolf,* the eponymous protagonist's hand "clasped like a steel trap" around Humphrey's hand, drawing him down in a "terrible grip" (London 273). In *Don't Look Now,* the narrator tells how the blind sister "held" John's hand "fast and would not let it go" (du Maurier 52). In *Snakewalk,* Patrick Todd remembers saving "some blind kid": "I damn near needed pliers to get his fingers off my arm" (Wheeler 17). Even Dinah, the young blind girl in King's *The Langoliers,* "imprinted on" Laurel with "scary intensity," "reaching with a timid sort of determination for her hand" (40), and later "reached out and grasped the cuff of Nick's jeans" (307).

20. The monstrous grip sometimes becomes more obviously sexual and thus resonant with eugenics. In *The Well of the Saints,* for instance, Molly Byrne shrinks away from Martin, who responds with "low, furious intensity," putting a hand on her shoulder and shaking her (Synge 89). Implicitly homoerotic illustration can be found in Lawrence's "The Blind Man," where Maurice is said to have "laid his hand on Bertie Reid's head, closing the dome of the skull in a soft, firm grasp" (363). The "hand of the blind man," says the narrator, "grasped the shoulder, the arm, the hand of the other man. He seemed to take him, in the soft, travelling grasp" (363–64).

Chapter 5

1. The fear motif is also illustrated in Conan Doyle's *Sir Nigel.* At one point, though outnumbered and held at knifepoint, the priest absolutely refuses to reveal the password that is sought by Nigel. When Andreas is summoned to the scene, however, this fearlessness dissipates immediately: "Keep him off me. Save me from blind Andreas! I will tell you everything" (290). Attention should be paid to this application of the third-person pronoun, to the fact that the priest does not address Andreas directly, instead assuming an identification with his sighted counterpart that resonates with the eye-to-eye complicity considered in chap. 6 of the present book. Other examples of the fear motif can be found in Lawrence's "The Blind Man," where more than being a "terrifying burden" to his wife (348), Maurice makes their guest Bertie feel a "quiver of horror" (363). Gazing "mute and terror-struck," says the narra-

tor, Bertie "had an unreasonable fear, lest the other man should suddenly destroy him" (364). Similarly, the narrator of "Cathedral" asserts, "I didn't want to be left alone with a blind man" (Carver 300), and in *The Insult,* Martin Blom is told, "Blind people—well, you know. They frighten people" (Thomson 78). Arguably evoking anticipation of the monstrous grip considered in chap. 4, the desire for avoidance is certainly implicit in all such applications of the fear motif.

2. Such dark spells are explored recurrently in twentieth-century writing. Kipling's "They" contains the "ginger-headed, canvas-gaitered giant" Mr. Turpin, who is "pushed" when beckoned into the room by Miss Florence (254). He was "like a frightened child," says the narrator, "in the grip of some almost overpowering fear" (254). The element of fear is manifest, but connotations of mysterious power are augmented when the narrator explains his return to the house by suggesting that his car "took the road of her own volition" (244). Though published a couple of decades on from Kipling, Lawrence's "The Blind Man" contains a comparable passage in which the "touch" of the title character, Maurice, is said to have an "almost hypnotising effect" on Isabel (355), when "unconscious, imprisoned" Bertie is depicted "under the power of the blind man, as if hypnotised" (364). Also, in Wolfe's *You Can't Go Home Again,* on meeting Judge Bland people are said to have been "instantly, even if they fought against it, captivated, drawn close to him, somehow made to like him" (62). Indeed, when asked to sit by Bland, George does so "like a child under the spell of the Pied Piper" (64). Moreover, in du Maurier's *Don't Look Now,* John tells his wife, Laura, of a "couple of old girls" who are "trying to hypnotise" him (7). The "twins were standing there," says the narrator, "the blind one still holding on to her sister's arm, her sightless eyes fixed firmly upon him. He felt himself held, unable to move, and an impending sense of doom, of tragedy, came upon him" (14). This hypnotic power may be thought of as a metaphysically monstrous grip.

3. A similar point is made by Langworthy (280).

4. The idea of Keller is not of a place where deaf-blind people can live a life that is a "sightless, soundless imitation of their unafflicted peers," but of a way of living that is "by and for the blind-deaf," that "accepts no convention just because that is the way it has always been done" (240). Accordingly, Varley's narrator claims to be "getting into the spirit of tactile seeing and understanding" (246), but in so doing he reveals that visual perception remains central. He refers, after all, to tactile *seeing* rather than tactile perception, as though the haptic must be framed in visual terms.

5. Many twentieth-century characterizations of blindness contain canine allusions, as illustrated in *The Sea Wolf,* where it is the "old Wolf Larsen and the tiger muscles" that save the protagonist from injury (London 252). More extensively, in Gide's *La Symphonie Pastorale,* asleep in the fireplace, Gertrude is initially perceived as a "nondescript-looking creature, whose face was entirely hidden by a thick mass of hair" (11). The allusions become less subtle when we are informed that she must have usually slept in a "corner under a staircase" (12), when the "sounds" that she makes are likened to the "plaintive whines of a puppy," and when she travels to the pastor's home "huddled up" at his feet (14). Gertrude's response to the attention of others, moreover, is to "groan and grunt like an animal," behavior that only ceases when she flings "herself on her food with a kind of bestial avidity" (19). An explicit canine reference can be found when the title character of Brecht's "The Blind Man" develops both an "aversion to water, like a dog with rabies," and an "inexplicable habit of wanting to lie on the ground like an animal" (23), much as in King's *The Langoliers,* Dinah's head is envisaged "cocked to one side," so that "for a moment she looked

strikingly like Nipper, the dog on the old RCA Victor labels" (169). These examples show that the canine trope is recurrent from the start to the end of the twentieth century.

6. The uncleanness of twentieth-century blind characters is both implicit and explicit. In *Ulysses,* the blind stripling is noted for having stains on his coat (Joyce 173), but in *La Symphonie Pastorale,* Gertrude is portrayed in a "state of unspeakable dirt" (Gide 16). Still more extreme are the examples found in the work of Brecht. The title character of "The Blind Man," for instance, is said to have lived "decently" until he lost his sight, at which point he could "no longer dress himself properly, and washing too proved difficult" (21). His "clothes were cleaned by his brothers," says the narrator, "but from then on the stains from the food which he spilt on his shirt grew worse and worse," until he "grew so dirty that his brothers could not take him anywhere" (23). The uncleanliness becomes yet more inexplicable when, having previously been "so clean" that his mother had "held him up as an example to his brothers," the protagonist is said to "foul himself by urinating into his clothes" and to have "put on his brother's trousers and soiled them" (23–24). A similar lack of regard for hygiene can be found in Brecht's "A Helping Hand," where Lorge is forced to "relieve himself beside the bed," and his brother is said to have noticed that he was "very dirty and had grown thin and blind" (27–28).

7. Several twentieth-century blind characters are ascribed beards: in *The Well of the Saints,* newly blind Martin Doul says, "I'll be letting my beard grow in a short while, a beautiful, long, white, silken, streamy beard, you wouldn't see the like of in the eastern world" (Synge 96); in "The Blind Man," the title character "grew a beard and could no longer recognise himself" (Brecht 23); in "Cathedral," Robert wears a "full beard! A beard on a blind man!" (Carver 296); and in *How Late it Was, How Late,* Sammy "wasnay gony shave at all, he was gony grow a beard" (Kelman 152). Though implicit in many instances, the rationale for the ascription is explicit in *How Late it Was, How Late,* where Sammy "didnay want to slice off his nose" (152).

8. A sense of psychological impingement is also evoked in *For Services Rendered,* where Eva refers to her brother Sydney by asking why she should be sacrificed, adding that she is "sick of being a drudge": "I'm very sorry he's blind. But it's not my fault" (Maugham 32).

9. As a characteristic of the blind, strangeness is something that blind characters may pass on to their sighted counterparts. In Lawrence's "The Blind Man," for example, numerous references are made to blind character Maurice's strangeness: his life is described as "strangely serene" (347); when he is joined in the stable by his wife, Isabel, the darkness seems to be in a "strange swirl of violent life" (353); at the dinner table, Bertie makes Isabel "conscious of a strangeness" in her husband (359); Isabel tells Bertie of "something strange in Maurice's presence" (361); and upon returning from the barn, Maurice is depicted "standing with his feet apart, like a strange colossus" (365). The key point to note is that after the barn scene, in which sighted character Bertie "lifted his hand, and laid the fingers on the scar, on the scarred eyes" of Maurice (364), it is not *his* but *their* footsteps that are thought to sound "strange" (364). Left with "sunken eyes" that are "glazed with misery," says the narrator, Bertie cannot "bear it" that he has been "touched by the blind man, his insane reserve broken in" (365).

10. Literary illustration can be found in *Ulysses,* where Miss Douce refers to the blind stripling by saying, "So sad to look at his face" (Joyce 252). That is to say, the assumed sadness of the blind stripling becomes the felt sadness of Miss Douce.

11. As well as in *The Well of the Saints,* where Timmy asserts that "the blind is wicked people" (Synge 90), numerous examples of malevolence are provided by twentieth-century writing: in *The Blind Barber,* Morgan finds a blood-soaked razor that is engraved with an "ugly and grotesque" figure, the head of which wears a bandage across the eyes (Dickinson-Carr 140); the narrator of *You Can't Go Home Again* refers to Judge Bland by saying, "Everyone who met him knew at once that the man was bad. No, 'bad' is not the word for it. Everyone knew that he was evil—genuinely, unfathomably evil" (Wolfe 62); and in *Wild Horse,* the dying words of blind character Valentine are "I killed the Cornish boy" (Frances 2).

12. The evil blind eye appears in many twentieth-century works of literature. For instance, in *The Well of the Saints,* when Martin loses his sight, Molly is "near afeard" of the "wild look he has come in his eyes" (Synge 92); in *You Can't Go Home Again,* people are said to have been "afraid" of Judge Bland "because his blind eyes saw straight through them" (Wolfe 67); and in du Maurier's *Don't Look Now,* the "blind sister" is depicted with "formidable" (23), "disconcerting" (52), "oddly penetrating" eyes that give protagonist John a "sudden feeling of discomfort" (10).

13. Given that the short white cane (sometimes known as a symbol cane) may be used quite specifically to indicate the visual impairment of its holder, the literary application of the stick as a signifier of blindness is hardly surprising. Hence, in *The Well of the Saints,* Martin Doul "gropes about for his stick" (Synge 94); in *Ulysses,* a "stripling, blind, with a tapping cane came taptaptapping" (Joyce 277); in *Night without Stars,* Giles Gordon recreates his past blindness by buying a "stick and a pair of sun-glasses" (Graham 176); in *Snakewalk,* Patrick Todd's inventory of his "starter kit" includes a "white cane, a braille pocket watch, and two braille books" (Wheeler 12); and in *How Late It Was, How Late,* Sammy says, "Even if the fucking sodjers grabbed him; he would just tell them man no fucking way, no without the stick, he wasnay going fucking poky unless they let him take the stick. It was an extension of himself" (Kelman 253). But illustrated in *The Well of the Saints,* when Timmy says, "Oh, God protect us, Molly, from the words of the blind" (Synge 91), some symbolism is quite inexplicable.

14. The metamorphosis from mobility aid to weapon is also illustrated in *The Well of the Saints,* when Mary Doul raises her "stick" to Martin and says, "Maybe if I hit you a strong blow you'd be blinded" (Synge 81), much as in *How Late It Was, How Late,* when Sammy reflects that he "would just have to use the stick. He could whirl it round his head. They wouldnay get near him that way" (Kelman 253). Indeed, the metamorphosis is supplemented in Thomson's *The Insult,* for not only does Martin Blom refer to an unhelpful doorman by saying, "I could have broken his nose with my stick" (117), but the reader is informed that Mazey "didn't know what a blind man was. He'd never seen one before. The dark glasses, the white stick. It worried him" (396). Perhaps implicit in all of these examples, but certainly manifest in Mary Doul's assertion about using the stick to blind Martin, there is a threat of contagiousness, whereby the signifier of blindness becomes a means of passing it from one person to another.

15. Blindness is passed from blind characters to their sighted counterparts in a number of ways. For instance, in *The Insult,* Martin presents Nina with a blindfold that is to be worn "in bed," so that the two of them can "be the same" (Thomson 100), equity that is less ardently desired in "The Girl in the Corner," when Ivy and her sighted husband are occupied with a newspaper on a train: "She'd only stay quiet when he read her big pieces from under the pictures, but sometimes there was only

a picture and hardly any writing, and you could see he wanted to look at it, but she'd laugh and turn over because he'd gone all quiet and didn't speak. Sometimes, he tried to turn back, just for a minute, to finish looking" (Norton 10). Thus, be it fetish or burden, both works render blindness as something that is shared.

Chapter 6

1. Perhaps, adds Sartre, "the objects of the world which I took for eyes were not eyes; perhaps it was only the wind which shook the bush behind me" (276).

2. The effect of such uncertainty is famously portrayed in Orwell's *Nineteen Eighty-Four* (1949). At any given moment the protagonist Winston Smith has no way of knowing if he is being observed via the telescreen, so it is perfectly conceivable that the observation is continuous. He has to live, therefore, in the assumption that every sound he makes is overheard and every movement scrutinized.

3. Proposed by Jeremy Bentham in the late eighteenth century, the philosophical aim of the panopticon was to challenge the conventions of institutionalism by suggesting that rather than residing in dungeons and darkness, rather than being kept out of sight, prisoners should occupy illuminated cells, should be put on display. Indeed, the architectural essence of the plan is asymmetrical insofar as the ring of cells is visible, while a central inspection tower is not.

4. Saramago's *Blindness* features a "grotesque spectacle" that would cause "the most restrained spectator to burst into howls of laughter, it was too funny for words, some of the blind internees advancing on all fours, their faces practically touching the ground as if they were pigs" (97). Another take on the theme can be found in Synge's *The Well of the Saints* when Martin's blindness is first cured, and to the delight of the villagers, he mistakes one woman after another for his wife, Mary. Although Martin is not blind at this point in the play, the jeering and laughter are nonetheless elicited by blindness.

5. Comparably routine activity becomes something of a spectacle when the narrator of "Cathedral" watches with "admiration" as Robert uses his knife and fork: "He'd cut two pieces of meat, fork the meat into his mouth, and then go all out for the scalloped potatoes, the beans next, and then he'd tear off a hunk of buttered bread and eat that. He'd follow this up with a big drink of milk. It didn't seem to bother him to use his fingers once in a while, either" (Carver 298–99). Any ascription of alterity serves the narrator's jealousy, as is suggested in the ocularnormative reference to Robert's use of his fingers. The admiring gaze is fueled by the narrator's need to draw a dividing line between his wife and Robert.

6. The overwhelming fascination is portrayed in *Invitation to the Waltz* when Olivia observes how one of the dancers is struck by Timmy's blindness: "She saw the girl's face alter suddenly, not in pity, but in a look of avid curiosity. She whispered something to her partner, they both turned to stare at him" (Lehmann 248). This example illustrates that this type of gaze, while being essentially masculine, is not adopted by men only.

7. In Saramago's *Blindness* it strikes the doctor's wife as "contemptible and obscene" that, as if from "behind a microscope," she finds herself observing a number of unsuspecting "human beings" (62), an assertion that reveals a pseudo-scientific aspect of the unseen gaze.

8. Literary manifestations of ontological negation can be found in Gide's *La Symphonie Pastorale,* in the assertion that Gertrude "allowed herself to be taken away like a

lifeless block" (12). This use of inanimation is bolstered when the pastor's wife refers to Gertrude by asking, "What do you mean to do with that?" (14), the assumptions being that Gertrude cannot *do* anything, that she is a thing with which something must be done, and that this something can only be done by a counterpart who does not have impaired vision. Other examples can be found in Synge's *The Well of the Saints,* where Molly "pushes" Martin Doul (75), the people "push him" and Timmy is "turning" him "round" (99); in Brecht's "The Blind Man," where the brothers of the title character "took him along to the theatre every now and again" (22); and in Green's *Blindness,* where Nanny's regard for newly blinded John Haye is articulated: "She could help him again bring him up his food and take him out for walks" (144). Of course a number of people who have visual impairments require visual assistance at one time or another. But the point to be noted is that assisting is distinct from taking, pushing, bringing, and so on. To assist a person who has a visual impairment, to offer, say, a guiding elbow, is to contribute to what is predominantly her or his activity, whereas to take, bring, or push is to ascribe passivity, to objectify, to possess—indeed, to construct Gide's lifeless block.

9. The inducement of self-consciousness is illustrated explicitly in *How Late It Was, How Late:* "It's just sometimes man ye see these cunts and the look they give ye can be different. It isnay just a look in passing, ye could be sitting there ye can imagine it, if okay ye're blind, ye're blind and ye're sitting there, just minding yer own business, relaxed, ye're enjoying a quiet pint. But cause ye're blind ye dont know it but every cunt's staring at ye, staring right into ye, like one of these terrible wee nightmare movies" (Kelman 274). Sammy's perspective clearly explores the profundity of the unseen gazer's presence.

10. Folk belief is invoked here, for the eye is sometimes "used as a sadistic weapon, and looking confers absolute power over the object looked at" (Kirtley 21).

11. This sense of authorship is illustrated in Lehmann's *Invitation to the Waltz* when Timmy's marriage is described: "She's sensible, she's matter-of-fact, she takes it for granted. How dare she . . . She keeps his life practical and orderly, keeps him cheerful. They've got a child. So he must love her. And it doesn't matter to him that she's not young or pretty" (255–56). The fact that Olivia has only just met Timmy has no bearing on her apparent appreciation of his life. Olivia can simply draw from ocularcentric notions of attraction and conclude accordingly.

12. More than being necessary, sight is sometimes posited as a sufficient condition of the doer, as in Brecht's "The Blind Man," where the narrator refers to the title character by saying, "When a child took him out for a walk it ran off to play and he was seized by a great fear and was not brought home till late at night" (22). *Taking* the blind man out and *bringing* him back home, the child evidently assumes charge.

13. A manifestly different scenario can be found in Green's *Blindness,* when an unnamed child refers to John Haye by plaintively asserting, "Look, Mumma, . . . blind, Mumma" (199, 204), providing a literary analogue to the way in which Fanon remembers being discussed: "Mama, see the Negro! I'm frightened!" (112). In both cases the adult is rendered Other by a child who thereby assumes authority, revealing much about the society in which he or she is reared. Fanon goes on to assert, "I could no longer laugh, because I already knew that there were legends, stories, history, and above all historicity" (112).

14. A comparably collective gaze is portrayed in Synge's *The Well of the Saints,* when Martin and Mary try to hide behind a bush, when they "kneel down, still clearly visible" (98); and in Lawrence's "The Blind Man," when the scent of some flowers causes

Maurice a moment of profound disturbance, for the "two watched the blind man smelling the violets. He bent his head and seemed to be thinking" (358). For different reasons, comedy in the one example and lament in the other, a spectacle of blindness is implied and confirmed by the shared silence of the unseen gazers.

15. In Lawrence's "The Blind Man," similar complicity can be found when Maurice tells Isabel that he and Bertie have become friends: "'Friends!' re-echoed Isabel. And she looked again at Bertie. He met her eyes with a furtive, haggard look; his eyes were as if glazed with misery" (365). Isabel takes hold of Maurice's hand and speaks to him, but her eyes are on Bertie: "She knew that he had one desire—to escape from this intimacy, this friendship, which had been thrust upon him" (365). In other words, a silent conversation takes place between the two sighted characters, communication from which Maurice is necessarily excluded.

Chapter 7

1. The idea that people mourn the loss of vision is portrayed explicitly in *The Insult,* for Martin Blom asserts that "like when someone close to you dies," blindness "draws a line through your life" (Thomson 48).

2. Indicative of the same notion of mourning, the longing for vision is often portrayed in twentieth-century writing. For instance, in "They," Miss Florence refers to the ghosts with whom she lives by saying that the narrator is "lucky" to "be able to see them" (Kipling 242); in *Happiness Is Blind,* Helen Bourne addresses Tony Street by saying, "I'm tired, darling—tired of being in the dark. I want to see. I want to look on the sunshine. I want to see my child" (Sava 176); and in *How Late It Was, How Late,* Sammy refers to the police interviewers by saying that "the two of them, they had the habit of moving about; ye didnay always know where they were talking from. He would like to have seen them, just fucking seen them" (Kelman 204). Notably, only one of these characters is in a period of adjustment; only Kelman's Sammy is newly blind when longing to see.

3. The story, according to Lyon's introduction, takes on an expressive, ironic strength as we gradually guess the secret of Whalley's blindness: "the slow-moving narrative comes to parallel Whalley's own slow-moving caution, and the lavishly accurate descriptions mock Whalley's own unseeing eyes" (xiv).

4. This expectation of fatal punishment is portrayed in "The Blind Man," when the narrator refers to the title character by saying, "death would have been a release" (Brecht 21); in *Invitation to the Waltz,* when Timmy is imagined "sitting alone downstairs in his house, waiting, and the doctor coming in to tell him it was all over" (Lehmann 285); and in *For Services Rendered,* when Sydney considers it "a matter of opinion" that he was "lucky not to have been killed" (Maugham 32). Consideration might also be given to *Under Milk Wood,* for, through the voyages of his tears, Captain Cat "sails to see the dead" (Thomas 87), a ghostly association echoed in *Blindness,* when men and women appear as "fluid as ghosts," like "ghosts attending a burial" (Saramago 285). There is no shortage of twentieth-century writing in which blindness heralds the end of life, be it through fatality, emptiness, or living as a ghost or some other bearer of death.

5. Literary examples of how blindness-darkness synonymy invokes melancholia can be found in *Invitation to the Waltz,* when Timmy Douglas is said to "sit in shadow," for light has "vanished not from his eyes alone but from his ruined brow and all his being" (Lehmann 285); in *How Late It Was, How Late,* when Sammy is "allowed to get

weary, lying in fucking blackness" (Kelman 172); and in *Blindness,* when an unnamed blind man is said to have "lost the habit of saying Good-day, not only because the days of the blind, strictly speaking are never likely to be good, but also because no one could be entirely sure whether it was afternoon or night" (Saramago 210).

6. The melancholia of blindness is portrayed explicitly in *La Symphonie Pastorale,* when the idea of a spectacle that Gertrude "could not behold" is said to have "begun by making her melancholy" (Gide 26); in *How Late It Was, How Late,* when "it couldnay get worse than this," Sammy "was really fuckt now," he "had fucking reached it now man the fucking dregs man the pits, the fucking black fucking limboland, purgatory" (Kelman 172); and in *The Insult,* when newly blinded Martin is informed that when the shock passes "depression sets in," that this can last for several years, becoming manifest, as it does, in hopelessness, self-pity and suicidal thoughts (Thomson 6).

7. In some representations suicide is deemed a viable option *for* the blind character. In *Invitation to the Waltz,* Marigold refers to Timmy by saying, "If it was me I'd shoot every one I could lay hands on and then myself" (Lehmann 289). In other representations the suicidal option is considered *by* the character. In *Night without Stars,* it seems like more of a probability than a possibility for Giles Gordon: "Till now it had been just a thought, a threat, a promise with a hint of bravado. Now it leered at me like a challenge to my own integrity and guts. You can't be so very sorry for yourself if all the time it's in your own hands to do something about it" (Graham 28). Similarly, in *Happiness Is Blind,* Helen is said to have "grown suddenly thoughtful. Her face was tense and her hands clenched hard. This desire in her was ridiculous, suicidal, but it was almost overwhelming" (Sava 187–88). It also proves relevant that the reader of Kelman's *How Late It Was, How Late* is informed that Sammy "would be as well parking the head in a gas oven" (29), for although this is a result of the combined loss of love and sight, the main concern becomes clear: "He couldnay even fucking see man know what I'm talking about, and he still had to listen to them, these fucking bampot bastards. And ye get angrier and angrier, angrier and angrier, till ye feel like ramming yer fist through the fucking kitchen window and with a bit a luck ye'll slice right through the main artery" (119). All such invocations work on the assumption that blindness may lead to suicide.

8. In accordance with the findings of chap. 5, suicide is sometimes rendered as a second order of contagious blindness. For example, in Sontag's *Death Kit,* it is not the blind character Hester but her sighted lover, Diddy, who attempts suicide by taking an overdose of sleeping tablets (6), who lies in his bed, on the verge of postcoital slumber, wanting to say, "Let's die together. Let's kill ourselves" (273). This may be said to illustrate the eugenic warning against relationships between people who have and people who do not have visual impairments or to imply that the suicidal tendencies of the blind are somehow transmittable.

9. Akin to the fate of Conrad's Captain Whalley, Wolf Larsen, in London's *The Sea Wolf,* sets fire to the mattress on which he sleeps (283); echoing the actions of Larson and Whalley, respectively, the title character in Brecht's "The Blind Man" sets fire to the house in which he lives (24), before descending toward his death in a stream (25), and the newly blind colonel, in Saramago's *Blindness,* initiates a similar end by shooting himself in the head (104). In these and other such examples suicide seems like a perfectly natural response to blindness.

10. Molly's disparaging references to Martin's physique are noteworthy because of the assumption that, when blind, Mary is unaware of her husband's anatomy. The ocularnormative implications are that the Douls' relationship is not a sexual one or that physical attributes can only be perceived by visual means.

11. Given the many comparisons Upton draws with Synge's *The Well of the Saints,* it is not surprising that a similar scenario can be found in Friel's *Molly Sweeney,* when Mr. Rice remembers the eponymous protagonist's stay in a psychiatric hospital: "I knew I had lost contact with her. She had moved away from us all. She wasn't in her old blind world—she was exiled from that. And the sighted world, which she had never found hospitable, wasn't available to her anymore" (59). But a less obvious comparison can be found in Sava's *Happiness Is Blind,* when Helen is rendered "depressed and worried" after her "first glimpse of the light," depression said to grow as her goal draws nearer, to culminate in a sense of gladness as her eyes are covered with bandages, the outcome being not a "brave new world," but a "cold, rather depressing world" (185–87).

12. Similarly, in *La Symphonie Pastorale,* subsequent to the restoration of her sight, Gertrude stoops and disappears while crossing the garden bridge and, though initially it seems that the suicide has been thwarted, dies after "a night of delirium and exhaustion" (Gide 66–70).

13. Wells's narrator comparably evokes differentiated worlds by contrasting a "city" with a "village," the "story of the outer world" with a "child's story," the "great world" of "sky and mountains and sight and such-like marvels" with the "darkness in the Country of the Blind" (131–32).

14. Friel's *Molly Sweeney* contains more than forty references and allusions to the notion of a blind world. For example, having read the philosophy of Berkeley, Molyneux, and Locke, Frank Sweeney argues that "most of us are born with all five senses; and with all the information they give us, we build up a sight world from the day we are born—a world of objects and ideas and meanings" (12). Frank's objectification of Molly is rivaled in the play by the medical profession. The ophthalmologist Mr Rice asserts that Molly has "lived in a blind world for forty years" (16) and poses many differentiating questions: "How do you think your world compares with the world the rest of us know, the world you would share with us if you had visual perception as well?" (14). The contrast between the solitariness of "your world" and the togetherness of "the world the rest of us know" is marked.

15. The antithetical scenarios that occur in the cultural imagination have both been reported to induce "temporary and longer term" psychopathology, "usually followed by psychosocial readjustment," but in some instances, "readjustment may not occur and suicide may result" (de Leo et al. 339).

Works Cited

Abraham, Karl. "Manifestations of the Female Castration Complex." 1920. *Selected Papers of Karl Abraham.* 1927. Trans. Douglas Bryan and Alix Strachey. London: Maresfield Library, 1988. 338–69. Print.

Allport, Gordon W. *The Nature of Prejudice.* London: Addison-Wesley, 1954. Print.

Amado, Jorge. *Gabriela, Clove and Cinnamon.* New York: Avon Books, 1962. Print.

Barnes, Colin. "Political Correctness, Language and Rights." *Rights Not Charity* (Winter 1993): 8. Print.

Barnes, Colin. "Visual Impairment and Disability." *Beyond Disability: Towards an Enabling Society.* Ed. Gerald Hales. London: Sage, 1996. 36–44. Print.

Barnes, Colin, and Geof Mercer. *Disability.* Cambridge: Polity P, 2003. Print.

Barthes, Roland. "The Metaphor of the Eye." 1963. Georges Bataille. *Story of the Eye by Lord Auch.* London: Penguin, 1982. 119–27. Print.

Barthes, Roland. "Right in the Eyes." 1982. *The Responsibility of Forms: Critical Essays on Music, Art, and Representation.* Trans. Richard Howard. Oxford: Basil Blackwell, 1986. 237–42. Print.

Bataille, Georges. *Story of the Eye by Lord Auch.* 1928. Trans. Joachim Neugroschal. London: Penguin, 1982. Print.

Beckett, Samuel. *Endgame.* 1957. London: Faber and Faber, 1964. Print.

Blank, H. Robert. "Psychoanalysis and Blindness." *Psychoanalytic Quarterly* 26.1 (1957): 1–24. Print.

Block, Lawrence. "Hot Eyes, Cold Eyes." 1980. *Love Kills.* Ed. Ed Gorman and Martin H. Greenberg. New York: Carroll and Graf Publishers, 1997. 295–302. Print.

Bolt, David. "Blindness and the Problems of Terminology." *Journal of Visual Impairment and Blindness* 97.9 (2003): 519–20. Print.

Bolt, David. "A Brief Introduction to Post-Disability Literary Criticism," *Disability Archive UK.* 21 Sept. 2004. Web. 18 July 2012.

Bolt, David. "Community, Controversy, and Compromise: The Language of Visual Impairment." *Language, Bodies, and Health.* Ed. Paul McPherron and Vaidehi Ramanathan. Berlin and New York: Mouton de Gruyter, 2011. 15–36. Print.

Bolt, David. "From Blindness to Visual Impairment: Terminological Typology and the Social Model of Disability." *Disability and Society* 20.5 (2005): 539–52. Print.

Bolt, David. “Social Encounters, Cultural Representation, and Critical Avoidance.” *Routledge Handbook of Disability Studies.* Ed. Nick Watson, Alan Roulstone, and Carol Thomas. London: Routledge, 2012. 287–97. Print.

Bolt, David. “Terminology and the Psychosocial Burden of Blindness.” *British Journal of Visual Impairment* 22.2 (2004): 52–54. Print.

Bolt, David. “The Terminology Debate Continues.” *Journal of Visual Impairment and Blindness* 98.3 (2004): 133–34. Print.

Borges, Jorge Luis. “The Other.” 1975. *The Book of Sand.* Trans. Andrew Hurley. London: Penguin, 2001. 3–11. Print.

Bozovic, Miran. Introduction. *The Panopticon Writings by Jeremy Bentham.* London: Verso, 1995. 1–27. Print.

Brecht, Bertolt. “The Blind Man.” 1920–24. *Collected Short Stories.* Ed. John Willet and Ralph Manheim. London: Minerva, 1992. 21–25. Print.

Brecht, Bertolt. “A Helping Hand.” 1920–24. *Collected Short Stories.* Ed. John Willet and Ralph Manheim. London: Minerva, 1992. 25–29. Print.

Bruce, Ian, Aubrey McKennell, and Errol Walker. *Blind and Partially Sighted Adults in Britain: The RNIB Survey.* London: HMSO, 1991. Print.

Campbell, Fiona. “Exploring Internalised Ableism Using Critical Race Theory.” *Disability and Society* 23.2 (2008): 151–62. Print.

Caplan, Lloyd M. “Pre-education of the Potentially Blind as a Deterrent to Suicide.” *Psychosomatics* 22.2 (1981): 165+. Print.

Carver, Raymond. “Cathedral.” 1983. *Where I’m Calling From: The Selected Stories.* London: Harvill, 1993. 292–307. Print.

Charlton, James. *Nothing about Us without Us: Disability Oppression and Empowerment.* Berkeley: U of California P, 1998. Print.

Cheyne, Ria. “Theorising Culture and Disability: Interdisciplinary Dialogues.” *Journal of Literary and Cultural Disability Studies* 3.1 (2009): 101–4. Print.

Clark, Lizzy. “Don’t Play Me, Pay Me.” Dontplaymepayme. Web. 16 January 2012.

Classen, Constance, ed. *The Book Of Touch.* Oxford and New York: Berg, 2005. Print.

Cole, Kevin L. “Saramago’s Blindness.” *Explicator* 64.2 (2006): 109–10. Print.

Coleman, Lerita M. “Stigma: An Enigma Demystified.” 1986. *The Disability Studies Reader.* Ed. Lennard J. Davis. New York and London: Routledge, 1997. 216–31. Print.

Conan Doyle, Arthur. *Sir Nigel.* 1906. London: John Murray, 1918. Print.

Conrad, Joseph. *The End of the Tether.* 1902. *Youth/Heart of Darkness/The End of the Tether.* London: Penguin, 1995. 151–299. Print.

Corker, Mairian, and Tom Shakespeare. *Disability/Postmodernity: Embodying Disability Theory.* London and New York: Continuum, 2002. Print.

Couser, G. Thomas. “Conflicting Paradigms: The Rhetorics of Disability Memoir.” *Embodied Rhetorics: Disability in Language and Culture.* Ed. James C. Wilson and Cynthia Lewiecki-Wilson. Carbondale and Edwardsville: Southern Illinois UP, 2001. 78–91. Print.

Couser, G. Thomas. “Signifying Bodies: Life Writing and Disability Studies.” *Disability Studies: Enabling the Humanities.* Ed. Sharon L. Snyder, Brenda Jo Brueggemann, and Rosemarie Garland-Thomson. New York: Modern Language Association of America, 2002. Print. 108–17.

Cushman, Keith. “Blind, Intertextual Love: ‘The Blind Man’ and Raymond Carver’s ‘Cathedral.’” *D. H. Lawrence’s Literary Inheritors.* Ed. Keith Cushman and Dennis Jackson. New York: St. Martin’s P, 1991. 155–66. Print.

Davidson, Michael. *Concerto for the Left Hand: Disability and the Defamiliar Body.* Ann Arbor: U of Michigan P, 2008. Print.

Davis, Lennard J. *Bending Over Backwards: Disability, Dismodernism and Other Difficult Positions.* New York and London: New York UP, 2002. Print.

Davis, Lennard J. *Enforcing Normalcy: Disability, Deafness, and the Body.* London and New York: Verso, 1995. Print.

Davis, Lennard J., ed. *The Disability Studies Reader.* New York and London: Routledge, 1997. Print.

de Leo, Diego, Portia A. Hickey, Gaia Meneghel, and Christopher H. Cantor. "Blindness, Fear of Sight Loss, and Suicide." *Psychosomatics* 40.4 (1999): 339–44. Print.

Derrida, Jacques. *Memoirs of the Blind: The Self-Portrait and Other Ruins.* 1990. Trans. Pascale-Anne Brault and Michael Naas. Chicago and London: U of Chicago P, 1993. Print.

Derrida, Jacques. "The Rhetoric of Drugs." *Points . . . Interviews, 1974–1994.* Ed. Elisabeth Weber. Trans. Peggy Kamuf. California: Stanford UP, 1995. 228–54. Print.

Descartes, René. *Meditations on the First Philosophy.* 1641. *Discourse on Method and The Meditations.* Trans. F. E. Sutcliffe. London: Penguin, 1968. 95–169. Print.

Devlieger, Patrick J. "Generating a Cultural Model of Disability." *Congress of the European Federation of Associations of Teachers of the Deaf.* 16 Oct. 2005. Web. 29 June 2011.

Dickinson-Carr, John. *The Blind Barber.* Bath: Lythway P, 1935. Print.

Disabled Peoples' International. "Proceedings of the First World Congress." The Disability Archive UK. 1981. Web. 29 June 2011.

Dobree, John H., and Eric Boulter. *Blindness and Visual Handicap: The Facts.* Oxford: Oxford UP, 1982. Print.

Dodds, Allan. *Rehabilitating Blind and Visually Impaired People: A Psychological Approach.* London: Chapman and Hall, 1993. Print.

Donaldson, Stephen. "The Lady in White." 1978. *Daughter of Regals.* Glasgow: Fontana, 1984. 129–61. Print.

du Maurier, Daphne. *Don't Look Now.* 1970. *Don't Look Now and Other Stories.* London: Penguin, 1973. 7–55. Print.

Encarta World English Dictionary. Microsoft Corporation. Bloomsbury Publishing, 1999. CD-ROM.

Etcoff, Nancy. *Survival of the Prettiest: The Science of Beauty.* London: Brown and Co., 1999. Print.

Fanon, Frantz. *Black Skin, White Masks.* 1952. London: Pluto, 1986. Print.

Ferenczi, Sandor. *First Contributions to Psychoanalysis.* 1916. Trans. Ernest Jones. London, New York: Karnes, 1994. Print.

Fink, Bruce. *The Lacanian Subject.* West Sussex: Princeton UP, 1995. Print.

Finkelstein, Vic. "The Social Model of Disability Repossessed." Disability Archive UK. 1 Dec. 2001. Web. 20 Nov. 2004.

Forster, E. M. *Aspects of the Novel.* 1927. London: Penguin, 2005. Print.

Foucault, Michel. *Discipline and Punish: The Birth of the Prison.* 1975. Trans. Alan Sheridan. London: Penguin, 1977. Print.

Frances, Dick. *Wild Horse.* London: Michael Joseph, 1994. Print.

French, Sally. "The Wind Gets in My Way." *Disability Discourse: Embodying Disability Theory.* Ed. Mairian Corker and Sally French. Buckingham, Philadelphia: Open UP, 1999. 21–27. Print.

Freud, Sigmund. *The Interpretation of Dreams.* 1900. Trans. James Strachey. Ed. James Strachey, Alan Tyson, and Angela Richards. London: Penguin, 1991. Print.

Freud, Sigmund. "Mourning and Melancholia." 1917. *On Metapsychology*. Trans. James Strachey. Comp. and ed. Angela Richards. London: Penguin, 1991. 251–68. Print.

Freud, Sigmund. *Three Essays on the Theory of Sexuality*. 1905. *On Sexuality*. Trans. James Strachey. Comp. and ed. Angela Richards. London: Penguin, 1991. 39–169. Print.

Freud, Sigmund. "The Uncanny." 1919. *Art and Literature*. Trans. Albert Dickson. London: Penguin, 1990. 335–76. Print.

Friedlander, Henry. *The Origins of Nazi Genocide: From Euthanasia to the Final Solution*. Chapel Hill: U of North Carolina P, 1997. Print.

Friel, Brian. *Molly Sweeney*. 1994. New York: Plume, 1995. Print.

Garland-Thomson, Rosemarie. *Extraordinary Bodies: Figuring Physical Disability in American Culture and Literature*. New York: Columbia UP, 1997. Print.

Garland-Thomson, Rosemarie. *Staring: How We Look*. New York: Oxford UP, 2009. Print.

Gide, André. *La Symphonie Pastorale*. 1919. Trans. Dorothy Bussy. London: Penguin, 1963. 9–71. Print.

Gillison, Samantha. "Too Close for Comfort." *Salon*. 18 Jan. 2000. Web. 9 July 2012.

Gilman, Sander L. *Difference and Pathology: Stereotypes of Sexuality, Race, and Madness*. Ithaca: Cornell UP, 1985. Print.

Goffman, Erving. *Stigma: Notes on the Management of Spoiled Identity*. 1963. Middlesex: Penguin, 1968. Print.

Graham, Winston. *Night without Stars*. 1950. London: Pan Books, 1997. Print.

Green, Henry. *Blindness*. 1926. London: Harvill P, 1996. Print.

Gross, Richard. *Psychology: The Science of Mind and Behaviour*. London: Hodder and Stoughton, 1996. Print.

Hubbard, Ruth. "Abortion and Disability: Who Should and Who Should Not Inhabit the World?" 1990. *The Disability Studies Reader*. Ed. Lennard J. Davis. New York and London: Routledge, 1997. 187–200. Print.

Hull, John M. *Touching the Rock: An Experience of Blindness*. London: SPCK, 1990. Print.

Humphries, Steve, and Pamela Gordon. *Out of Sight: The Experience of Disability 1900–1950*. Plymouth: Northcote House, 1992. Print.

Hunt, Paul, ed. *Stigma: The Experience of Disability*. London: Geoffrey Chapman, 1966. Print.

James, Phyllis Dorothy, and Harriet Harvey Wood, eds. *Sightlines*. London: Vintage, 2001. Print.

Jay, Martin. *Downcast Eyes: The Denigration of Vision in Twentieth-Century French Thought*. Berkeley, Los Angeles, and London: U of California P, 1994. Print.

Jernigan, Kenneth. "Blindness: Is Literature against Us?" National Federation of the Blind. The Banquet of the Annual Convention. Chicago. 3 July 1974. Address.

Jernigan, Kenneth. "The Pitfalls of Political Correctness: Euphemisms Excoriated." *Braille Monitor* 36.8 (1993): n. p. National Federation of the Blind. Web. 29 June 2011.

Jernigan, Kenneth. "To Man The Barricades." National Federation of the Blind. The Banquet of the Annual Convention. Houston. July 1971. Address.

Joyce, James. *Ulysses*. 1922. Ed. Jeri Johnson. Oxford: Oxford UP, 1998. Print.

Kelman, James. *How Late It Was, How Late*. Leicester: Minerva, 1995. Print.

Kent, Deborah. "Shackled Imagination: Literary Illusions about Blindness." *Braille Monitor* 33.1 (1990): n.p. National Federation of the Blind. Web. 28 Oct. 2007.

King, Stephen. "The Langoliers." *Four Past Midnight*. Vol. 1. Bath: Chivers P, 1990. 3–373. Print.

Kipling, Rudyard. "They." 1904. *A Choice of Kipling's Prose.* Comp. Craig Raine. London: Faber and Faber, 1987. 239–57. Print.

Kirtley, Donald. D. *The Psychology of Blindness.* Chicago: Nelson-Hall, 1975. Print.

Kleege, Georgina. *Sight Unseen.* New Haven and London: Yale UP, 1999. Print.

Kühl, Stefan. *The Nazi Connection: Eugenics, American Racism, and German National Socialism.* 1994. New York and Oxford: Oxford UP, 2002. Print.

Kuusisto, Stephen. *Eavesdropping: A Life by Ear.* New York: W. W. Norton, 2006. Print.

Kuusisto, Stephen. *Planet of the Blind.* New York: Dial P, 1998. Print.

Kuusisto, Stephen, and Petra Kuppers. "Auto-Graphein or 'The Blind Man's Pencil': Notes on the Making of a Poem." *Disability and/as Poetry.* Ed. Jim Ferris. Spec. issue of *Journal of Literary and Cultural Disability Studies* 1.1 (2007): 74–80. *Metapress.* Web. 1 Jan. 2008.

Langworthy, Jessica L. "Blindness in Fiction: A Study of the Attitude of Authors toward Their Blind Characters." *Journal of Applied Psychology* 14.282 (1930): 269–84. Print.

Lawrence, D. H. "The Blind Man." 1920. *The Complete Short Stories of D. H. Lawrence.* Vol. 2. London: William Heinemann, 1955. 347–65. Print.

Lee, Irving J. *How Do You Talk about People?* New York: Freedom Pamphlet, Anti-Defamation League, 1950. Print.

Lehmann, Rosamond. *Invitation to the Waltz.* 1932. London: Virago, 1981. Print.

Leitch, Vincent B., William E. Cain, Laurie Fink, Barbara Johnson, John McGowan, and Jeffrey J. Williams, eds. *The Norton Anthology of Theory and Criticism.* New York: W. W. Norton and Company, 2001. Print.

Lester, David. "Suicide after Restoration of Sight." *JAMA* 216 (1971): 678–97. Print.

Lester, David. "Suicide after Restoration of Sight (continued)." *JAMA* 219 (1972): 757. Print.

London, Jack. *The Sea Wolf.* 1904. South Africa: Reader's Digest Association, 1993. Print.

Lowenfeld, Berthold. "The Case for the Exceptional." 1946. *Berthold Lowenfeld on Blindness and Blind People: Selected Papers by Berthold Lowenfeld.* New York: American Foundation for the Blind, 1981. 205–9. Print.

Lowenfeld, Berthold. "Effects of Blindness on the Cognitive Functions of Children." 1948. *Berthold Lowenfeld on Blindness and Blind People: Selected Papers by Berthold Lowenfeld.* New York: American Foundation for the Blind, 1981. 67–78. Print.

Lowenfeld, Berthold. "A Psychological Approach to Blindness." 1949. *Berthold Lowenfeld on Blindness and Blind People: Selected Papers by Berthold Lowenfeld.* New York: American Foundation for the Blind, 1981. 79–86. Print.

Lowenfeld, Berthold. "What Is Blindness?" 1974. *Berthold Lowenfeld on Blindness and Blind People: Selected Papers by Berthold Lowenfeld.* New York: American Foundation for the Blind, 1981. 221–30. Print.

Lunsford, Scott. "The Debate Within: Authority and the Discourse of Blindness." *Journal of Visual Impairment and Blindness* 100.1 (2006): 26–35. Print.

Lyon, John. Introduction. *Youth / Heart of Darkness / The End of the Tether.* By Joseph Conrad. London: Penguin, 1995. vii–xiv. Print.

Macey, David. *The Penguin Dictionary of Critical Theory.* London: Penguin, 2001. Print.

Maugham, W. Somerset. *For Services Rendered.* 1932. *Plays: Two.* London: Methuen Drama, 1999. 2–83. Print.

McRuer, Robert. *Crip Theory: Cultural Signs of Queerness and Disability.* New York: New York P, 2006. Print.

Memmi, Albert. *Dependence: A Sketch for a Portrait of the Dependent.* Boston: Beacon P, 1984. Print.

Merleau-Ponty, Maurice. *The Visible and the Invisible.* Chicago: Northwestern UP, 1968. Print.

Michalko, Rod. "Blindness Enters the Classroom." *Disability and Society* 16.3 (2001): 349–59. Print.

Michalko, Rod. *The Mystery of the Eye and the Shadow of Blindness.* Toronto: Toronto UP, 1998. Print.

Michalko, Rod. *The Two-In-One: Walking with Smokie, Walking with Blindness.* Philadelphia: Temple UP, 1999. Print.

Mitchell, David T., and Sharon L. Snyder. Introduction. *The Body and Physical Differences: Discourses of Disability.* 1997. Ann Arbor: U of Michigan P, 2000. 1–33. Print.

Mitchell, David T., and Sharon L. Snyder. *Narrative Prosthesis: Disability and the Dependencies of Discourse.* Ann Arbor: U of Michigan P, 2000. Print.

Monbeck, Michael E. *The Meaning of Blindness: Attitudes Toward Blindness and Blind People.* London: Indiana UP, 1973. Print.

Murray, Stuart. *Representing Autism: Culture, Narrative, Fascination.* Liverpool: Liverpool UP, 2008. Print.

Norton, Mary. "The Girl in the Corner." 1951. *The Bread and Butter Stories.* London: Virago, 1998. 1–15. Print.

Oliver, Mike. "Defining Impairment and Disability: Issues at Stake." *Exploring the Divide.* Ed. Colin Barnes and Geof Mercer. Leeds: Disability P, 1996. 29–54. Print.

Orwell, George. *Nineteen Eighty-Four.* 1949. London: Penguin, 2000. Print.

Price, Alan. *Synge and Anglo-Irish Drama.* London: Methuen, 1961. Print.

Price, Janet, and Margrit Shildrick. "Bodies Together: Touch, Ethics and Disability." *Disability/Postmodernity: Embodying Disability Theory.* Ed. Mairian Corker and Tom Shakespeare. London: Continuum, 2002. 62–75. Print.

Quayson, Ato. *Aesthetic Nervousness: Disability and the Crisis of Representation.* New York: Columbia UP, 2007. Print.

Rao, Shridevi. "'A Little Inconvenience': Perspectives of Bengali Families of Children with Disabilities on Labelling and Inclusion." *Disability and Society* 16.4 (2001): 531–48. Print.

Rée, Jonathan. *I See A Voice: A Philosophical History of Language, Deafness and the Senses.* London: Harper Collins, 1999. Print.

Roaf, Caroline. "Le Mot Juste: Learning the Language of Equality." *Curricula for Diversity in Education.* Ed. T. Booth, W. Swann, M. Masterton, and P. Potts. London and New York: Routledge, 1992. 340–44. Print.

Rodas, Julia Miele. "On Blindness." *Journal of Literary and Cultural Disability Studies* 3.2 (2009): 115–30. Print.

Rycroft, Charles. *A Critical Dictionary of Psychoanalysis.* 1968. London: Penguin, 1985. Print.

Saramago, José. *Blindness.* London: Harvill P, 1995. Print.

Sartre, Jean-Paul. *Being and Nothingness: An Essay on Phenomenological Ontology.* 1943. Trans. Hazel E. Barnes. London: Methuen, 1957. Print.

Sava, George. *Happiness Is Blind.* London: Robert Hale, 1987. Print.

Schor, Naomi. "Blindness as Metaphor." *Differences: A Journal of Feminist Cultural Studies* 11.2 (1999): 76–104. Print.

Scott, Robert A. *The Making of Blind Men: A Study of Adult Socialization.* 1969. New Brunswick: Transaction, 1991. Print.

Shakespeare, Tom. *Disability Rights and Wrongs.* Oxon: Routledge, 2006. Print.

Shakespeare, Tom, and Nicholas Watson "The Social Model of Disability: An Outdated Ideology?" *Research in Social Science and Disability* 2 (2002): 9–28. Print.

Shreve, Anita. *Eden Close*. London: Abacaus, 1994. Print.

Skelton, Robin. *The Writings of J.M. Synge*. London: Camelot P, 1971. Print.

Snyder, Sharon L. and David T. Mitchell. *Cultural Locations of Disability*. Chicago: U of Chicago P, 2006. Print.

Sontag, Susan. *Death Kit*. London: Vintage, 1967. Print.

Strindberg, August. *A Dream Play*. 1901. *Plays: Two*. Trans. Michael Meyer. London: Methuen Drama, 2000. 178–254. Print.

Synge, John Millington. *The Well of the Saints*. 1905. *Collected Plays and Poems and The Aran Islands*. London: Everyman, 1996. 66–108. Print.

Thomas, Dylan. *Under Milk Wood*. 1954. London: Orion Books, 1992. Print.

Thomson, Rupert. *The Insult*. London: Bloomsbury, 1996. Print.

Titchkosky, Tanya. "Cultural Maps: Which Way to Disability?" *Disability/Postmodernity: Embodying Disability Theory*. Ed. Mairian Corker and Tom Shakespeare. London, and New York: Continuum, 2002. 101–11. Print.

Tremain, Shelley. "On the Subject of Impairment." *Disability/Postmodernity: Embodying Disability Theory*. Ed. Mairian Corker and Tom Shakespeare. London and New York: Continuum, 2002. 32–47. Print.

Tuttle, Dean W. *Self-Esteem and Adjusting with Blindness: The Process of Responding to Life's Demands*. Springfield, IL, 1984. Print.

Twersky, Jacob. *Blindness in Literature: Examples of Depictions and Attitudes*. New York: American Foundation for the Blind, 1955. Print.

Upton, Carole-Anne. "Visions of the Sightless in Friel's *Molly Sweeney* and Synge's *The Well of the Saints*." *Modern Drama* 40.3 (1997): 347–58. Print.

Valentine, James. "Naming and Narrating Disability in Japan." *Disability/Postmodernity: Embodying Disability Theory*. Ed. Mairian Corker and Tom Shakespeare. London and New York: Continuum, 2002. 213–27. Print.

Van Weelden, Jacob. *On Being Blind: An Ontological Approach to the Problem of Blindness*. Amsterdam: Netherlands Society for the Blind, 1967. Print.

Varley, John. "The Persistence of Vision." 1978. *The John Varley Reader*. New York: Penguin, 2004. 228–70. Print.

Vidali, Amy. "Seeing What We Know: Disability and Theories of Metaphor." *Journal of Literary and Cultural Disability Studies* 4.1 (2010): 33–54. Print.

Wagner-Lampl, A., and G. W. Oliver. "Folklore of Blindness." *Journal of Visual Impairment and Blindness* 88 (1994): 267–76. Print.

Webster's Third New International Dictionary. Unabridged. Springfield: G. and C. Merriam, 1966. Print.

Wells, H. G. "The Country of the Blind." 1904. *Selected Short Stories*. Middlesex: Penguin Books , 1958. 123–46. Print.

Wheeler, Charles. *Snakewalk*. New York: Harmony Books, 1989. Print.

White, Peter. *See It My Way*. London: Little, Brown and Company, 1999. Print.

Wittenstein, Stuart. Letter to the editor. *Journal of Visual Impairment and Blindness* 98.3 (2004): 133. Print.

Wolfe, Thomas. *You Can't Go Home Again*. 1940. London and Toronto: William Heinemann, 1947. Print.

Wood, Philip. *International Classification of Impairments, Disabilities and Handicaps*. Geneva: World Health Organisation, 1980. Print.

World Health Organisation. "International Classification of Functioning and Disability. ICIDH-2." World Health Organisation. 2001. Web. 3 Dec. 2004.

Wyndham, John. *The Day of the Triffids*. 1951. London: Book Club Associates, 1981. Print.

Yeats, W. B. *On Baile's Strand*. 1904. *Selected Plays*. London: Penguin, 1997. 49–72. Print.

Index